James Bain, Hugh Hornby Langton

A Joint Catalogue of the Periodicals, Publications and Transactions of Societies

.

James Bain, Hugh Hornby Langton

A Joint Catalogue of the Periodicals, Publications and Transactions of Societies

ISBN/EAN: 9783337188962

Printed in Europe, USA, Canada, Australia, Japan

Cover: Foto ©Andreas Hilbeck / pixelio.de

More available books at **www.hansebooks.com**

TORONTO

.. A ..

JOINT CATALOGUE

OF THE

PERIODICALS, PUBLICATIONS AND TRANSACTIONS OF SOCIETIES

And Other Books Published at Intervals

TO BE FOUND IN THE VARIOUS LIBRARIES

OF THE

CITY OF TORONTO

TORONTO :
THE BRYANT PRESS,
1898.

List of Libraries contributing to this Catalogue,
with the abbreviation used to denote them.

PREFATORY NOTE

A T a recent conference of the Librarians of this city, a resolution was passed expressive of the desire for co-operation, both as a means of extending the usefulness of the libraries and of economizing their funds, by preventing the purchase of duplicate sets or valuable volumes. As a preliminary step it was agreed to prepare a Joint Catalogue of the sets of Periodicals, Transactions of Societies, Almanacs and other sets of books published at intervals, with the exception of daily newspapers, in the twelve contributing libraries, and after some delay arising from difficulties over which the editors have had no control, the catalogue is now complete.

The entries have been furnished by the librarians in charge of the various libraries, and have been collated and condensed by Miss Grace K. Andrews, Cataloguing Clerk, Public Library. Each book, or set of books, appears under the first word of the title, and in cases where changes in the title have taken place, cross-references have been made. As far as possible missing volumes have been indicated both as a guide to readers and to those whose duty it is to purchase or procure the missing parts. A summary under subjects appears at the end as a guide to those who are desirous of knowing what sets are available for the pursuit of any special branch of study.

With all its imperfections the Editors hope that, as a preliminary effort to combine and make serviceable, so many different libraries, it may meet with the approval of all who are anxious to facilitate the work of the student and the seeker after information.

JOINT CATALOGUE

····● OF ●····

PERIODICALS, TRANSACTIONS

AND

Books Published at Intervals

IN THE LIBRARIES OF THE
.....CITY OF TORONTO.

Aargauische Naturforschende Gesell-schaft.
Mittheilungen. Heft. 1-5. *Aarau*, 1878-89. U
Abbotsford Club.
Publications. Nos. 1-10, 12-35. *Edinburgh*, 1835-66. P
Abeille (L') Canadienne, Journal de littéra-ture et de sciences. *Montreal*, 1819. P
Aberdeen Philosophical Society.
Transactions. Vol. I. *Aberdeen*, 1884. C
Aborigines' Friend. *See* Colonial Intelligencer.
Aborigines Protection Society.
Annual Reports, 1-10, with extracts from Papers and Proceedings. *London*, 1838-47. U
Academia Cæsarea (Leopoldino-Caro-lina Germanica) NaturæCuriosorum.
(Also called : Kaiserliche Leopoldinisch-Carolinische (deutsche) Akademie der Naturforscher.)
Miscellanea Curiosa medico-physica. Dec. 2, ann. 1-9. *Jenae*, 1682-90. U
Nova Acta (*or* Verhandlungen). Tom. 21-64. *Breslau, Bonn, Dresden, Halle*, 1845-96. *In progress.* U
Academia Georgia Augusta. *See* Königliche Gesellschaft der Wissenschaften zu Göttingen.
Academia Nacional de Ciencias de la Republica Argentina en Cordoba.
Acta. Tom. 6, and Atlas to Tom. 6. *Buenos Aires,* 1889. C
Boletin. Tom. 6 13. *Buenos Aires*, 1884-93. C

Academia Real das Sciencias de Lis-boa.
Jornal de Sciencias Mathematicas, Physicas e Naturaes. Ser. 1. No. 1-48. *Lisboa*, 1866-88. M
Ser. 2. No. 1-11. *Lisboa*, 1889-94. *In progress.* M
Ser. 2. Tom. 1-3. *Lisboa*, 1890-95. *In progress.* C
Memorias. Tom. 1-6. *Lisboa*, 1854-1885. M
Sessão Publica, em 12 de Decembro de 1875.
em 15 de Maio de 1877.
em 9 de Junho de 1880.
em 17 de Decembro 1893. M
Academia Scientiarum Imperialis Petropolitana. (*Or* Académie Impériale des Sciences de St. Pétersbourg.)
Bulletin. Série 5. Tom. 1-4. *St. Pétersbourg,* 1894-6. *In progress.* C
Commentarii. Tom. 1-10, (1726-1738). *Petropoli*, 1728-39. U
Mélanges Biologiques tirés du Bulletin Physico-mathématique. Tom. 1-13. *St. Pétersbourg,* 1850-94. *In progress.* U
Mélanges Mathématiques et Astronomiques tirés du Bulletin Physico-mathématique.
Tom. 5, 6. *St. Pétersbourg*, 1874-88. U
Mémoires, Classe Physico-mathématique. Série 7. Tom. 39-42. *St. Pétersbourg,* 1889-94. *In progress.* C
Série 8. Tom. 2. *St. Pétersbourg*, 1895. *In progress.* C

Academie de la Rochelle. Société des Sciences Naturelles. Annales. Vols. 19-28, 30. *La Rochelle*, 1882 91, 1893. *In prog. ess.* C

Academie (Royale) de Medecine. Mémoires. Tom. 1-2, 14, 17-21. *Paris*, 1828-57. U

Academie des Inscriptions et Belles-Lettres. Histoire de l'Académie....avec les Mémoires de Littérature tirez des Registres....Tom. 1-44. *Paris*, 1717 93. U Histoire et Mémoires de l'Institut Royal de France. Classe d'Histoire et de Littérature ancienne. Tom. 1 4. *Paris*, 1815 18. U Continued as : Mémoires de l'Institut Royal de France, Académie des Inscriptions et Belles-Lettres. Tom. 5-8. *Paris*, 1821-27. U

Academie (Royale) des Sciences. Comptes-rendus hebdomadaires des Séances. Tom. 1-123. *Paris*, 1835-96. *In progress.* U Mémoires. Tom. 1-44 (1816-89). *Paris*, 1818-89. *In progress.* U Mémoires présentés par divers savans. Sciences mathématiques et physiques. Tom. 1-24. *Paris*, 1827-77. Continued as : Mémoires présentés par divers savants. 2 me Série. Tom. 25-31. *Paris*, 1877-94. *In progress.* Philosophical History and Memoirs....or an abridgement of all the papers relating to Natural Philosophy....from 1699-1720, by Martyn & Chambers, 5 vols. *London.* 1742. U

Academie des Sciences, Arts, et Belles-Lettres de Dijon. Mémoires. 2 me Série. Tom. 13. *Dijon*, 1866. U 3 me Série. Tom. 1-3, *Dijon*. 1873 6. U 3 me Série. Tom. 9-10 ; 4 me Série, Tom. 1-4. *Dijon*, 1885-94. *In progress.* C

Academie des Sciences de Cracovie. Bulletin International. Comptes rendus. *Cracovie*, 1889-91, 1895. *In progress.* C

Academie des Sciences, Inscriptions et Belles-Lettres de Toulouse. Mémoires. 8 me Série. Tom. 7-10 ; 9 me Série. Tom. 1-7. *Toulouse*, 1885-95. *In progress.* C

Academie d'Hippone. Bulletin. Nos. 9-12, 14-15, 17, 19-21, 23-27. *Bône*, 1870 95. *In progress.* C Comptes-rendus des Réunions. *Bône*, 1895. *In progress.* C

Academie Imperiale des Sciences. *See* Academia Scientiarum Imperialis Petropolitana.

Academie Imperiale (or Nationale) des Sciences, Arts, et Belles-Lettres de Caen. Mémoires. 16 vols. (of various dates). *Caen*, 1855 86. U " *Caen*, 1885 95. *In progress.* C

Academie (Imperiale et) Royale des Sciences et Belles-Lettres de Bruxelles. (After 1845 : Acad. Roy. des Sciences, des Lettres et des B aux-Arts de Belgique). Annuaire. Années 1 36. *Bruxelles*, 1835-70. U " 44-60. *Bruxelles*, 1877-93. C

Bulletin. 1 ère Série. 23 tom. (1832-56); 2 me Série. Tom. 1-28. , *Bruxelles*, 1832 69. U 2 me Série. Tom. 41-44, 46-50 ; 3 me Série. Tom. 1-29. C *Bruxelles*, 1876-95. *In progress* C Mémoires. 5 tom. *Bruxelles*, 1777-88. U Nouveaux Mémoires. Tom. 1-19. Continued as : Mémoires. Tom. 20 52. *Bruxelles*, 1820-94. *In progress.* U Mémoires couronnés et mémoires des Savant, étrangers. Tom. 17-53 (1843 93). *Bruxelle*C 1845-94, 4to. *In progress.* U Mémoires couronnés et mémoires des Savants étrangers. (After Tom. 6 : Mémoires couronnés et autres mémoires.) Collection in 8vo. Tom. 1-47. *Bruxelles*, 1840 93. *In prog ess.* U (Tomes 1-3, 1840-49, have no common title and are not numbered.)

Academy. Vols. 10-12. *London*, 1876-77. L Vols. 11-16, 23-24. *Londo* , 1877-9, 1883. E Vols. 17-23, 37-51. *London*, 1880-83, 1890-97. *In progress.* U Vols. 25-51. *London*, 1884-97. *In progress.* P Vols. 29-51. *London*, 1886-97. *In progress.* T Vols. 37-51. *London*, 1890-97. *In progress.* V

Academy of Natural Sciences of Philadelphia. Journal. Vols. 2-8. *Philadelphia*, 1821-42. U Series 2. 1-9. *Philade'phia*, 1847-95. (Wanting Vol. 3). *In progress.* C Do. Vols. 1-4. *Philadelphia*, 1847-60. C Proceedings. 1844-95. *Philadelphia*, 1846-96. (Wanting Vols. 6, 15 and 22). *In progress.* C Do. 1857-96. *Philadelphia*, 1888-97. *In progress.* C

Academy of Science of St. Louis. Transactions. Vols. 2-5. *St. Louis*, 1861-88. U Do. Vols. 3-5. *St. Louis*, 1868-88. C

(Reale) Accademia delle Scienze. (Earlier volumes : Société Royale de Turin, or Académie [royale or impériale] des Sciences). Atti. Tom. 14-15, 17, 19-27. *Torino*, 1878-92. C

Miscellanea philosophico-mathematica (Mélanges de Philosophie et de Mathématique). 5 tomi. *Turin*, 1759-73. Continued as : Mémoires (Memorie). Tom. 6-40 ; Serie 2. Tom. 1-42. *Torino*, 1784-1892. U Do. Tom. 24-40 ; Serie 2. Tom. 21-29, 31, 34-43. *Torino*, 1820 93. *In progress.* C

Accademia di Scienze, Lettere e Arti. Atti Rendiconti. Nuova Serie. Tom. 6. *Acireale*, 1894. *In progress.* C

Accademia Pontificia de' Nuovi Lincei. Atti. Tom. 42-49. *Roma*, 1888-96. *In progress.* C

Acta Mathematica. Bd. 8-18. *Berlin*,] *Stockholm* and *Paris*, 1884-94. *In progress.* C

Acta Universitatis Lundensis. *See* Lunds Universitet.

Acta Victoriana. Vols. 1-19. *Cobourg* and *Toronto*, 1878-96 (Vol. 2 incomplete). *In progress.* V

Adelaide Philosophical Society.
Transactions and Proceedings and Report, 1877-79. *Adelaide*, 1878-9. Continued as : Royal Society of South Australia. Transactions, Proceedings and Report. Vols. 3-12. *Adelaide*, 1880-9 (Wanting Vol. 4). U Do Vols. 14-20. *Adelaide*, 1890-6. *In progress.* C

Adress-Buch deutscher Export-Firmen. Bd. 1-4. *Berlin*, 1883-5. P

Adventurer (By J. Hawkesworth, Samuel Johnson and others). 4 vols. in 1. *London*, 1752-4. U

Advocate of Moral Reform.
New York, 1837-39. V

Aelfric Society.
Publications. 4 vols. *London*, 1843-48. U

Aerztlicher Verein zu Wien.
Mittheilungen. Bd. 1-3. *Wien*, 1872-74. U

Africa. Meteorological Reports. *See* Observatories : Africa.

Agricultural Society of England. *See* Royal Agricultural Society.

Akademia Umiejetnosci.
Sprawozdania Komisyi Jezykowéj. Tom. 4. *Krakow*, 1891. U
Rozprawy i sprawozdania z posiedzen wydzialu filologicznego. Tom. 15. *Krakow*, 1891. U

Albany. School Reports. 1 vol., 1872-9. E

Albany Institute.
Transactions. Vol. 1. *Albany*, 1828-30. P

Albion. N.S. Vols. 8, 10-16. *New York*, 1849, 1851-7. P

Album des Familles, revue mensuelle.
Ottawa, 1883. P

Album Litteraire et Musical de la Revue Canadienne. Tom. 1-3. *Montreal*, 1846-8. P

Alemannia, Zeitschrift fuer Sprache, Litteratur und Volkskunde des Elsasses. Bd. 1-24. *Bonn*, 1873-96. *In progress.* U

All the Year Round. Vols. 1-20 ; 2nd Series. Vols. 1-43 ; 3rd Series. Vols. 1-13. *London*, 1859-95. P
(Continuation incorporated with Household Words).

Allgemeine deutsche ornithologische Gesellschaft zu Berlin.
Journal für Ornithologie. Separat-Abdruck : Jahresbericht des Ausschusses für Beobachtungsstationen der Vögel Deutschlands. Jahresb. 8-11 (1883-6). Naumburg, 1885-8. U

Allgemeine medizinische Annalen.
See Medizinische National-Zeitung für Deutschland.

Allgemeine Schweizerische Gesellschaft fuer die gesammten Naturwissenschaften. (Also called Société Helvétique des Sciences Naturelles).
Neue Denkschriften (*or* Nouveaux Mémoires). Bd. 3-30. *Neuchatel, Neuenberg, Zürich*, 1839-88. U
Verhandlungen (*or* Actes). Jahresberichte, 1861, 1864, 1872-89. *V.P.*, 1861-90. U
Do. 1887-94. *In progress.* C

Allgemeine Zeitschrift fuer Psychiatrie und psychisch-gerichtliche Medicin. Bd. 50-52. *Berlin*, 1894-96. *In progress.* U

Almanach Americain. *Paris*, 1784. P

Almanach de Gotha. *Gotha*, 1884-98. *In progress.* P

Almanach der Bellettristen und Bellettristinnen. *Ulielet*, 1782. U

Almanach des Maris et Conseiller des Celibataires. *Paris*, 1877. P

Almanach Royal (et National). *Paris*, 1826, 1832, 1840. U

Amateur Photography. Vols. 10-11. *London*, 1889-90. P

Amateur Work. N.S. Vols. 1-3. *London*, n.d. P

American Academy of Arts and Sciences.
Proceedings. Vols. 21-31. *Boston*, 1885-94. C

American Academy of Political and Social Science.
Annals. Vols. 1-9 and Supplements. *Philadelphia*, 1890-98. *In progress.* C.L.P.U.

American Agriculturist. Vols. 40-41. *New York*, 1881-2. L

American Almanac and Repository of Useful Knowledge.
Boston, 1830-61 (Wanting Vol. 2). U

American Almanac and Treasury of Facts.
New York, 1850, 1861, 1878-80, 1884-9. P
New York, 1878, 1885, 1887, 1889. L

American Analyst. Vols. 2-8. *New York*, 1886-1890. L

American Annual of Photography.
New York, 1890-98. *In progress.* P

American Annual Register, 1825-33. *New York*, 1825-36. U

American Anthropologist. *See* Anthropological Society of Washington.

American Antiquarian and Oriental Journal. Vols. 8, 13, 16-19. *Chicago*, 1886, 1891, 1894-7. *In progress.* C

American Antiquarian Society.
Archæologia Americana. Vols. 1-7. *Worcester, Mass.*, 1820-85. P.U
Proceedings. *Worcester, Cambridge, Boston*, 1813-90. (Imperfect). U
Do. 1861-95. *In progress.* C

American Architect and Building News. Vols. 3-55. *Boston*, 1878-97. *In progress.* S.

American Art Review. 2 vols. *Boston*, 1880-1. P

American Association for the Advancement of Science.
Memoirs. *Salem*, 1875. P
Proceedings. Vols. 1-45. *Philadelphia, Boston, Cambridge, Salem*, 1849-97. *In progress.* P.U
American Bookmaker. Vols. 11-12. *New York*, 1890-91. P

American Cabinet Maker and Upholsterer. Vols. 29-38, 41-45, 47, 49-54. *New York*, 1884-97. *In progress.* P

American Catholic Historical Society. P
Records. Vols. 1-4. *Philadelphia*, 1884-91. P
Do. Vol. 6. *Philadelphia*, 1895. *In progress.* C

American Catholic Quarterly Review.
Vols. 11-22. *Philadelphia*, 1886-97. *In progress.*   C
Vols. 20-22. *Philadelphia*, 1895-7. *In progress.*   P

American Chemical Journal, Vols. 1-19.
Baltimore, 1879-97 (Wanting Vols. 12 and 13). *In progress.*   U
Vols. 8-9, 11-19. *New York*, 1886 97. *In progress.*   C

American Church Almanac and Year Book. Vol. 65. *New York*, 1895.   T

American Dialect Society.
Dialect Notes. Vol. 1. *Norwood, Mass.*, 1896. *In progress.*   P

American Economic Association.
Publications. Vols. 1-12. *New York*, 1886-97. *In progress.*   L. U

American Educational Monthly.
11 vols. *New York*, 1866-76.   E

American Engineer and Railroad Journal. Vol. 69. *New York*, 1895.   C

American Ephemeris and Nautical Almanac, 1856, 1858, 1875, 1884, 1889-99. *Washington*, 1853-96. *In progress.*   U

American Ethnological Society.
Transactions. Vols. 1-2. *New York*, 1845-8. P
Bulletin. Vol. 1. *New York*, 1860-61.   P

American Folk-Lore Society.
Memoirs. Vols. 1-5. *Boston* and *New York*, 1894-7.   P

American Garden. Vols. 11-12. *New York*, 1890-91. Continued as :
American Gardening. Vol. 13. *New York*, 1892.   P

American Geographical Society (of New York).
Bulletin. 1878-81. *New York*, 1878-81.   U
Journal. Vols. 3-21 (1870-89). *New York, London, Paris*, 1873-[89] (Wanting Vols. 6 and 7). U

American Geographical and Statistical Society.
Bulletin. Vols. 1, 17-25, 27-9. *New York*, 1852-97. *In progress.*   C
Proceedings. *New York*, 1862-5.   C

American Geologist. Vols. 1-19. *Minneapolis*, 1888-97. *In progress.*   U

American Historical Association.
Annual Reports, 1889-95. *Washington*, 1890-96. *In progress.*   C.P.U
Papers. Vols. 1-5. *New York*, 1886-91. *In Progress.*   P.U

American Historical Register.
Vols. 2-4. *Philadelphia*, 1895-7. *In progress.* L

American Historical Review. Vols. 1-2. *New York*, 1896-7. *In progress.* L.P.T.U.V

American History. Vol. 11. *New York* 1884-92.   L

American History Leaflets, Colonial and Constitutional (bi-monthly). Nos. 1-30. *New York*, 1892-6. *In progress.*   O.P

American Institute (of the City of New York).
Annual Reports, 1846, 1848, 1850, 1855, 1857, 1858, 1861, 1863, 1865-72. *Albany*, 1847-72. U
Do. *Albany*, 1846-54.   C
Do. *Albany*, 1846-57.   P

American Institute of Mining Engineers.
Transactions. Vols. 1-17. *Philadelphia, Easton, New York*, 1872-89.   U
Index to Vols. 1-15.
Do. Vols. 1-9, 11-16, 24. *New York*, 1871-94.   C

American Journal of Archæology.
Vols. 1-12. *Baltimore* and *Princeton*, 1885-97. *In progress* (Wanting Vols. 2-5).   U
Vols. 1-5. *Baltimore*, 1885-9.   P
Vols. 10-12. *Princeton*, 1895-6. *In progress.* V

American Journal of Education.
Vols. 1-23. *Hartford*, 1856-72.   U
Vols. 10-11. *St. Louis*, 1877-8.   E

American Journal of Mathematics.
Vols. 1-19. *Baltimore*, 1878-97. *In progress.* U

American Journal of Obstetrics.
Vol. 20. *New York*, 1887.   P

American Journal of Philology.
Vols. 1-18. *Baltimore*, 1880-97. *In progress.* U.V

American Journal of Politics (American Magazine of Civics). Vols. 4-6. *New York*, 1894-5.   L

American Journal of Psychology.
Vols. 1-7. *Baltimore* and *Worcester*, 1887-95. *In progress.*   U

American Journal of Science and Arts.
1st Series. Vols. 1-49. *New Haven*, 1820-45. E
2nd Series. Vols. 1-50. *New Haven*, 1846-70.   C.E
Vols. 16-50. *New Haven*, 1853 70 M
3rd Series. Vols. 1-50. *New Haven*, 1871-95.   C.M.U
4th Series. Vols. 1-3. *New Haven*, 1896-7. *In progress.*   C.M.U

American Journal of Semitic Languages. *See* Hebraica.

American Journal of the Medical Sciences.
Vols. 40-62. *Philadelphia*, 1860-71.   U
Vols. 69-74, 92-98. *Philadelphia*, 1875-7, 1888-9.   P

American Lancet. Vols. 10-16. *Detroit*, 1886-92.   L

American Law Review. Vols. 1-16. *Boston*, 1866-82.   U

American Machinist. Vols. 7, 9-20. *New York*, 1884, 1886-97. *In progress.*   P

American Magazine of Civics. *See* American Journal of Politics.

American Mathematical Society.
Bulletin. Vols. 1-2. *New York*, 1894-6. *In progress.*   L

American Medical and Philosophical Register. 4 vols. *New York*, 1810-13. U

American Medical Association. Journal. Vol. 16. *Chicago*, 1891.   L

American Medico-Surgical Bulletin.
Vols. 6-9. *New York*, 1893-6. *In progress.* U

American Monthly Magazine and Critical Review. Vol. 2. *New York*, 1817-8.   P

American Monthly Microscopical Journal. Vols. 1-3. *New York*, 1880-2. U
Continued as :
American Monthly Micro-opical Journal containing Contributions to Biology. Vols. 10-17. *Washington*, 1889-96. *In progress.* C

American Museum of Natural History.
Bulletin. Vols. 1-8. *New York*, 1881-96. *In progress.* C.U
Reports. Vols. 1-27. *New York*, 1870-95. *In progress.* U

American Naturalist. Vols. 1-31. *Salem, Mass*, and *Philadelphia*, 1867-97. *In progress.* (Wanting Vol. 26, U) (Wanting Vols. 10-13, 15-17, P). P.U
Do. Vols. 19-27, *New York*, 1887-95. *In progress.* C

American Newspaper Catalogue. *Cincinnati*, 1883, 1891-2. P

American Newspaper Directory. *New York*, 1880. T

American Oriental Society.
Journal. Vols. 1-14. *New Haven*, 1850-90. U

American Pharmaceutical Association.
Proceedings. Vols. 6-41. *Philadelphia*, 1857-93 (Wanting Vol. 10). U

American Philological Association.
Transactions. Vols. 1-27. *Hartford, Boston*, 1869 [96] *In progress.* U

American Philosophical Society.
Early Proceedings (1744-1838). *Philadelphia*, 1844. C.U
Proceedings. Vols. 15-34. *Philadelphia*, 1876-95 (Wanting Vol. 15, C). *In progress.* C.U
Transactions. New Series. Vol. 12. *Philadelphia*, 1863. U

American Pioneer. Vols. 1-2. *Cincinnati*, 1842-3. P

American Practitioner. Vols. 1-2. *Louisville, Ky*, 1870. U
Continued as :
American Practitioner and News. Vols. 1-2. *Louisville, Ky.*, 1886. L

American Public Health Association.
Public Health : Reports and Papers, 1873-5. *New York*, 1875. U

American Publishers' Circular and Literary Gazette. Vols. 4-5. *New York*, 1858-9. E

American Quarterly Church Review. *See* Church Review.

American Quarterly Microscopical Journal. Vol. 1. *New York*, 1878. U

American Quarterly Register and Magazine. Vols. 3-6. *Philadelphia*, 1849-52. U

American Quarterly Review. Vols. 1-21. *Philadelphia*, 1827-37. P

American Railway Master Mechanics' Association.
Reports of Proceedings. *Cincinnati*, 1883-7. C

American Review. Vols. 1-2. *Philadelphia*, 1811. T

American Society for Psychical Research.
Proceedings Vol. 1 (1885-9). *Boston* [1889]. C.U

American Society of Civil Engineers.
Proceedings. Vols. 10-18, 20-21. *New York*, 1884-95. *In progress.* Vol. 17. C
Do. Vols. 19-23. *New York*, 1893-6. *In progress.* S
Transactions Vols. 13-30, 32-4. *New York*, 1884-95. *In progress.* C
Index to Vols. 1-27.
Reference Maps of the United States, 1893. C

American Statistical Association.
Publications, N.S., Vols. 1-5. *Boston*, 1889-96. *In progress.* (Wanting Vol. 1, C). C.P.U

American Swedenborg Printing and Publishing Society. *See* Swedenborg Printing and Publishing Society.

American Teacher. Vols. 11-18. *Boston*, 1887-95. *In progress.* E

Analectic Magazine. Vols. 1-14. *Philadelphia*, 1813-19. P

Anatomische Gesellschaft.
Verhandlungen (Published as Ergänzungshefte to the Anatomischer Anzeiger, q.v.)

Anatomischer Anzeiger. Jahrg 1-12. *Jena*, 1886-97. *In progress.* U

Ancient Order of Foresters' Friendly Society, Directory. *London*, 1891-3. P

Andover Review. Vols. 1, 5-12, 14-15, 18-19. *Boston*, 1884-93. V

Anecdota Oxoniensia : Texts, documents and extracts, chiefly from Manuscripts in the Bodleian and other Oxford Libraries.
Semitic Series, Pts. 1-4. *Oxford*, 1882-9. P.U
Aryan Series, Pts. 1-5. *Oxford*, 1881-6. P.U
Classical Series. Pts. 1-6. *Oxford*, 1882-92. U
Mediæval and Modern Series, Vol. 1, Pts. 1-5. *Oxford*, 1882-94. *In progress.* U
Do. Vol. 1, Pts. 1-8, 10. *Oxford*, 1882-94. *In progress.* P

Anglia, Zeitschrift fuer englische Philologie. Bd. 1-20. *Halle*, 1878-97. *In progress.*
Mittheilungen aus dem gesammten Gebiete der englischen Sprache und Litteratur, Beiblatt zur "Anglia." Jahrg. 1-7. *Halle*, 1891-7. *In progress.* U

Anglo-American Magazine. Vols. 1-5. *Toronto*, 1852-4. E.L
Vols. 1-6. 1852-5. U
Vols. 1-2, 7. 1853-5. U

Annaes de Sciencias Naturaes.
Tom. 3. *Porto*, 1896. *In progress.* C

Annalen der (Chemie und) Pharmacie.
Bd. 1-76. Neue Reihe, Bd. 1-92 (Bd. 77-168.) *Lemgo, Heidelberg, Leipzig*, 1832-73.
Continued as :
Justus Liebig's Annalen der Chemie (und Pharmacie). Bd. 169-290 (continuing the original numeration of volumes) and Supplementbände 1-8. *Leipzig* and *Heidelberg*, 1874-96. *In progress.* U
General-Register, Bd. 1-276, in 4 vols.

Annalen der Physik (hrsg. von L. W. Gilbert). 76 Bde. *Halle, Leipzig*, 1799-1824. Continued as :
Annalen der Physik und Chemie (hrsg. von J. C. Poggendorff). 160 Bde, 8 Ergänzungsbde und Jubelband. *Leipzig*, 1824-77. *In progress.* U

Neue Folge (hrsg. von G. Wiedemann), Bd.
1-58 *Leipzig*, 1877-96. *In progress.* U
Beiblatter zu den Annalen, &c. Bd. 1-20.
Leipzig, 1877-96. *In progress.* U
Sach-Register zu Gilbert's Annalen, Bd. 1-76.
Namen und Sach-Register zu Poggendorff's
Folge, Bd. 1-160, &c., in 4 vols. Namen-
Register zu Wiedemann's Reihe, Bd. 1-50.

**Annalen des Charite-Krankenhauses
zu Berlin.** Bd. 4-6. *Berlin*, 1853-55. U

Annales de Chimie (et de Physique.)
1 ère Série, 96 tom.
2 me   "   75   "
3 me   "   69   "
4 me   "   30   "
5 me   "   30   "
6 me   "   30   "
7 me   "   Tom. 1-7.
Tables, 8 tom.
Paris, 1789-1896. *In progress.* U

Annales des Mines. *See* Journal des Mines.

Annales des Ponts et Chaussees.
Lois, Décrets, Arrêtés, etc.   Série 6, tom.
7-10. *Paris*, 1887-90.   C
Série 7, Tom. 3. *Paris*, 1893.   C
Personnel. 1886-89, 1891-6. *In progress.* C
Mémoires et documents.   Série 6, Tom 11-
20. Tables Générales. *Paris*. 1886-90.   C
Série 7, Tom. 1-12. *Paris*, 1886-96. *In progress.*
                               C

Annales des Sciences Naturelles
30 tomes and 2 tomes of Plates.

2 me Série, Botanique. 20 tom.
2 me   "   Zoologie. 20   "
3 me   "   Botanique. 20   "
3 me   "   Zoologie. 20   "
4 me   "   Botanique. 20   "
4 me   "   Zoologie. 20   "
5 me   "   Botanique. 20   "
5 me   "   Zoologie. 20   "
6 me   "   Botanique. 20   "
6 me   "   Zoologie. 20   "
7 me   "   Botanique. 20   "
7 me   "   Zoologie. 20   "
8 me   "   Botanique. Tom. 1-2.
8 me Série, Zoologie. Tom 1-2.
Paris, 1824-96. *In progress.* U

**Annales d' Hygiene Publique et de
Medecine Legale.**
2 me Série. Tom. 15-36. *Paris*, 1861-72. U

Annales Medico-psychologiques.
7 me Série. Tom. 17-20. 8 me Série. Tom. 1-5.
Paris, 1893-7. *In progress.* U

**Annals and Magazine of Natural
History.** *See* Annals of Natural History.

**Annals of Agriculture and Other Use-
ful Arts** (ed. by Arthur Young). Vols. 1, 3, 5
and 8. *Bury St. Edmund's*, *London*, 1784
(1790)-87.

Annals of Botany. Vols. 1-11. *London*, 1887-
97. *In progress*   P

Annals of Hygiene. Vols 4-7. *Philadelphia*,
1889-92.   L

Annals of Mathematics, published at University of Virginia. Vols. 1-6, 8-10. *Charlottes-
ville*, 1884-96. *In progress.*   C

**Annals of Natural History, or Maga-
zine of Zoology, Botany and Geology**
(conducted by Sir W. Jardine, etc.). Vols. 1-5.
London, 1838-50. Continued as :
Annals and Magazine of Natural History,
Vols. 6-17. *London*, 1841-7.
Second Series. 20 vols. *London*, 1848-57.
Third   "   20 vols   "   1858-67.
Fourth   "   Vols. 9-20   "   1872-77.
Sixth   "   Vols 4-19   "   1888-97.
In progress.   U

Annals of the American Academy. *See*
American Academy.

**Annee geographique, revue annuelle
des voyages de terre et de mer, etc.**
Tom. 13 (1875). 2 me Série. Tom. 1-3 (1876-8).
Paris, 1876-80.   U

Annuaire de Legislation etrangere.
See Société de Législation Comparée, Annuaire,
etc.

Annuaire de Legislation francaise.
See Société de Législation Comparée, Annuaire,
etc.

Annuaire de Quebec. *Quebec*, 1881-2.   P

Annuaire des Deux Mondes.
Années 1850-67. *Paris*, 1851-68.   U

**Annuaire geologique (Universel et
Guide du Geologue).** 12 tom. *Paris*,
1885-96. *In progress.*   U

Annuaire historique universel. 1829-44.
Paris, 1830-45 (Wanting Vols for 1833, 1842 and
1843).   U

**Annuaire Statistique de la Province
de Buenos Aires.** Vol. 8. *La Plata*, 1883. C

Annual Cyclopædia. N.S. Vols. 1-20 (1876-
95). *New York*, 1883-95. *In progress.*
Index to Vols 1-20.   P

Annual Literary Index. 1892-6. *New
York*, 1893-7. *In progress.*   P. U

Annual of Scientific Discovery. *Boston*
1850-68.
Do. *Boston*, 1870.   L

**Annual Record of Science and In-
dustry.** *New York*, 1871-5, 1877.   E
Do. *New York*, 1372-5, 1877-8.   P

Annual Register. *London*, 1758-1897. *In
progress.* Index, 1758-1792, 2 vols. L.O.P
Do. *London*, 1758-1829, 1890-96. *In pre-
gress.*   U
Index, 1758-1819, 1 vol.

Anthony's Photographic Annual. *New
York*, 1891.   P

**Anthropological Institute of Great
Britain and Ireland.**
Journal. Vols. 1-18, 20, 22-26. *London*. 1871-
97.   C
Do Vols. 4, 19-26. *London*, 1875-97.
In progress.   C
Index to Publications for years 1843-91.

Anthropological Review. Vols. 1-9. *London*, 1863-71.   C

Anthropological Society of London.
Memoirs. Vols. 1-3 (1863-69). *London*, 1865-9.
                                  C.U.P
Publications. 5 vols. *London*, 1863-5.   U.P

Anthropological Society of Washington.
Transactions. Vols. 1-3. *Washington*, 1879-85. U
American Anthropologist. Vols 1-10. *Washington*, 1889-97 *In progress.* C.P

Anthropologische Gesellschaft in Wien.
Mittheilungen Bd 3-26. *Wien*, 1873 1896. *In progress.* C

Anti-Jacobin Review. Vols. 26 61. *London*, 1807-21. T

Antiquarian Magazine and Bibliographer. Vols. 1-6. *London*, 1882 4. P

Antiquarische Gesellschaft in Zuerich. (Gesellschaft für vaterländische Alterthümer) Mittheilungen. Bd. 1 22. *Zürich* and *Leipzig*, 1841 89 (Wanting Bd. 4, 5 and 8). U

Antivarisk Tidskrift for Sverige. *See* Kongliga Vitterhets. Historie och Antiqvitets Akademi. Antiqvarisk Tidskrift, etc.

Antiquary. Vols. 1 33. *London*, 1880 97. *In progress.* P

Appleton's Annual Cyclopædia. *See* Annual Cyclopædia.

Appleton's Journal. Vols. 6-11. *New York*, 1879-81. L

Appleton's Mechanic's Magazine.
Vol 1. *New York*, 1851. E
Vols 2 3. *New York*, 1852-3. C

Archæologia, or miscellaneous tracts relating to Antiquity. *See* Society of Antiquaries of London. Archæologia.

Archæologia Aeliana. *See* Newcastle-upon-Tyne Society of Antiquaries. Archæologia .Eliana.

Archæologia Americana. *See* American Antiquarian Society. Archæologia Americana.

Archæologia Cambrensis. *See* Cambrian Archæological Association. Archæologia Cambrensis.

Archæologia Scotica. *See* Society of Antiquaries of Scotland. Transactions (Archæologia Scotica, etc).

Archæological Institute of America. Papers of the American School of Classical Studies at Athens. Vol. 1 (1882 3). *Boston*, 1885. U

(Royal) Archæological Institute of Great Britain and Ireland (Vol. 1 under name of British Archæological Association). Archæological Journal. Vols. 1-50. 2nd Series. Vols. 1 3. *London*, 1845-94. *In progress.* U.P
Index to Vols. 1-25.
Proceedings. Annual Reports. *London*, 1845-53. P

Archæological Journal. *See* Archæological Institute of Great Britain and Ireland. Archæological Journal.

Archæological Review. 4 vols. *London*, 1887-90. U

Architect. Vols. 31 57. *London*, 1884-97. *In progress.* P

Architectural Publication Society.
Detached essays and illustrations, issued 1848-52. *London*, 1853. C.P
Dictionary of architecture. 8 vols. *London*, n.d. P
Essays. *London*, 1848-52. C.P

Architectural Record. Vols 1 6. *New York*, 1891-7. *In progress.* S

Architectural Review. Vols. 1-4. *Boston*, 1894-7. *In progress.* S

Architectural Societies (associated) [of the Midland Counties of England]. Reports and Papers. Vols. 1-20. *London*, 1850-9-. Indexes to Vols. 1-19. P

Architecture and Building. Vols. 4 17- *New York*, 1886-92. L

Archiv der Mathematik und Physik. Reihe 2, Teil 4. *Leipzig*, 1886. C

Archiv fuer Anatomie, Physiologie und wissenschaftliche Medicin. Jahrg.. 1861-70. *Berlin*, *Leipzig*, 1861-70. U
Continued as:
Archiv für Anatomie und Physiologie. Jahrg. 1877-96. *Leipzig*, 1877 96. *In progress.* U

Archiv fuer das Studium der neueren Sprachen und Literaturen (hrsg. von Herrig). Bd. 1 97. *Elberfeld u. Eiserlohn*, *Braunschweig*, 1846-96. *In progress*

Archiv fuer die gesammte Physiologie des Menschen und der Thiere. Bd. 1-63. *Bonn*, 1868 96. *In progress.* U

Archiv fuer Geschichte der Philosophie. Bd. 1-10. *Berlin*, 1888 97. *In progress.* U

Archiv fuer Kunde oesterreichischer Geschichts-Quellen. *See* Kaiserliche Akademie der Wissenschaften. Archiv, etc.

Archiv fuer lateinische Lexikographie und Grammatik. Bd. 1-9. *Leipzig*, 1884-96. *In progress.* U

Archiv fuer Litteraturgeschichte. 15 Bde. *Leipzig*, 1870-87. U

Archiv fuer mikroskopische Anatomie (und Entwickelungsgeschichte). Bd. 1 47. *Bonn*, 1865 96. *In progress.* U
Namen-und Sach-Register, Bd. 1-40, in 2 vols.

Archiv fuer Naturgeschichte. Jahrg 1-62. *Berlin*, 1835-96. *In progress.* U
Register, Jahrg. 1-60, in 2 vols.

Archiv fuer pathologische Anatomie und Physiologie, und fuer klinische Medicin. Bd. 1-144. *Berlin*, 1847-96. *In progress.* U

Archiv fuer Psychiatrie und Nervenkrankheiten. Bd. 1-29. *Berlin*, 1868-97. *In progress.* U

Archiv fuer soziale Gesetzgebung. Bd. 1-10. *Tubingen*, *Berlin*, 1888 97. *In progress.* U

Archives de Biologie. Tom. 1-14. *Gand* and *Leipzig*, *Paris*, 1880-96. *In progress.* U

Archives de la Commission scientifique du Mexique. *See* Commission Scientifique, etc.

Archives de Medecine experimentale et d'Anatomie pathologique. 1 ère Série. Tom. 5-9. *Paris*, 1893-7. *In progress.* U

Archives de Physiologie normale et pathologique.

1 ère Série. 5 tom.
2 me   "   10   "
3 me   "   10   "
4 me   "   2   "
5 me   "   Tom. 1-9.
Tables 1 re et 2 me Série, 1868-82.
Paris, 1868-97. *In progress.*   U

Archives de Zoologie experimentale et generale.

1 ère Série. 10 tom.
2 me   "   10 tom.
3 me   "   Tom. 1-5.
Paris, 1872-97. *In progress.*   U

Archives des Missions scientifiques et litteraires.

1 ère Série. 6 tom.
2 me   "   6   "
3 me   "   15   "
Paris, 1850 90.   U
(Publication was discontinued from 1857 to 1863).
Continued as :
Nouvelles Archives, etc. Tom. 1-6. *Paris*, 1891-6. *In progress.*   U

Archives des Sciences Physiques et Naturelles. *See* Bibliothèque Universelle (de Genève). Archives, etc.

Archives Generales de Medecine.

5 me Série. Tom. 17-20 ; 6 me Série, Tom. 1-18.
Paris, 1861-71.   U

Archivio Glottologico Italiano.

Vol. 1-13. *Roma*, 1873-96. *In progress.*   U

Arcturus. Vol. 1. *Toronto*, 1887.   P

Arena. Vols. 1-17. *Boston*, 1890-7 (Wanting Vols. 1-2, L). *In progress.*   L, P

Argosy. Vols. 1-32. *London*, 1866-81.   P

Arkansas. School Reports, annual, 1879-92. E

Armana Prouvencau, 1855-97. *Avignoun* and *Paris*, 1855-97. *In progress.*   U

Arminian Magazine. Vols. 1-35. *London*, 1778-1812. Continued as :
The Methodist Magazine and Wesleyan Methodist Magazine. Vols. 35-97. *London*, 1812-74 (Wanting Vols. for 1863-8, 1870 and 1872). V

Army List. *See* Hart's Army List.

Arrow. Vol. 1. *Toronto*, 1886.   P

Art (L'). *Paris*, 1875-94.   P

Art Amateur. Vols. 9-35. *New York*, 1883-97. *In progress.*   P

Art Decorator. Series 2-6. *London*, 1891-5. P

Art for All. Vol 1. *New York*, 1888-9.   P

Art Interchange. Vols. 17-38. *New York*, 1886-97. *In progress.*   P

Art Journal (commenced as Art Union, 10 vols. 1839-48)
London, 1839-97. *In progress.*   P

Art (L') pour Tous. Vols. 1-12. *Paris*, 1861-73.   P

Art Union. *See* Art Journal.

Artistic Japan. Vols. 1-6. *London*, n.d. P

Artists' Repository and Drawing Magazine. Vols. 1-4. *London*, n.d.   P

Artizan.

Vols. 8-10, 13-25. *London*, 1850-67.   P
Vols. 9-18. *London*, 1851-61.   C
Vols. 11, 15-18, 20-28. *London*, 1853-70.   U

Arundel Society.

Annual and occasional publications. *London*, 1849-88.   P
Supplementary volumes. *London*, 1854-82.   P

Ashlar (The). Vols. 1-3. *Detroit*, 1855-8. P

Asiatic Annual Register, 1799-1801. *London*, 1800-1802.   U

Asiatic Society of Bengal.

Asiatic Researches, or Transactions Vols. 1-7, 9-10. *London*, 1799-1811.   L
Index to papers in the Journal and Proceedings of Asiatic Society of Bengal. Appendix D. pp. 106-195 of Centenary Review of the Researches of the Society, 1784-1883. *Calcutta*, 1885.   C
Journal. Vols. 52-55, 58-61, 62 (pt. 2), 63 (pts. 1-2), 64 (pts. 1-2). *Calcutta*, 1883-95. *In progress.*   C
Proceedings. *Calcutta*, 1883-87, 1889-96. *In progress.*

Asiatic Society of Japan.

Transactions. Vols. 1-19. *Yokohama*, 1882-91. U
Do. Vols. 13-15, 17-18, 20-3. *Yokohama*, 1885-94. *In progress.*   C
General index to Vols. 1-23.

Associated Architectural Societies.

See Architectural Societies.

Association Francaise pour l'Avancement des Sciences.

Comptes-Rendus des Sessions 14-22. *Paris*, 1885 93. *In progress.*   C

Association geodesique internationale.

Comptes rendus des Séances des Conférences générales, 7-9. *Berlin*, 1884-9.
Comptes- rendus des Séances de la Commission permanente, 1887-8. *Berlin*, 1888 9.   U

Association of Dominion Land Surveyors.

Proceedings. *Montreal*, 1888-90.   C

Association of Engineering Societies.

Journal. Vols. 9-17. *Chicago*, 1890-7. *In progress.*   S

Association of Provincial Land Surveyors.

Proceedings. *Toronto*, 1886-97. *In progress.*   P.S

Association pour l'Encouragement des Etudes Grecques.

Revue des tudes Grecques. Tom. 1-10. *Paris*, 1888 97. *In progress.*   P

Assurance Magazine. Vols. 1-25. *London*, 1851 86. Index to Vols 1-20.   P

Astronomical and Physical Society of Toronto.

Transactions and Reports. *Toronto*, 1890-7. *In progress.*   C.P
Do. 1894-7. *In progress.*   U

Astronomical Papers prepared for the use of the American Ephemeris.

Vols. 1-4. *Washington*, 1882-91.   U

(Royal) Astronomical Society of London.
Memoirs. Vols. 2-51. *London*, 1826-95. *In progress* (Vols. 17 and subsequent Vols. are called half vols., the Vols. of monthly notices for the same dates being considered supplementary to them). U
Monthly Notices. Vols. 1, 6, 8, 10-19, 28-55. *London*, 1831-95. *In progress*. U
Index to Vols. 1-52, in 2 vols.

Astronomisch-meteorologisches Jahrbuch fuer Prag. Jahrg. 2-4. *Prag.* 1843-5. U

Astronomische Nachrichten Bd. 125-135. *Kiel*, 1890-5. *In progress*. S

Astronomischer Kalender. *See* Observatories : Germany.

Astronomisches Jahrbuch. *See* Königliche (preussische) Akademie der Wissenschaften zu Berlin.

Astronomisches Jahrbuch fuer physische und naturhistorische Himmelsforscher und Geologen (after Jahrg. 4: Naturwissenschaftlich astronomisches Jahrbuch). Jahrgang 1-9 (1839-47). *München*, 1838-47. U

Astronomy and Astro-Physics. Vols. 11-16. *Northfield, Minn.*, 1892-7. *In progress*. S

Astrophysical Journal. Vols. 1-5. *Chicago*, 1895-7. *In progress*. P.S

Asylum Journal of Mental Science. Vols. 1-3. *London*, 1855-7. Continued as :
Journal of Mental Science. Vols. 4-42. *London*, 1858-96 *In progress*. U
Index to Vols. 1-24.

Atalanta. Vols. 1-11. *London*, 1887-97. *In progress*. P

Ateneo di Brescia. Commentari, 1885-95. *Brescia*, 1885-95. *In progress*. C

Athenæum, 1830-83, and 1890-6. *London*, 1830-96. *In progress*. U
1873-83, 1888-91. L
1884-97. *In progress*. P
1886-97. *In progress*. T

Athenee Louisianais. Comptes rendus.
3 me Série. Tom. 6 ; 4 me Série, Tom. 1-4 ; 5 me Série. Tom. 1-3.
New Orleans, 1889-96. *In progress*. C

Atlantic Monthly. Vols. 1-80. *Boston*, 1857-97. *In progress*. P
Index to Vols. 1-62.
Vols. 1-26, 30-80. *Boston*, 1858-97. *In progress*. L

Attisches Museum (hrsg. von Wieland). 4 Bde. *Zürich, Leipzig, Lucerne*, 1796-1803. Continued as :
Neues Attisches Museum. 3 Bde. *Zürich, Leipzig*, 1805-11. U

Auk (The). *See* Nuttall Ornithological Club.

Australasian Association for Advancement of Science.
Reports. Vols. 1-4. *Sydney*, 1888-95. *In progress*. C

Australia. Meteorological reports. *See* Observatories : Australia.

Australia Year Book, 1894. *Sydney*. C

Australian Journal of Education. 2 vols. *Sydney*, 1869-70. E

Austria. Meteorological reports. *See* Observatories : Austria.

Babylonian and Oriental Record. Vols. 1-5. *London*, 1886-91. U

Badminton Magazine. Vols. 1-4, *London*, 1895-7. *In progress*. P

Baird Lectures. 11 vols. *Edinburgh* and *London*, 1873-91. K
1895, 1897. *In progress*. P

Baldwin Lectures. *Chicago*, 1888, 1896. *In progress*. P

Ballad Society.
Publications, Nos. 1-34, *London*, 1868-95. *In progress*. U

Ballou's Pictorial. Vols. 12-17. *Boston*, 1857-59. P

Baltimore. School Reports, annual. 1856-64, 1869-80, and 1882-4. E

Bampton Lectures. 107 vols. *Oxford* and *London*, 1780-1894 (Wanting Vols. for 1834-5, 1841, 1850, 1859, 1880, 1886, 1888, 1891, 1893). K
Do. 1859, 1866, 1872-4, 1877, 1883, 1885-6, 1889-97. *In progress*. P

Band of Hope Review. First Series, 1 vol., 1851-60. *London*, n.d. P

Banking Almanac, Directory, Year-Book and Diary. *London*, 1884. P

Banking Law Journal. Vols. 1-13. *New York*, 1889-96. *In progress*. L

Banks and Savings' Institutions of Pennsylvania.
Reports. *Harrisburg*, 1887-92, 1895. *In progress*. C

Banner. 1 vol. *Toronto*, 1843-4. K

Banner of Israel. Vols. 11-20. *London*, 1887-96. *In progress*. P

Barker's Facts and Pictures. *London*, 1891. P

Bataviaasch Genootschap van Kunsten en Wetenschappen.
Notulen van de Algemeene en Bestuursvergaderingen, Deel 24-32. *Batavia*, 1886-94. *In progress*. C
Register, 1879-95.
Tijdschrift voor Indische Taal Land en Volkenkunde. Deel 13, 14, 16, and 18. *Batavia*, 1863-72. U
Do. Deel 31-37, 40-41. *Batavia*, 1886-94. P
Verhandelingen. Deel 46-7. *Batavia*, 1891-2. *In progress*. C

Baumgarten's Jahresbericht. *See* Jahresbericht über die Fortschritte in der Lehre von den pathogenen Mikroorganismen

Bay State Monthly. Vols. 1-3. *Boston*, 1884-5. Continued as :
New England Magazine. Vols. 4-6. New Series. Vols. 1-13. *Boston*, 1886-96. *In progress*. P

Bayerische Botanische Gesellschaft zur Erforschung der heimischen Flora.
Berichte. Bd. 1-4. *München*, 1891-6. *In progress*. C

Beeton's Boy's Annual. Vols. 1-5, 9. *London*, 1862-66, 1870. P

Beitraege zur Assyriologie und vergleichenden semitischen Sprachwissenschaft (hrsg. von F. Delitzsch und P. Haupt). Bd. 1-2. *Leipzig*, 1890-4. *In progress.* U

Beitraege zur Geschichte der deutschen Sprache und Literatur. Bd. 1-20. *Halle*, 1874 95. *In progress,* U

Beitraege zur Kunde der indogermanischen Sprachen. 16 Bde., *and* Supplement-Band. *Göttingen*, 1877-90. U

Beitraege zur pathologischen Anatomie und zur allgemeinen Pathologie. Bd. 1-20. *Jena*, 1886-96. *In progress.* U

Beitraege zur Statistik der Stadt Frankfurt. *See* Frankfurter Verein für Geographie und Statistik. Beiträge, etc.

Beytraege zur kritischen Historie der deutschen Sprache, Poesie und Beredsamkeit. 8 Bde. *Leipzig*, 1732-42. U

Belfast Magazine. *Belfast*, 1825. P

Belfast Natural History and Philosophical Society. Report and Proceedings. *Belfast*, 1888-96. *In progress.* C

Belfast Naturalists' Field Club. Annual Reports and Proceedings. *Belfast*, 1865-73, 1880-7, 1893-4. C

Belford's Monthly Magazine. *See* Canadian Monthly and National Review.

Belgium. Meteorological reports. *See* Observatories : Belgium.

Belgravia. Vols. 1-94. *London*, 1867-97. *In progress.* P

Bell, B. T. A. *See* Canadian Mining Manual.

Bengal Asiatic Society. *See* Asiatic Society of Bengal.

Berg-und Huettenmaennische Zeitung. Bd 51. *Berlin*, 1892 3. S

Bergen Museum. Aarsberetning. *Bergen*, 1885-91. C Aarbog *Bergen*, 1886 96. *In progress.* M Do. *Bergen*, 1892-96. *In progress.* C U

Berghaus' Physikalischer Atlas. *See* Physikalischer Atlas.

Berlin Academy of Science. *See* Königliche (preussische) Akademie der Wissenschaften zu Berlin.

Berlin–Gesellschaft fuer Erdkunde. *See* Gesellschaft fur Erdkunde zu Berlin.

Berlin–Gesellschaft naturforschender Freunde. *See* Gesellschaft naturforschender Freunde zu Berlin.

Berlin–Koenigliche Sternwarte. *See* Observatories : Germany.

Berliner Gesellschaft fuer Anthropologie, Ethnologie und Urgeschichte. Verhandlungen. *Berlin*, 1883-95. C Zeitschrift für Ethnologie. Bd. 21-28. *Berlin*, 1889 96. *In progress.* Do. General-Register zu Bd. 1-20 (1869-88). C

Bern—Naturforschende Gesellschaft. *See* Naturforschende Gesellschaft in Bern.

Bezzenberger's Beitraege. *See* Beiträge zur Kunde der Indogermanischen Sprachen.

Bible Society Recorder. Vols. 1-2. *Toronto*, 1870-1. P

Biblical Repertory and Classical Review. 3rd Series Vols. 3-4. *New York*, 1847-48. V
Continued as :
Biblical Repertory and Princeton Review, 12 vols. *Philadelphia*, 1848 66. K
Continued as :
Presbyterian Quarterly and Princeton Review. 4 vols. *New York*, 1873-6. K
Continued as :
Princeton Review. Vols. 1-19. *New York*, 1872 84. P
Continued as :
New Princeton Review. Vols. 1-6. *New York*, 1886-8. P.U

Biblical World. *See* Old Testament Student.

Bibliographer. Vols. 1-6. *London*, 1881-4. P

Bibliographica. 3 vols. *London*, 1895-7. P

Bibliographisch-kritischer Anzeiger fuer romanische Sprachen und Literaturen. N F., Bd. 2. *Berlin*, 1890. U

Bibliotheca Sacra. Vols. 1-41, 52-53. *Andover and Oberlin* 1844-84, 1895-6. *In progress.* V Vols. 39 40. 42 53 *Oberlin*, 1882 96. *In progress.* L

Bibliothek der deutschen Medicin und Chirurgie. Jahrg. 1-4. *Würzburg*, 1828-31. U

Bibliothek des literarischen Vereins in Stuttgart. *See* Literarischer Verein in Stuttgart.

Bibliothek der schoenen Wissenschaften und der freyen Kuenste. 12 Bde., *and* Anhang zu dem 1 ten und 2 ten (*and* 3 ten und 4 ten) Bände. *Leipzig*, 1757-65. Continued as :
Neue Bibliothek, etc. 72 Bde. *Leipzig*, 1770-1806. U
Allgemeines Register, Bibliothek, Bd. 1-12 *and* Neue Bibliothek, Bd. 1 60, 5 vols

Bibliotheque Canadienne. Tom. 1-9. *Montreal*, 1825-9. P
Continued as :
L'Observateur. Tom. 1-2. *Montreal*, 1830-31. P
Continued as :
Magasin du Bas-Canada. Tom. 1-2. *Montreal*, 1832. P

Bibliotheque de l'Ecole des Chartes. *See* École des Chartes. Bibliothèque.

Bibliotheque de l'Ecole des hautes Etudes. *See* École (pratique) des hautes Etudes. Bibliothèque, etc.

Bibliotheque des Ecoles francaises d'Athenes et de Rome. *See* Écoles françaises, etc. Bibliothèque

Bibliotheque du Code Civil, Quebec. Vols. 5-9. *Montreal*, 1880 3. E

Bibliotheque Universelle (de Geneve). Archives des Sciences physiques et naturelles. 36 tom ; Nouvelle période, 62 tom ; 3me période. Tom. 1-36. *Genève*, 1846 96. Table 1846-78. *In progress.* U

Bidrag till Finlands Naturkaenne-dom, Etnografi och Statistik. *See* Finska Vetenskaps Societet. Bidrag, etc.

Bidrag till Kaennedom om Finlands Natur och Folk. *See* Finska Vetenskaps Societet. Bidrag, etc

Biographisches Jahrbuch fuer Alter-thumskunde. Bd. 11. *Berlin,* 1888. U

Biological Society of Washington.
Proceedings. Vols. 1 10. *Washington,* 1880-96. *In progress* (Vols. 2 3 wanting, C).   · C.U

Biologisches Centralblatt. Bd. 1-16 [1881-96]. *Erlangen, Leipzig* [1882] 96. *In progress.*   U

Birmingham Natural History and ~~Microscopical Society,~~ *Philos: So-* Reports and Transactions. *Birmingham,* 1880-3.   C
Proceedings. Vol. 9. *Birmingham,* 1894-5. *In progress.*   C

Bizarre Notes and Queries. Vols. 2-4. *Manchester, N.H.,* 1884-7.   P

Black and White. Vols. 2-9. *London,* 1892-5.   L

Blackwood's Magazine. Vols. 1-162. *Edinburgh,* 1817-97. *In progress.*   L
Vols. 1-99. *Edinburgh,* 1817-66.   O
Index to Vols. 1-50.
Vols. 45-160. *New York,* 1839 96. *In progress.*   P

Bollettino di Bibliografia e di Storia delle Scienze Matematiche e Fisiche. Tom. 19 20. *Roma,* 1886 7.   C

Bollettino Industriale del Regno d'Italia. (After Vol. 7 of the 2nd Series : Bollettino delle Privative Industriali del regno d'Italia). 6 vols. and atlases, N.P., 1864-69.
2a Serie. Vol. 1-20. *Torino,* 1870-89.   U

Bombay Medical Transactions. *See* Medical and Physical Society of Bombay. Transactions.

Bon (Le) Jardinier Almanach. *Paris,* 1853-4.   P

Bonn—Naturhistorischer Verein. *See* Naturhistorischer Verein der preussischen Rheinlande und Westphalens.

Bookman, American Edition. Vols. 1-4. *New York,* 1895-7. *In progress.*   V

Bookman. English Edition. Vols. 1-11. *London,* 1891-7. *In progress.*   P.V

Boston. School Reports, annual, 1851-84.   E

Boston Almanac, 1857. *Boston,* 1857.   U

Boston Browning Society Papers, 1886 97. *New York,* 1897.   P.U

Boston Society of Natural History.
Annual reports. *Boston,* 1865-9.   C
Boston Journal of Natural History. Vols. 1, 2, 6. 7. *Boston,* 1834-63.   U
Memoirs. Vols. 1-5. *Boston,* 1866-95. *In progress.*   U
Occasional Papers. Vols. 1-3. *Boston,* 1869-80.   U
Proceedings. Vols. 1, 3-8, 10-27. *Boston,* 1841-97. *In progress.*   U
Do. Vols. 5-13, 15-27. *Boston,* 1856 97. *In progress.*   C

Botanical Gazette. Vols. 1-22 (imperfect). *Logansport, Crawfordsville, Madison, Chicago,* 1875-97. *In progress.*   U
Vols. 19-22. *Madison,* 1894-7. *In progress.* S

Botanical Magazine. Vols. 1-14. *London,* 1787-1800. Continued as :
Curtis's Botanical Magazine. 3rd Series, Vols. 40-53. *London,* 1884-97. *In progress.*   P

Botanical Society of Canada. Annals. Vol. 1 (n.t.), 1860-2.   P

Botanical Society of Edinburgh. Transactions and Proceedings. Vols. 13-20. *Edinburgh,* 1876-96. *In progress.*   C

Botanische Zeitung. Jahrg. 51-4. *Berlin,* 1893-6. *In progress.*   U

(Just's) Botanischer Jahresbericht. Jahrg. 6-21 (1878-93). *Berlin,* 1880-96. *In progress.*   U

Botanisches Centralblatt. Bd. 1-68. *Cassel,* 1880-96. *In progress.*   U
Beihefte. Jahrg. 1-6. *Cassel,* 1891-6. *In progress.*   U

Boyle Lectures. *London,* 1692, 1697, 1704-5, 1711 14, 1719-20, 1736. 1738 1750, 1752, 1756-8, 1802-5, 1846, 1861, 1864-6, 1868-9, 1870-5. 1878, 1891-3, 1895. In 34 vols.   K
Do. *London,* 1820, 1871-4, 1882.   T

Brain, a Journal of Neurology (after Vol. 9 : Brain, etc. edited for the Neurological Society of London). Vols. 1-19. *London,* 1878-96. *In progress.*   U

Braunschweig—Verein fuer Naturwissenschaft. *See* Verein für Naturwissenschaft zu Braunschweig.

Brazilian Biographical Annual. Vols. 1-3. *Rio de Janeiro,* 1876.   C

Bremen—Naturwissenschaftlicher Verein. *See* Naturwissenschaftlicher Verein zu Bremen.

Bremisches Jahrbuch. *See* Künstlerverein-Abtheilung für Bremische Geschichte, etc. Bremisches Jahrbuch.

Bristol Naturalists' Society. Proceedings. New Series. Vols. 3, 5-7. *Bristol,* 1879, 1885-94.   C
(Botanical Section) : Flora of the Bristol Coal Fields. *Bristol,* 1881.   U

Britannic Magazine. Vols. 1-12. *London,* n.d.   P

British Almanac and Companion. 1828-77. *London* (1828-77).   U

British American. Nos. 1-2. *Toronto,* 1863. T

British American Cultivator. N.S., Vols. 1-2. *Toronto,* 1845-6.   L.P

British American Journal.
Vols. 1-3. *Montreal,* 1860-2.   E
Vols. 1-2. *Montreal,* 1860-1.   L

British American Journal. Vol. 1. *St. Catharines,* 1834.   P

British American Journal of Medical and Physical Science. 3 vols. *Montreal,* 1849-51.   E

British American Magazine.
Vols. 1-2. *Toronto*, 1863-4.   E.L.P

British and Foreign Bible Society.
Reports, 1-14. *London*, 1805-18.   U

British and Foreign Evangelical Review. 37 vols. *Edinburgh*, 1852-88.   K

British and Foreign Medical Review.
Vols. 1-12. *London*, 1836-41.   U

British and Foreign Medico-Chirurgical Review. Vols. 1-60. *Lon on.* 1848-77.   U

British Archæological Association.
Journal. Vols. 1-50. *London*, 1846-94.
N.S., Vol. 1. *London*, 1895. *In progress.* P
General Indices to Vols. 1-42.
Collectanea Archæologica. Vols. 1-2. *London*, 1861-3.   P

British Association for the Advancement of Science.
Reports. Vols. 1-65. *London*, 1831-96.
In progress.   U.L
Do. Vols. 1-16, 18-26, 41-4, 50-65. *London*, 1853-96. *In progress.*   M
Do. Vols. 1-27. *London*, 1831-58.   C

British Chronicle. Vols. 1-2. *New York*, 1842-3.   P

British Colonial Magazine.
Vol. 1. *Toronto*, 1853.   P

British Columbia.
Journals of the Legislative Assembly, 1872, 1875-96. *In progress.*   O
Do. 1872-96. *In progress.*   L
Sessional Papers, 1875-5, 1878-81, 1883-93. *In progress.*   O
Do. 1872-96. *In progress.*   L
Gazette. Vols. 35-6. *Victoria*, 1895-6. *In progress.*   O
Educational Reports. *Victoria*, 1872-95. *In progress.*   E

British Columbia Board of Trade.
Annual Reports. Nos. 3-5, 7, 10-11. *Victoria*, 1882-90.   C

British Columbia Directory.
Victoria, 1882-3, 1892, 1897-8.   P

British Controversialist.
London, 1850-72.   L

British Critic. 1st Series. 42 vols. ; 2nd Series. 23 vols. ; 3rd Series. Vols. 1-2. *London*, 1793-1826.
General Index to the 1st series, 2 vols.   U
Continued as :
British Critic and Quarterly Theological Review and Ecclesiastical Record. Vols. 8-34. *London*, 1830-43.   T

British Economic Association.
Economic Journal. Vols. 1-6. *London*, 1891-96. *In progress.*   U

British Journal of Photography.
Vols. 31-44. *London*, 1884-97. *In progress.* P

British Journal Photographic Almanac. *London*, 1884-97. *In progress.*   P

British Lithographer. Vols. 2-3. *London*, 1892-4.   P

British Magazine. Vols. 1-24, 32. *London*, 1832-43, 1847.   T

British Medical Association.
British Medical Journal. *London*, 1860-72.
(Wanting Vol. 1 of 1869, and Vol. 2 of 1872).   U
Do 13 vols. *London*, 1884-90.   P

British Medical Journal. *See* British Medical Association. British Medical Journal.

British Meteorological Society.
Proceedings. *London*, 1855-8, 1861-71.   M
Quarterly Journal, Vols. 1-23. *London*, 1871-97. *In progress.*   M
Meteorological Record. Vols. 6-16. *London*, 1886-96. *In progress.*   M
List of Fellows. *Lon lon*, 1878 9, 1886, 1888, 1890.   M

British Mothers' Journal.
London, 1856-64.   E

British North American Almanac.
Montreal, 1864.   P

Brit sh Quarterly Review. Vols. 53-56, 59-86. *New York* and *Philadelphia*, 1871-2, 1874-86.   P
Vols. 53-78. *London*, 1871-83.   L

British Review. 4 vols. *London*, 1812-5. K

British Workman. 1 vol. *London*, 1855-63. P

Brooklyn. School Reports, annual, 1 vol. 1856-62.   E

Brussels Academy of Science. *See* Académie (Impériale) et royale des Sciences et Belles-Lettres de Bruxelles.

Buffalo. School Reports, annual. 1863-74. E

Buffalo Historical Society.
Annual Reports. *Buffalo*, 1875-95.   P
Do. 1885-95.   C
Miscellaneous Papers. *Buffalo*, 1868, 1882, 1885-6, 1890-1.   P
Publications. Vols. 1-3, 4. *Buffalo*, 1879-80, 1896. *In progress.*   P

Buffalo Society of Natural Sciences.
Bulletin. Vols. 1-5. *Buffalo*, 1873-91. *In progress.*   U
Do. Vols. 1-4. *Buffalo*, 1873-83.   C

Builder. Vols. 1-20. *London*, 1843-62.   C
Vols. 8-72. *Lon'on*, 1850-97. *In prog'ess.*   P

Builder and Wood-Worker.
Vols. 20-21. *New York*, 1884-5.   P

Bulletin Archeologique. *See* Comité des Travaux historiques et scientifiques, etc Bulletin archéologique.

Bulletin de Correspondance Hellenique. *See* Ecole Française d'Athènes. Bulletin, etc.

Bulletin de Geographie, historique et descriptive. *See* Comité des Travaux historiques et scientifiques, etc. Bulletin de Géographie.

Bulletin des Recherches Historiques.
See Société des Etudes Historiques.

Bulletin des Sciences Naturelles et de Geologie. *See* Bulletin Universel des Sciences et de l'Industrie. Section 2. Bulletin des Sciences Naturelles.

Bulletin d' Histoire Ecclesiastique et d' Archeologie Religieuse.
Années 6-14. *Valence*, 1885-94. *In progress.* C

Bulletin Historique et Philologique.
See Comité des Travaux historiques et scientifiques, etc. Bulletin.

Bulletin Scientifique de la France et de la Belgique. (For Vols. 1-17 : Bulletin Scientifique, historique, et littéraire du Département du Nord et des Pays Voisins.)
Tom 1-25. *Lille, Paris,* 1869-93. U

Bulletin Universel des Sciences et de l'Industrie. Section 2 : Bulletin des Sciences Naturelles et de Géologie. 27 tom.
Paris, 1824-31. U

Bulwark. 6 vols. *Edinburgh,* 1852-6. K

Bureau fuer Bremische Statistik.
Jahrbuch für Bremische Statistik. Jahrg. 1889-96. *Bremen,* 1890-97. *In progress.* U

Bureau International des Poids et Mesures.
Travaux et Mémoires. Tom. 1-6. *Paris,* 1881-8. U

Bursian's Jahresbericht. See Jahresbericht über die Fortschritte der classischen Alterthumswissenschaft.

Butler's Educational Review.
Vols. 1-10. *New York,* 1891-95. *In progress.* E

Bystander. Vols. 1-3. *Toronto,* 1880-83. L
Vols. 1-2. *Toronto,* 1880-81. P.V
N.S., Vol. 1. *Toronto,* 1889-90. P.V

Caen - Academie des Sciences. See Académie (Impériale) des Sciences, etc. de Caen.

Calcutta Review. Vols. 1-19, 21-29. *Calcutta,* 1844-57. L

Calendars of State Papers. 186 vols. *London,* 1859-96. *In progress.* U

California.
School Reports, annual, 1851-60, 1864-5, 1870-80, 1883-84, 1891-93. E
State Horticultural Commissioners. Reports.
Sacramento 1882. C
State Viticultural Commissioners. Reports 1-2.
Sacramento, 1881-84. C

California Academy of Sciences.
Bulletin. Vols. 1-2. *San Francisco,* 1884-7. C
Occasional Papers. Vols. 1, 3-4. *San Francisco,* 1890-93. C
Proceedings. 2nd Series. Vols. 1-5. *San Francisco,* 1888-96. *In progress.* C

California Teacher. 10 vols. *Sacramento,* 1865-76. E

Californian. Vol. 3. *San Francisco,* 1892-3. I.

Calvin Translation Society. 52 vols. *Edinburgh,* 1843-55. K

Cambrian Archæological Association.
Archæologia Cambrensis, a record of the antiquities of Wales and the Marches, and the Journal of the Cambrian Archæo'ogical Association. 4th Series. 14 vols.; 5th Series. Vols. 1-13. *London,* 1870-96. *In progress.* P

Cambrian Journal. 11 vols. *Tenby,* 1854-64. P

Cambrian Register. Vols. 1-2 (1795-96). *London,* 1796-99. U

Cambridge and Dublin Mathematical Journal. See Cambridge Mathematical Journal.

Cambridge Classical Researches. See Museum Criticum.

Cambridge Mathematical Journal.
4 vols. *Cambridge,* 1839-45. U
Continued as :
Cambridge and Dublin Mathematical Journal.
9 vols. *Cambridge,* 1846-54. C.U

Cambridge Philological Society.
Proceedings. Pts. 7, 8, 10-42. *Cambridge,* 1884-95.
Transactions. Vols. 3, 8, 11-12, 14-15. *London,* 1871-95. C

Cambridge Philosophical Society.
Proceedings. Vols. 1-7. *Cambridge,* 1843-92. C
Transactions. Vols. 1-5. " 1822-34. U

Cambridge, Mass. School Reports, 1867-79. E

Camden Society.
1st Series. Nos. 1-105. *London,* 1838-72. P
2nd Series. Nos. 1-56. " 1871-96. *In progress.* P
Descriptive Catalogue of First Series, 2nd edition, *London,* 1872. (Camden Miscellany. 7 vols.
1st Series. Nos. 39, 55, 61, 73, 87, 104. 2nd Series. No. 14). P

Canada.
Lower Canada, 1792-1841.
Journals of the House of Assembly.
1st Parliament, Se-sions 2-4. 1793-6.
2nd " " 1-4. 1797-1800.
3rd " " 1-2. 1801-2.
4th " Session 1. 1805.
6th " " 1. 1810.
7th " Sessions 2, 4-5. 1812-13.
11th " Session 2. 1821-2. P
Proclamations, English and French, 1792-1836. I.
Proceedings of the Provincial Parliament, 1828-9. P
Journals of the Special Council. Vols. 1-6, 1838-41. P
Report of Select Committee on Civil Government of Canada, 1829. P.T
Review of the Proceedings of the Legislature in 1831. *Montreal* 1832. P.T
Upper Canada, 1792-1841.
Journal of the House of Assembly, 1792-1824.
1st Parliament, 1792-3.
2nd " Sessions 2-4. 1798-1800.
3rd " " 1-4. 1801-4.
4th " " 1-4. 1805-8.
5th " " 2-4. 1810-12.
6th " " 3. 5. 1814, 16.
7th " " 1-4, 6. 1817-19, 1820.
8th " " 1-3 (1st Session printed).
1821-3.
(*Type written from the original MSS. Where gap occurs no known copies exist.*)
Journals of the House of Assembly and Appendices. 24 vols. (Printed).
9th Parliament. Sessions 1-4. 1825-8.
10th " " 1-2. 1829-30.
11th " " 1-4. 1831-4.
12th " " 1-4. 1835-6.
13th " " 1-5. 1836-40.
28 vols. E.L.O.P
Index 1825-40. O.P.
Journals of the Legislative Council, 1792-3, 1798-1840. L
1825-40. O.T
Report on Internal Navigation, 1826. P
Reports on Public Departments, 1839. P

Canada (Upper and Lower), 1841-65.
Journals of the Legislative Assembly and Appen-
dices and Sessional Papers, 1841-66.   E. L. O. P
Do. 1854-66.   U
Index. 1841-66   2 vols.   P
Journals of the Legislative Council, 1841 66.
                                        E. L. O. P
Do. 1854-66.   U
Debates on Confederation, 1865.   E. P. T
Mirror of Parliament, 1846.   P
Thompson's Mirror of Parliament, 1860.   P
Board of Agriculture, Upper Canada. Trans-
actions.   *Toronto*, 1855 68.   P
See Ontario Agriculture and Arts Association.
Board of Registration and Statistics, Upper
Canada, Appendix to 1st Report, 1849.   T
Municipal Reports. Vol. 1, 1863. *Toronto*.   E
Report and Proceedings of the Select Committee
on charges against the late Administration.
Quebec, 1855.   P
Reports of Superintendent of Education, 1849-65.
                                                E. P
Reports of the Financial and Departmental
Commission. *Quebec*, 1863-4.   P
Canada (Dominion of), 1866-96.
Reports on Canadian Archives. (Brymner.)
1872 4. 1881-96. *In progress*.   O. P
1881-96. *In progress*.   E
1882-96. *In progress*.   C
1883-96. *In progress*.   L
1884-96. *In progress*.   U
Journals of the Senate. 36 vols. 1867-96.
In progress.   E. L. O. P. T. U
Journals of the House of Commons, with Appendices. 40 vols., 1867-96. *In progress*.
                                    E. L. O. P. T. U
Index, 1867-90. 2 vols.   O. P
Sessional Papers, House of Commons. 325 vols.
1867-96. *In progress*.   E L O P. U. V

The Sessional Papers contain the annual reports
of the following departments, as well as all important returns and statements made to the Parliament of
the Dominion of Canada :

Auditor-general.   Post Office.
Public Accounts.   Department of the
                              Interior.
Insurance.   Geological Survey.
Trade and Commerce.   Indians.
Inland Revenues.   North - West Mounted
                              Police.
Agriculture.   Secretary of State.
Archives.   Civil Service List.
Criminal Statistics.   Library of Parliament.
Public Works.   Minister of Justice.
Railways and Canals.   Militia and Defence of
                              Canada.
Marine and Fisheries.   Penitentiaries.
Steamboat Inspection. Trade and Navigation.
Debates of the House of Commons, 1870-72,
1875-96. *In progress*.   L O. P
Debates of the Senate, 1872, 1874-7, 1878-93,
1896. *In progress*.   P
Do. 1879-86. *In progress*.   L. O
Votes and Proceedings of the House of Com-
mons, 1867-8. 1870 2, 1879-82, 1885-91.   P
Budget Speeches. *Ottawa*, 1876-96. *In pro-
gress*.   P

Census.
1608-1871. 1 vol. *Ottawa*.   E. P
1851-2.   2 vols.   "   E. P. T. U
1861. *Quebec*.   E. P. U
1870 1. 4 vols. *Ottawa*, 1872. C. E. P. U. V
1880-1. 4 vols.   E. P. U. V
1890-1. Vols. 1-4. *In progress*. E. P. U. V
Geological and Natural History Survey. See
Geological.
Meteorological Reports. See Observatories :
Canada.
Patent Office.
Canadian Patents, 1824-55. 2 vols. *Toronto*,
1860-65.   P
Canadian Patent Office Record and Register of
Copyrights and Trade Marks. Vols. 1-25.
Ottawa, 1873-97. *In progress*.   O. P
Vols. 6-11, 14-25. *Ottawa*, 1878-97. *In
progress*.   L
See also Great Britain, United States, and
Victoria—Patents.
Statistical Abstract and Record of Canada,
Continued as :
Statistical Year-book of Canada. See Statistical
Year-book of Canada, 1890 96.
Official Post Office Guide, *Ottawa*.   P
See also names of Provinces of Canada.

Canada. A journal of religion, patriotism, science
and literature. Vol. 1. *Benton, N. B.*, 1891.   P

Canada Baptist Magazine. Vols. 1 and 3.
Montreal, 1837, 1840.   Mc.

Canada Business Directory.
Montreal and *Toronto*, 1851, 1853, 1857-8, 1864-
66, 1871, 1890.   P

Canada Ecclesiastique. Almanach annuaire
du clergé Canadien. *Montreal*, 1893.   P

Canada Educational Directory.
Toronto, 1876.   P

Canada Educational Monthly.
Vols. 1-19. *Toronto*, 1879-97. *In progress*. E. P
(Wanting Vols. 4, 7, E).
(Wanting Vol. 2, P).

Canada Farmer. Vols. 1-4. *Toronto*, 1864-67.
                                                  P

Canada Francais. Vols. 1-4 *Quebec*, 1888-91.
                                                  P

Canada Gazette. Commenced as Upper
Canada Gazette or American Oracle. 1793-1809
(imperfect).   L
Continued as : Upper Canada Gazette, New
Series. 1822, 1824, 1826-29, 1830-41.   P
Do. 1826-7, 1828-41, 1841.   L
Continued as : Canada Gazette. 1841-4, 1846-9,
1851-97. *In progress*.   P
1841-4, 1858, 1859 (part 2), 1865-97. *In
progress*.   L
See also Ontario Gazette, Quebec Gazette.

Canada, House of Commons. Alphabetical
list of members. *Ottawa*, 1890-91.   P

Canada Lancet. Vols. 3-5, 7, 9, 12. *Toronto*,
1871-7, 1879-80.   P
Vols. 15, 18, 20, 22-24. *Toronto*, 1883-91.   L
Vols. 21-29. *Toronto*, 1889 97. *In progress*. T. U

Canada Law Journal. *See* Upper Canada Law Journal.

Canada Lumberman. Vols. 1 3. *Toronto,* 1880 82. L

Canada Medical Association. Transactions. Vol. 1. *Montreal,* 1877. C.P

Canada Medical Journal. Vols. 4-5. *Montreal,* 1868 9. E

Canada School Journal. Vols. 1-12. *Toronto,* 1877 87. E

Canadian Agriculturist. Vols. 1-9, 12. *Toronto,* 1849-57, 1860. P
Vols. 13-15. *Toronto,* 1860-63. E

Canadian Almanac. *Toronto,* 1848-70, 1872 98. *In progress.* P
Toronto, 1848-90. *In progress.* E
Toronto, 1848-80. C

Canadian American. Vols. 2-5. *Minneapolis,* 1884-8. P

Canadian Antiquarian and Numismatic Journal.
1st Series. Vols. 1-13. *Montreal,* 1872-86.
2nd Series. Vols. 1-3. " 1889 94. P

Canadian Architect and Builder. Vols. 1-10. *Toronto,* 1888 97. *In progress.* P.S (Wanting Vol. 1, S).

Canadian Baptist *Toronto,* 1859, 1860-69, 1870 76, 1878, 1879, 1882-9. Mc.

Canadian Bee Journal. Vols. 1-8. *Beeton, Ont.,* 1885-93. P

Canadian, British American and West Indian Magazine. Vol. 1. *London,* 1839. P

Canadian Christian Examiner. Vols. 1-4. *Niagara,* 1837-40. K.P

Canadian Church Magazine. *See* Our Mission News.

Canadian Church Missionary Gleaner. Vol. 2. *Toronto,* 1897. *In progress.* T

Canadian Church Press. *Toronto,* May-Sept., 186 . V

Canadian Ecclesiastical Gazette. Vols. 1-9 *Toronto,* 1854-62. T

Canadian Electrical News and Steam Engineering Journal. N.S. Vol. 6. *Montreal* and *Toronto,* 1896. C

Canadian Engineer. Vols. 1-4. *Toronto,* 1893-7. *In progress.* P

Canadian Entomologist. Vols. 1-29 *Toronto,* 1869-97. *In progress.* C.P
(Wanting Vol. 17, C).

Canadian Gem and Family Visitor. Vol. 2. *Toronto,* 1849. P

Canadian Illustrated News. Vols. 1-28. *Montreal,* 1869-83. L.P (Wanting Vol. 12, L).

Canadian Independent. Vols. 4 6, 10-21. *Toronto,* 1858-75. Mc.
Vols. 6-7. *Toronto,* 1860-1. P

Canadian Independent Magazine. Vols. 5-31. *Toronto,* 1879-81. N.S. Vols. 1-6. *Toronto,* 1882-7. E

Canadian Indian. Vol. 1. *Owen Sound,* 1890 1. P.U

Canadian Institute.
Canadian Journal and Proceedings of the Canadian Institute.
1st Series. Vols. 1-3. *Toronto,* 1852-5. C.E.L.P.T.U
2nd Series. Vols. 1-15. *Toronto,* 1856 78. C.E.L.T.U
(Wanting Vol. 15, E).
3rd Series. Vols. 1 7. *Toronto.* 1879 90. C.P.T.U
Transactions. Vols. 1 5. *Toronto,* 1889 96. *In progress.* C.L.P.U
N.B.—Vol. 3, pp. 317-336 of the Transactions contains a classified index of the original papers from 1852-92.
Reports. *See* Ontario, Minister of Education, appendix to reports.

Canadian Journal. *See* Canadian Institute.

Canadian Journal of Medical Science. Vols. 1-6 *Toronto,* 1876-81. P
Vol. 7. *Toronto,* 1882. P
Continued as :
Canadian Practitioner. Vols. 8-10. *Toronto,* 1883-5. P
Vols. 13-14, 17-22. *Toronto,* 1889, 1891-7. *In progress.* E
Vols. 9-17. *Toronto,* 1884-92. L
Vols. 14-22. *Toronto,* 1891-7. *In progress.* U
Vols. 15-16, 19-22. *Toronto,* 1890-91, 1894-7. *In progress.* C

Canadian Journal of Oddfellowship. Vols. 1-2. *Stratford,* 1875 6. P

Canadian Law Times. Vols. 1-9. *Toronto,* 1881-89. U
Vols. 9-17. *Toronto,* 1889-97. *In progress.* E

Canadian Magazine. Vol. 1. *Toronto,* 1871. P

Canadian Magazine. Vols. 1 9. *Toronto,* 1893-97. *In progress.* E.L.O.P

Canadian Magazine and Literary Repository. Vols. 1, 4. *Montreal,* 1823, 1825. E

Canadian Manufacturer. Vol. 18. *Toronto,* 1890. E
Vols. 32-33. *Toronto,* 1895. *In progress.* C

Canadian Merchants' Magazine.
Vols. 1-3. *Toronto,* 1857-8. C
Vols. 2-4. *Toronto,* 1857-9. E
Vols. 1-4. *Toronto,* 1857-9. P

Canadian Methodist Magazine. Vols. 1-45. *Toronto,* 1875-97. *In progress.* E L.P.V
(Wanting Vols. 21-34, L).

Canadian Methodist Quarterly. Vols. 1-5. *Toronto,* 1889 93.
Continued as :
Canadian Methodist Review. Vols. 6-7. 1894-95. V
(Amalgamated with Canadian Methodist Magazine).

Canadian Military Institute. Selected papers from the Transactions. Nos. 1-5. *Toronto*, 1890-94. *In progress.* P

Canadian Mining Manual. *Ottawa*, 1890-91. P
Continued as : Canadian Mining, Iron and Steel Manual. *Ottawa*, 1894-97. *In progress.* P.S (Wanting 1894, P).

Canadian Mining Review. Vols. 5-6, 8-15. *Ottawa*, 1887-8, 1889-96. *In progress.* P
Vol. 15. *Ottawa*, 1896. *In progress.* C

Canadian Monthly and National Review. Vols. 1-13. *Toronto*, 1872-77.
Continued as :
Belford's Monthly Magazine. Vols. 1-3. *Toronto*, 1877-8.
Continued as :
Rose-Belford's Canadian Monthly and National Review. Vols. 1-8. *Toronto*, 1878-82. E.L.O P

Canadian Naturalist. See Natural History Society of Montreal. Canadian Naturalist, etc.

Canadian Parliamentary Companion. *Ottawa*, 1862, 1864, 1867, 1871-2, 1874, 1876-81, 1883, 1885, 1887, 1889, 1897. *In progress.* P
Do. *Ottawa*, 1869-84, 1891. E
Do. *Ottawa*, 1869, 1875, 1878, 1881, 1883, 1885, 1887, 1889. L

Canadian Photographic Journal. Vols. 1-6. *Toronto*, 1892-7. *In progress.* P

Canadian Poultry Chronicle. Vols. 1-2. *Toronto*, 1870-72. P

Canadian Presbyter. Vols. 1-2. *Montreal*, 1857-8. P

Canadian Record of Science. See Natural History Society of Montreal.

Canadian Review. Vols. 1-2. *Montreal*, 1824-6. L

Canadian Shoe and Leather Directory. *Toronto*, 1892.

Canadian Society of Civil Engineers. Transactions. Vols. 1-11. *Montreal*, 1887-97. *In progress.* C.S

Canadiana. A collection of Canadian notes. Vols. 1-2. *Montreal*, 1889-90. P

Canadien Illustre. Vol. 1. *Montreal*, 1881. P

Cape of Good Hope.
Votes and Proceedings of Parliament, with Appendices. 1882-1893. L
Annual reports on education. *Cape Town*, 1891-95. *In progress.* E

Caroline Almanac. *Rochester, N.Y.*, 1840. P

Carlsberg Laboratori.
Meddelelser. Bk. 1-2. *Kjobenhavn*, 1879-88. U

Carpenter and Builder. See Illustrated Carpenter and Builder.

Carpentry and Building. Vols. 7-8. *New York*, 1885-6. P

Cassel-Verein fuer Naturkunde. See Verein für Naturkunde zu Cassel. U

Cassell's Family Magazine. *London*, 1873-97. *In progress.* P

Cassell's Magazine. N.S. Vols. 1-19. *London*, n d.

Catalogue of Canadian Publications : Newspapers and periodicals. *Toronto*, 1890. P

Catholic, The. *Kingston, U.C.*, 1830. P

Catholic Presbyterian. Vols. 1-10. *London*, 1879-83. K.P

Catholic Weekly Register. Vols. 1-6. *Toronto*, 1887-92. Continued as :
Catholic Register. Vols. 1-5. *Toronto*, 1893-7. *In progress.* P

Catholic World. Vols. 6-52, 56-65. *New York*, 1867-97. *In progress.* P

Cellule (La), Recueil de Cytologie et d'Histologie generale. Tom. 1-13. *Lierre, Gand & Louvain* [1884-97]. *In progress.* U

Celtic Magazine. Vols. 3-4. *Inverness*, 1877-9. P

Celtic Society. Publications. *Dublin*, 1847-52. P (United in 1853 with Irish Archæological Society).

Celtic Society of Montreal. Transactions. *Montreal*, 1884-91. P

Central America. Meteorological reports. See Observatories : Central America.

Central-Organ fuer die Interessen des Realschulwesens. Jahrg. 1-13. *Berlin*, 1873-85. (Wanting Bd. 5). U

Centralblatt fuer allgemeine Pathologie und pathologische Anatomie. Bd. 4-7. *Jena*, 1893-6. *In progress.* U

Centralblatt fuer Bacteriologie und Parasitenkunde. Bd. 1-20. *Jena*, 1887-96. *In progress.* U

Centralblatt fuer Bibliothekswesen. Jahrg. 6-14, and Beihefte 9-17. *Leipzig*, 1889-97. *In progress.* (Wanting Jahrg. 7-9). U
Register, Jahrg. 1-10.

Centralblatt fuer die medicinischen Wissenschaften. Jahrg. 31-34. *Berlin*, 1893-6. *In progress.* U

Centralblatt fuer Physiologie. Bd. 1-9. *Leipzig* and *Wien*, 1888-96. *In progress.* U

Centralblatt fuer Rechtswissenschaft. Bd. 1-9. *Stuttgart*, 1882-9. U

Century Magazine.
Vols. 1-54. *New York*, 1870-97. *In progress.* P
Vols. 23-54. *New York*, 1881-97. *In progress.* L
Vols. 33-54. *New York*, 1886-97. *In progress.* E

Ceylon. Meteorological reports. See Observatories : Ceylon.

Chambers's Journal. *London*, 1832. L
Do. *London*, 1833-97. *In progress.*

Chap-Book. Vols. 1-7. *Chicago*, 1893-7. *In progress.* P

Chapman's Magazine of Fiction. Vols. 1-8. *London*, 1895-7. *In progress.* P

Charities Review. See Charity Organization Society. Charities Review.

Charity Organization Society. Charities Review. Vols. 1-5. *New York*, 1892-96. *In progress.* U

Chaucer Society.
Publications. 1st Series. Nos. 1-88.   U
    2nd "   " 1-29. *London*, 1867-
96. *In progress.*   U
Do.   1st Series. Nos. 1-76.   P
    2nd "   " 1-24. *London*, 1867-
87. *In progress.*   P

Chautauquan. Vols. 1-17, 19-25. *Meadville,
Pa.*, 1880-97. *In progress.*   L

Chemical Gazette.
Vol. 12-16. *London*, 1854-8.
2nd Series. Vol. 4. *London*, 1866.   C

Chemical News.
Vols. 1-12, 14, 57-76. *London*, 1860-97. *In
progress.*   U
Vols. 49-76. *London*, 1884-97. *In progress.* P
Vols. 70-76. *London*, 1894-7. *In progress.* T
Vols. 5, 53-76. *London*, 1862-97. *In progress.* C

Chemical Society of London.
Memoirs and Proceedings. Vols. 2-3. *London*,
1843-8.   U
(Quarterly) Journal. Vols. 1-70. *London*, 1849-96.
In progress.   U
  (Wanting Vols. 11 and 18).
Quarterly Journal. Vols. 7-12, 14, 18-19. *London*,
1855-60, 1862, 1866-7.   C

**Chemisch-pharmaceutisches Central-
blatt.** *See* Pharmaceutisches Centralblatt.

Chemisches Centralblatt. *See* Pharmaceutisches Centralblatt.

Chemist and Druggist. Vols. 14-15. *London*, 1873-4.   T

Chercheur (Le). Vols. 1-2. *Quebec*, 1888-9. P

Chetham Society.
Remains historical and literary connected with
the Palatine counties of Lancaster and Chester.
Vols. 1-114. *Manchester*, 1844-86.   P
  General Index to Vols. 1-32.
Vols. 32-114. *Manchester*, 1854-86.   U
  (Wanting Vols. 33, 35-7, 39-45, 47-8,
  50-1, 53-4).   U
2nd Series. Vols. 1-32. *Manchester*, 1883-
94. *In progress.*   P
2nd Series. Vols. 1-19, 23-36. *Manchester*,
1883-96.   U

Chicago.
Board of Public Works. Annual Reports.
Chicago, 1865, 1869.   C
Board of Trade. Annual reports of trade and
commerce. *Chicago*, 1858, 1865, 1888-93,
1895.   C
Department of Public Instruction. Annual re-
ports of Board of Education. *Chicago*, 1869-70.
                                                     C
School Reports, annual. *Chicago*, 1854-65,
1867-8, 1872-82, 1884, 1889, 1894-5.   E

Chicago Academy of Sciences.
Annual Reports. Nos. 38-39. *Chicago*, 1895-6.
In progress.   C

Chicago City Directory. *Chicago*, 1860.   P

Chicago Historical Society.
Collections. Vols. 1-3. *Chicago*, 1882-4.   P.U
Do. Vol. 4. *Chicago*, 1890.   C
Report of Annual Meeting. *Chicago*, 1888.   C
Reports of Quarterly Meetings. Jan.-Apr. 1889.
Chicago.   C

Child Garden, or Kindergarten.
Vol. 1. *Chicago*, 1892-3.   E

Chili. Meteorological Reports. *See* Observatories:
Chili.

China. Decennial Reports on Trade, Navigation,
etc., of Ports Open to Foreign Commerce, 1882-
1891.   L
Meteorological Reports. *See* Observatories : China.

Christian Advocate. *New York*, 1866-68. V

**Christian Examiner and Theological
Review.** Vols. 1-5. *Boston*, 1824-7.
Continued as :
Christian Examiner and General Review.
2nd Series. Vols. 1-13. *Boston*, 1829-35.
3rd series. Vols 1-17. *Boston*, 1836-44.
Continued as :
Christian Examiner and Religious Miscellany.
4th Series. Vol. 1. *Boston*, 1844.   Mc.

Christian Guardian. *Toronto*, 1829-96.
In progress.   Methodist Book Room.

**Christian Journal and Literary Reg-
ister.** Vols. 1-4, 7-14. *New York*, 1817-1830. T

Christian Magazine. Vol. 10. *Edinburgh*,
1806.   T

Christian Mirror. Vols. 1-3. *Montreal*,
1841-43.   P

**Christian Miscellany and Family
Visitor.** 1st Series. Vols. 1-4; 2nd Series. Vols.
2, 13-15 ; 3rd Series. Vol. 4. *London*, 1846-80. V

Christian Observer. Vols. 18-20, 22-37.
London, 1818-1837.   T

Christian Recorder. Vols. 1-2. *York, U.C.*,
1819-21.   P.T

Christian Remembrancer. Vols. 1-54.
London, 1819-1867.   T

Christian Review. Vols. 1-26. *Boston, New
York*, and *Baltimore*, 1836-61.   Mc.

**Christian Sentinel, and Anglo-Cana-
dian Churchman's Magazine.**
Vols. 1-3. *Montreal*, 1827-9.   P

Christian Social Union (Oxford University Branch).
Economic Review. Vols. 1-7. *London*, 1891-
97. *In progress.*   P.U

Christian Thought. *New York*, 1889-91. V

Christian Witness. Vols. 3-4, 6-7. *London*,
1846-1850.   V

Christian Work. *London*, 1864-72.   Mc.

Christian World Pulpit. Vols. 1-42.
London, 1871-92.   V

Chromolithograph. Vols. 1-2. *London*,
1867-9.   P

**Chronicles and Memorials of Great
Britain and Ireland during the
Middle Ages.** ("Rolls Chronicles.") Nos.
1-98 in 239 vols. *London*, 1858-96. *In progress.* U

Church (The). Vols. 1-11. *Cobourg, U.C.*, 1837-
1848.   T

Church Bells. Vols. 1-20, 22-26. *London*,
1871, 1890, 1891-6. *In progress.*   T

Church Chronicle. Vols. 1-3. *Toronto*, 1863-
1865.   T

Church Club Lectures, 1892. *New York*,
1893.   T

Church Missionary Intelligencer and Record. N.S. Vols. 6-8. *London*, 1881-3. T

Church of England.
Australia and Tasmania, Proceedings of the General Synod of Dioceses. *Sydney*, 1891. T
Canada.
Authorized Report of the First and Second Congress of the Church of England in Canada. *Hamilton*, 1883-4. T
General Synod. Journal of Proceedings of the 1st Session held at Toronto. *Kingston*, 1894. T
Provincial Synod, Proceedings. *Montreal* and *Quebec*, 1861-2, 1865, 1868, 1871-2, 1883, 1889, 1893, 1895. T
Year Book and Clergy List of the Church of England in Canada. *Toronto*, 1892, 1894-7. *In progress.* T

LOCAL REPORTS.

Algoma, Missionary Bishop of. Report, 1895-7. *In progress.* T
British Columbia, Report of Second Session of Fifth Synod, and of the Special Session of the Synod. *Victoria, B.C.*, 1891, 1893. T
Huron, Diocese of. Journal of Proceedings. *London*, 1896. T
Niagara, Synod of. Journal of Proceedings. *Hamilton*, 1885-6, 1896. T
Ontario, Synod of Diocese. Journals. *Kingston*, 1862-87, 1889, 1896. T
Ottawa, Synod of Diocese. Journal. *Ottawa*, 1896. T
Rupert's Land, Report of the Synod of the Diocese, with appendixes. *Winnipeg*, 1895. T
Outlook of Indian Missions in Rupert's Land. *Winnipeg*, 1893. T
Report of a Regular Meeting of the Provincial Synod. *Winnipeg*, 1891. T
Triennial Report to the Provincial Synod of the Indian Missions of the Ecclesiastical Province. *Winnipeg*, 1893. T
Toronto, Diocese of.
Canons and Resolutions. *Toronto*, 1851-71. T
Church Society, Constitution and Annual Reports. *Cobourg* and *Toronto*, 1842-68. T
Do., 1843-65. P
Synod, Proceedings of. *Toronto*, 1854, 1856-73, 1884. 1886, 1893-6. T
Holy Trinity, Church of. Report of Parochial Association Committee. *Toronto*, 1859. T
England.
Missionary Conference of the Anglican Communion. *London*, 1894. T
Official Year Book of the Church of England. *London*, 1883-91. T
United States.
Protestant Episcopal Church. Journals of Convention. *Philadelphia* and *Boston*, 1857, 1865, 1880. T
Reports of Congress. *New York*, 1881, 1885. T
New Jersey, Journal of Diocese. *Burlington*, etc., 1837, 1860, 1864-5, 1869-74, 1883. T
Journal of Diocese of Northern New Jersey. *Newark* and *Princeton*, 1875, 1879-81. T

Journal of Diocese of Newark. *Newark*, 1895. T
New York, Journal of Proceedings at Annual Convention. *New York*, 1817-8, 1828, 1868-72, 1890. T

Church of England Magazine.
Vols. 1-21. *London*, 1836-51. T

Church of England Quarterly Review.
Nos. 1-68 ; New Series. Nos. 1-17. *London*, 1837-58. (Incomplete. T). Mc.T

Church Quarterly Review.
Vols. 5-8, 27. *Boston*, 1877-9, 1889. Mc.

Church Quarterly Review.
Vols. 1-44. *London*, 1875-97. *In progress.* P
"   3-44. *London*, 1876-97. *In progress.* T

Church Review and Ecclesiastical Register.
Vols. 1-10. *New Haven*, 1848-58. P.T
Continued as :
American Quarterly Church Review.
Vols. 11-18, 20-23. *New Haven* and *New York*, 1858 71. P
Vols. 11-19. *New Haven* and *New York*, 1858-67. T
Continued as :
American Church Review. Vols. 27-30, 32-38, 41-2, 45. *New York*, 1875-84. T
Continued as :
Church Review. Vols. 46-50, 55-60. *New York*, 1885-91. P
Vols. 50-1, 54-7. *New York*, 1887, 1889-90. T

Churchman's Family Magazine.
Vols. 1-8. *London*, 1863-6. P

Churchman's Remembrancer.
York, U.C., 1827. T

Cincinnati. School Reports, annual. 1836-86. (Wanting 1865, 1874, and 1877). E

Cincinnati Society of Natural History.
Journal. Vols. 1-19. *Cincinnati*, 1878-97. *In progress.* P
Do. Vols. 4-19. *Cincinnati*, 1881-97. *In progress.* C

Circolo Matematico di Palermo.
Annuario. *Palermo*, 1896. C
Rendiconti. Tom. 1-10. *Palermo*, 1884-96. *In progress.* C
General index to Tom. 1-10 in Tom. 10.

Civil Engineer and Architects' Journal. Vols. 1-7, 20-26, 28-29. *London*, 1837-44, 1857-63, 1865-6. P
Vols. 1-19, 22-25. *London*, 1837-1862. C
Vols. 26, 28-30. *London*, 1863-67. U

Classical Journal. Vols. 1-22. *London*, 1810-20. U
(Wanting Vols. 17 and 18).

Classical Museum. 7 vols. *London*, 1844-1850. U

Classical Review. Vols. 1-11. *London*, 1887-97. *In progress.* U.V
Do. Vols. 8-11. *London*, 1894-7. Mc.

Claus's Arbeiten. *See* Zoologisches Institut der Universität Wien und der zoologischen Station in Triest. Arbeiten.

Clergy Lists. 9 vols. *London*, 1840, 1846·
1848, 1858, 1865 6, 1876, 1884.   T
Clerical Directory. *See* Crockford.
Cleveland. School Reports, annual. 1869-80. E
Clinical Society of London.
Transactions. Vols. 1-29. *London*, 1868-96.
In progress.   U
Index. Vols. 1-12.
Cobden Club. Publications. *London*, 1870·
1880.   L
[**Colburn's**] **New Monthly Magazine.**
See New Monthly Magazine.
**Collection de Documents inedits sur
l'Histoire de France.** 236 vol·. *Paris*,
1835-96. *In progress.*   U
**Colonial Church Chronicle and Mis-
sionary Journal.**
London, 1847 60, 1865-73.   P
London, 1856 67.   T
Colonial Enterprise. Vols. 1-6. *London*,
1894-1897. *In progress.*   T
Colonial Gazette. Vols. 6-7. *London*, 1844-45·
                                                  U
**Colonial Intelligencer and Abori-
gines' Friend.** Vols. 1-4. *London*, 1847-54·
Continued as :
Aborigines' Friend and Colonial Intelligencer.
Vol. 1. *London*, 1855-58.   U
Colonial Journal. Vols. 1-3. *London*, 1816-
17.   P
Colonial Magazine (Martin's). Vols. 1-8.
London, 1840-42. Continued as :
Fisher's Colonial Magazine. Vols. 1-4.
London, 1842-3.
Continued as :
Simmond's Colonial Magazine. Vols. 1-19,
21-23. *London*, 1844-50, 1851-2.
Continued as :
Colonial and Asiatic Review. Vols. 1-2,
London, 1852-3   P
Colonial Office List. 1874-77, 1879 80,
1882-89. *London*, 1874-89.   U
Colorado College Scientific Society.
Papers. Vols. 3, 5-6. *Colorado Springs*, 1892.
1895-6. *In progress.*   C
Colorado Scientific Society.
Proceedings. Vols. 1 4. *Denver*, 1883-93.   C
Columbia, District of. School Reports, annual.
1874-8.   E
Columbia College University Studies
Vols. 1 4. *New York*, 1891-1894.   L
**Comite des Travaux Historiques et
Scientifiques.**
Revue des Travaux Scientifiques. Tom. 1-15.
Paris, 1881-95. *In progress.*   U
Section des Sciences Économiques et Sociales,
Bulletin. 1883-91, 1893-5. *Paris*, 1883-96.
In progress.   U
Section d'Histoire et de Philologie.
Bulletin Archéologique. Années 1885-95.
Paris, 1885 95. *In progress.*   U
Bulletin de Géographie, historique et descrip-
tive. Années 1886-95. *Paris*, 1886-95. *In
progress.*   U
Bulletin (Historique et Philologique). Années
1884-95. *Paris*, 1884-95. *In progress.*   U

Table générale des Bulletins du Comité . . .
et de la Revue des Sociétés Savantes (to 1893).
                                                  U
Comite Geologique de Russie.
Bulletins. Vols. 1-14. *St. Péterbourg*, 1882-95.
In progress.   C
Mémoires. Vols. 1-2, 4-6, 8, 10. *St. Péterbourg*,
1883-6, 1887 95. *In progress.*   C
Commercial Year Book. Vols. 1-2. *New
York*, 1896-7. *In progress.*   P
Commission Scientifique du Mexique.
Archives. 3 tom. *Paris*, 1864-69.   U
**Companion to the Newspaper, and
Journal of Facts.** *London*, 1833.   P
Conchologist. Vols. 1-2. *London*, 1891-3.
Continued as :
Journal of Malacology. Vol. 3. *London*, 1894. P
**Conference of Charities and Correc-
tion.** Proceedings. 1874, 1877 8, 1881.
Continued as : National Conference of Charities
and Correction. 1882 97. *Boston* and *Madi-
son*, 1877 97. *In progress.*   P
Congregational Lectures. 13 vols. *Lon-
don*, 1852-4. (Wanting Vols. 6 and 8).   K
**Congres Periodique International des
Sciences Medicales.**
8me session, Copenhague, 1884 ; Compte-rendu.
4 tom. *Copenhague*, 1886.   U
Conjuror's Magazine. Vols. 1 2. *London*,
1792.   U
Connaisance des Temps. *See* Observa-
tories : France.
Connecticut. Legislative documents, 1879-96. L
Journals of the Senate, 1879-96.   L
Colonial Records. Vols. 7-15. *Hartford*, 1726-76.
                                                  L
Records of the State. Vols. 1-2. *Hartford*,
1776-80.   L
School Reports, annual. 1855-95. *In progress.*
                                                  E
**Connecticut Academy of Arts and
Sciences.**
Transactions. Vols. 1-8. *New Haven*, 1866-90.
                                                  U
Do. Vols. 1-8, 9 (pt. 1). *New Haven*, 1866 92.
                                                  U
Connecticut Common School Journal.
Hartford, 1838-74.   E
Connecticut Historical Society. Public
Records of the Colony of Connecticut, 1636 1677.
Hartford, 1850-2.   U
Connoisseur. Vols. 1-2. *n.T.*, 1887.   P
Contemporary Review. Vols. 1-72. *Lon-
don*, 1866 97. *In progress.*   L.P.U
(Wanting Vols. 1 9, 29-38, 45-50, U).
Continent. Vols. 5 6. *New York*, 1883-4.   P
Co-operative Wholesale Society. An-
nual. *Manchester*, 1884-5, 1889.   P
**Copenhagen—Royal Danish Scientific
Society.** *See* Kongeligt Dansk videnskabernes
Selskab.
**Copernicus-Verein fuer Wissenschaft
und Kunst zu Thorn.** Hefte 1-4 and 6.
Leipzig, Thorn, 1878-87.   U

Cornhill Magazine. Vols. 1-47. *London*, 1860-83.
N.S. Vols. 1-26. *London*, 1883-96.
3rd Series, Vols. 1-3. *London*, 1896-7.
In progress.   P

Cosmopolis. Vol. 4. *London*, 1896. *In progress.*   V

Cosmopolitan. Vols. 2-23. *New York*, 1886-97. *In progress.*   P
Vols. 12-23. *New York*, 1891-7. *In progress.*   L

✠ **Cosmos, Revue des Sciences et de leurs applications.** N.S. Tom. 12, 15-16, 39-42. *Paris*, 1889-1893.   C

Cosmos, Revue encyclopedique hebdomadaire des Progres des Sciences. Tom. 8-18. *Paris*, 1856-61.   U

Cosmos di Guido Cora. Sui Progressi piu recenti e notevoli della Geografia e delle scienze affini. Tom. 1-3, 5. *Torino*, 1873-79.   C

Courrier du Livre. Vol. 1. *Quebec*, 1896-7. *In progress.*   P

Craftsman and British Masonic Record. Vols. 1-3. *Hamilton*, 1866-69.
Continued as :
Craftsman and Canadian Masonic Record. Vols. 4-5. *Hamilton*, 1869-70.
Continued as :
Canadian Craftsman and Masonic Record. Vols. 24-28. *Hamilton*, 1889-94. *In progress.*   P

Crelle's Journal fuer Mathematik. *See* Journal für die reine und angewandte Mathematik.

Critic. N.S. Vols. 13-14, 16, 18-28. *New York*, 1890-97. *In progress.*   P

Critical Review. 1st Series. Vols. 1-40. *London*, 1756-1775.   L
2nd Series. Vols. 31-33. *London*, 1801.   T
3rd Series. Vols. 4-24. *London*, 1805-11.   U
4th Series. Vols. 1-4. *London*, 1812-13.   U

Critical Review. Vols. 1-7. *Edinburgh*, 1891-97. *In progress.*   T.V
Vols. 6-7. *Edinburgh*, 1896-7. *In progress.* U

Critical Review of Theological and Philosophical Literature.
Vols. 6-7. *Edinburgh*, 1896-7. *In progress.* Mc.

Crockford's Clerical Directory. *London*, 1882, 1891.   T

Cuba. Meteorological reports. *See* Observatories : Cuba.

Cumberland and Westmorland Antiquarian and Archæological Society. Publications. Extra Series. Vol. 8. *Kendal*, 1892.   P

Cunningham Lectures. 13 vols. *Edinburgh*, 1865-92.   K

Curio. Vol. 1. *New York*, 1887-8.   P

Current History. *Buffalo*, 1891-6. *In progress.*   L

Current Literature. Vols. 12-13. *New York*, 1893.   V

Dante Society.
Annual Reports, 1-15. *Cambridge*, (*Mass.*), 1882-96. *In progress.*   U

Dantzig—Naturfo: schaft. *See* Natur Dantzig.

Davenport Acad Sciences.
Proceedings.   Vols
Davenport, Iowa,
Do. Vols. 1 and 5.
1 — 6.

Day of Rest.   1 vol.

Decoration.   New
15-17. *London*, 1881-

Decorator and F
21-30. *New York*, 188

Demorest's Montl
Vols. 16-20. *New*

Denison Universi
Bulletin of Scientific
Granville, O., 1887-94.

Denmark. Meteoro
vatories : Denmark.

Dental Cosmos.
1888-9.

Detroit.   School I
1855-72.

Deutsche Anthre schaft in Nuern
grüssung der XVIII. K

Deutsche Chemis
Berichte. Jahrg. 1-
progress. (Wantin
General Register, 18

Deutsche Geogra;
Geographische Gesells

Deutsche Gesell pologie, Ethno chichte.
Correspondenzblatt,
1880-90.
Do., Jahrg. 14-

Deutsche Gesellsc Voelkerkunde O
Mittheilungen. Bd.

Deutsche Literatı
Berlin, 1892.

Deutsche Morge schaft.
Jahresbericht für d
Leipzig, 1846 [-47]
Wissenschaftlicher J
genländischen Stud
1867 [Hft 1 only],
zig, 1868-85.
Zeitschrift. Bd. 1-5
progress. Registe

Deutsche Rundsc
1889-96. *In progress*

Deutsche Shakes
Jahrbuch. Jahrg. 1-3
progress. (Wantin

Deutschen Mund
Nürnberg, Nordling
3-4).

Deutscher Palaestina-Verein.
Zeitschrift. Bd. 16 19. *Leipzig*, 1893-96.
Mittheilungen und Nachrichten, 1895. *Leipzig*,
1895. *In progress.* U

Dialect Notes. *See* American Dialect Society.

Diario de los Literatos de Espana.
7 tom. *Madrid*, 1737-42. U

Dietrichsen and Hannay's Royal Almanack and Nautical and Astronomical Ephemeris. 1843, 1845-71. *London*, [1843 71]. U

Dijon—Academie des Sciences, etc. *See* Académie des Sciences, Arts et Belles-Lettres de Dijon.

Dingler's Polytechnisches Journal. *See* Polytechnisches Journal.

Diogenes. Vols. 1-3. *Montreal*, 1868-70. P

Dissertationes philologicæ Argentoratenses selectæ. Vols. 4-10. *Argentorati*, 1880-86. (Wanting Vol. 5). U

Dolman's Magazine. Vols. 1-8. *London*, 1845-8.
New Series. Vol. 1. *London*, 1849. P

Dominion Annual Register. *Montreal* and *Toronto*, 1863-90. P
Do., 1878-1891. L
Do., 1878-1886. T

Dominion Educational Association.
Addresses and Proceedings. *Montreal*, 1893. P.T

Dominion Illustrated. Vols. 1-7. *Montreal*, 1888, 1891. P
Vols. 1, 3, 6. *Montreal*, 1888-9, 1890. L

Dominion Illustrated Monthly.
Vols. 1-3. *Montreal*, 1892-3. P

Dominion Medical Monthly and Ontario Medical Journal. Vol. 5. *Toronto*, 1895. C

Dominion Review. Vol. 1. *Toronto*, 1896. P

Douglas Jerrold's Shilling Magazine.
London, 1845. P

Dresden Museum. *See* Königliches zoologisches, etc. Museum zu Dresden.

Dresden—Verein fuer Erdkunde. *See* Verein für Erdkunde zu Dresden.

Dublin Magazine, or General Repertory of Philosophy, Belles-Lettres, etc. 2 vols. *Dublin*, 1820. U

Dublin Penny Journal. Vols. 1-4. 1832-36. V

Dublin Quarterly Journal of Medical Science. Vols. 30-52. *Dublin*, 1861-71. U

Dublin Review. New Series. Vols. 14-31. *London*, 1870-78. P
3rd Series. Vols. 1-5, 11-38. *London*, 1884-97. *In progress.* P

Dublin University Magazine. Vols. 1-90. *Dublin*, 1833-77. L
Vols. 20 28, 47-62. 67, 69-90. *Dublin*, 1842-6, 1856 63, 1866, 1867-77. P

Duluth, Minn. Board of Public Works. Annual Reports, 1890 91. *Duluth, Minn.*, 1890-91. P

Dumfriesshire and Galloway Natural History and Antiquarian Society.
Transactions. *Dumfries*, 1886-95. C

Early English Text Society.
Publications.
Original Series. Nos. 1-108. P.U
Extra Series. " 1-71. P.U
London, 1864-97. *In progress.*
(Wanting, Original Series, Nos. 13 and 14. U)

Eason's Almanac for Ireland. *Dublin*, 1884-7. P

Ecclesiologist.
Vols. 1-29. *London*, 1843-68. P
Vols. 1-3. *Cambridge*, 1843 4. Mc.

Echo (L') de la France. Vols. 1-9. *Montreal*, 1865-9. P

Echo (L') du Cabinet de Lecture Paroissial. *Montreal*, 1865-7. P

Eclectic Magazine. Vols. 13-70, 72-91. *New York*, 1848-78. L
Vols. 60-62, 72-119. *New York*, 1863-92. P

Eclectic Review.
1st Series. Vol. 4. *London*, 1808. T
" " Vol. 9. " 1813. V
2nd " Vols. 2-10. " 1815-23. V
4th " " 1-15. " 1837-44. U
" " Vol. 27. " 1850. P
5th " Vols. 1-12. " 1851-56. P
6th " " 1-4. " 1857-8. P
7th " " 1-5. " 1859-61. P
8th " " 1-3, 5. " 1861-62, 1863. P

Ecole Centrale des Travaux Publics (afterwards .cole Polytechnique).
Journal, Cahiers 1-64. *Paris*, [1795]-1894.
2 me Série. Cah. 1. *Paris*, 1895. *In progress.*
Table, Cah. 1-45. P

Ecole des Chartes.
Bibliothèque. Tom. 1-57. *Paris*, 1839-96. *In progress.* U

Ecole (Pratique) des hautes Etudes.
Annuaire : Section des Sciences historiques et philologiques, 1895-97. *Paris*, 1895-97. *In progress.* U
Bibliothèque : Sciences philologiques et historiques. Fasc. 1-113. *Paris*, 1869 (1872)-96. *In progress.* U
Bibliothèque : Section des Sciences naturelles.
Tom. 1-37. *Paris*, 1869 90. U
Physiologie expérimentale. Travaux du Laboratoire de M. Marey. Années 1875-79. *Paris*, 1876-80. U

Ecole (Speciale) des Langues Orientales vivantes.
Recueil de Textes et de Traductions. Vols. 1-2. *Paris*, 1889. U

Ecole Francaise d'Athenes et de Rome.
Bibliothèque. Fasc. 1-74. *Paris*, 1877-96. *In progress.* U

Ecole Francaise d'Athenes.
Bulletin de Correspondance Hellénique. Années 1-20. 'Αθηναι and *Paris*, (1877)-95. *In progress.* Table générale, 1877-86. U

Ecole Francaise de Rome.
Mélanges d'Archéologie et d'Historie. Années 3-16. *Paris, Rome*, 1883-96. *In progress.* U

Ecole libre des Sciences Politiques.
Annales. Années 1-11. *Paris*, 1886-96. *In progress.* U

Ecole Normale Superieure.
Annales Scientifiques. 8 tom. *Paris*, 1864-70.
  2 me Série. 12 tom. *Paris*, 1872-83.
  3 me "   12 "   "   1884-95.
  In progress.   U

Ecole Polytechnique. *See* École Centrale des Travaux publics.

Ecole Polytechnique de Delft.
Annales. Vols. 1-7. *Leiden*, 1885-91.   C

Economic Journal. *See* British Economic Association. Economic Journal.

Economic Review. *See* Christian Social Union (Oxford University branch). Economic Review.

Economist. Vols. 46-9, 55. *London*, 1888-1891, 1896. *In progress.*   L
  Vols. 50-55. *London*, 1892-96. *In progress.* P.U

Edinburgh Almanac. *Edinburgh*, 1828, 1838.   L

Edinburgh Annual Register.
Vols. 1-17. *Edinburgh*, 1808-24.   L
Vols. 17-19. *Edinburgh*, 1824-26.   T

Edinburgh Christian Instructor.
Vols. 10-30. *Edinburgh*, 1811-31.   K
Vols. 18-36. *Edinburgh*, 1819-37.   T

Edinburgh Geological Society. Transactions. Vols. 1-5. *Edinburgh*, 1866-88. C

Edinburgh Magazine. *See* Scots Magazine.

Edinburgh Medical Journal. Vols. 1-17 and 24 *Edinburgh*, 1855-78.   U
  (Wanting Vol. 17, part 2 ; and Vol. 24, part 2).

Edinburgh New Journal, Sciences and Arts. N.S. Vols. 2-13, 15-17. *Edinburgh*, 1855-63.   C

Edinburgh New Philosophical Magazine. 68 vols. *Edinburgh*, 1827-45.   K
  (Wanting Vols. 1, 3, 5, 7, 15-16, 43).

Edinburgh Review. Vols. 1-147. *Edinburgh*, 1802-1878.   O
  Index, Vols. 1, 80.
Vols. 1-80, 143, 146-153, 156-160, 164-9, 171-2. *Edinburgh*, 1802-90.   Mc
Vols. 1-186. *Edinburgh*, 1802-97. *In progress.*
  General index to Vols. 1-50.   P
  (Wanting Vols. 81-2, 89-90, 99-100, 103-6, 127-8, 137-140, 143-4).
Vols. 1-136, 139-159, 161-186. *Edinburgh*, 1802-1897. *In progress.*   U
Vols. 1-136 and 170-186. *Edinburgh* and *New York*, 1802 (1814)-97. *In progress.* U
  (Wanting Vols. 76, 122, 123, 126-130, 132-134). General Index to Vols. 1-80, in 3 vols.

Education. Vols. 1-15. *Boston*, 1880-95. *In progress.* (Wanting Vols. 2, 4-6).   E

Educational Expositor. Vols. 2-3. *London*, 1854-5.   E

Educational Journal. Vols. 1-9. *Toronto*, 1887-96. *In progress.*   E

Educational Record, Quebec. Vols. 1-14. *Montreal*, 1886-94.   E

Educational Review. Vols. 1-4. *New York*, 1891-92.   U

Educational Review, New Brunswick. *St. John, N.B.*, 1887-97. *In progress.*   E

Educational Times. *London*, 1849-83. U
  See also Mathematical Questions.

Educational Weekly. Vols. 1-5. *Toronto*, 1885-7.   E

Educationalist. Vol. 1. *Brighton, Canada*, 1860.   E

Egyptian Exploration Fund. 12 vols. *London*, 1880-94.   K

Electrical Engineer. Vols. 5-8, 10-19, 21-22. *New York*, 1886-96.   C

Electrical World. Vols. 17-29. *New York*, 1891-97.   S

Electrician. Vols. 12-37. *London*, 1883-96. *In progress.*   P
  Vols. 25, 27-8, 37. *London*, 1890, 1891-2, 1896. C
  In progress.

Elisha Mitchell Scientific Society.
Journal. Vols. 1, 3-6. *Raleigh*, 1883-90. U
  Do. Vols 1-5, 7-12. *Raleigh*, 1883-8, 1890-5. C

Emden—Naturforschende Gesellschaft. *See* Naturforschende Gesellschaft in Emden.

Encyclopedie Canadienne. Tom. 1. *Montreal*, 1842-3.   P

Encyclopedie d' Architecture, Journal mensuel. Tom. 1-12. *Paris*, 1851-62.
  Continued as :
  Gazette des Architectes et du Bâtiment. Tom. 1. *Paris*, 1863.   U

Engineer. Vols. 57-82. *London*, 1884-96. *In progress.*   P

Engineering. Vols. 1-59. *London*, 1866-95. L
Vols. 29-64. *London*, 1880-97. *In progress.* S
Vols. 59-64. *London*, 1895-7. *In progress.* P

Engineering and Building Record. *See* Sanitary Engineer.

Engineering and Mining Journal.
Vols. 30, 34, 36-7. *New York*, 1877, 1881, 1883, 1889-90.   T
Vols. 37-63. *New York*, 1884-97. *In progress.* P
Vols. 54-63. *New York*, 1892-97. *In progress.* S

Engineering Magazine. Vols. 7-12. *New York*, 1894-97. *In progress.*   S

Engineering News. Vols. 17-37. *New York*, 1887-97. *In progress.*   S

Engineering Record. Vols. 15-26. *New York*, 1886-92.   L

Engineering Societies. *See* Association of Engineering Societies.

Engineering Society of the School of Practical Science. Papers. Nos. 1-9. *Toronto*, 1885-96. *In progress.*   P.S.U

England. *See* Great Britain.

Englische Studien. Bd. 1-21. *Heilbronn*, 1877-96. *In progress.*   U

English Catalogue of Books. 1885-97. *London*, 1886-98. *In progress.*   E

English Dialect Society.
Publications. Nos. 1-73. *London*, 1873-96. *In progress.*   P.U

English Historical Review. Vols. 1-12. *London*, 1886-97. *In progress.*   P.U
Vols. 1, 3, 6-12. *London*, 1886, 1888, 1891-7. *In progress.*   T

English Historical Society.
Publications. 26 vols. *London*, 1838-56. P

English Illustrated Magazine.
Vols. 1-17. *London*, 1883-97. *In progress.* L.P

English Journal of Education. *London*, 1849-59, 1861. E

English Mechanic. Vols. 17-37, 40-65. *London*, 1873-83, 1885-97. *In progress.* P
Vols. 20-27, 29-30, 32-33. *London*, 1874-81. L

English Review. Nos. 1-35. *London*, 1844-1852. (*Incomplete*). T

Englishwoman's Review. Vols. 18-26. *Lonuon*, 1887-95. P

Entomological Society of Ontario. *See* Ontario Sessional Papers.

Entomologiske Foreningen i Stockholm.
Entomologisk Tidskrift. Vols. 13-18. *Stockholm*, 1892-7. *In progress.* C

Entomologist. Vol. 9. *London*, 1876. P

Ephemeris Epigraphica: Corporis Inscriptionum Latinarum Supplementum. Vols. 1-8. *Romae*, *Berolini*, 1872-92. *In progress.* U

Escola de Minas de Ouro Preto.
Annals. *Rio de Janeiro*, 1881-85. C

Essex Institute.
Bulletin. Vols. 1-19, 22-26. *Salem*, 1869-87, 1890-94.
Communications. Vols. 5-6. *Salem*, 1866-70.
Historical Collections. Vols. 1-31. *Salem*, 1859-95.
Proceedings. Vols. 1-4. *Salem*, 1848-65. C

Ethical Record. 3 vols. *Philadelphia*, 1888-90. U
Continued as:
International Journal of Ethics. Vols. 1-7. *Philadelphia*, 1891-97. *In progress.* U.V
Do. Vols. 4-7. *Philadelphia*, 1894-7. *In progress.* Mc

Etonian. Vols. 1-2. *Windsor*, 1820-21. P

Euphorion, Zeitschrift fuer Litteraturgeschichte. *See* Vierteljahrsschrift für Litteraturgeschichte.

Europa. (hrsg. von F. Schlegel). Bd. 1. *Frankfurt-am-Main*, 1803. U

Evangelical Christendom.
London, 1851-1876. Mc

Evangelical Magazine. Vols. 2-24. *London*, 1797-1816. T
Continued as:
Evangelical Magazine and Missionary Chronicle. Vols. 12, 15, 21-22. *London*, 1834-43. Mc

Evangelical Magazine and Theological Review. Vols. 1-9. *London*, 1815-23. Mc

Ex Libris Society. Journal. Vols. 1-7. 1891-7. *London*, 1892-8. *In progress.* P

Exeter Hall Lectures. *London*, 1845-65. L

Exposition des Beaux Arts. Salon de 1880-97. *Paris*, 1881-98. *In progress.* P

Expositor. 1st, 2nd and 3rd Series. *London*, 1875-1889. T
4th Series. Vols. 1-4, 6-14. *London*, 1882, 1890-96. *In progress.* Indexes to Vols. 1-10. V

Expository Times. Vol. 1. *Edinburgh*, 1889-90. T
Vols. 3-8. *Edinburgh*, 1891-7. *In progress.* V
Vols. 7-8. *Edinburgh*, 1896-7. *In progress.* Mc

Family Herald. Vols. 1-78. *London*, 1843-97. *In progress.* P

Farmer and Mechanic. Vols. 4, 10. *New York*, 1850, 1852. P

Farmer's Advocate. Vol. 21. *London, Ont.*, 1886. E

Farmers' Journal. Vol. 11. *Montreal*, 1858-9. E

Farmer's Magazine. Vols. 11-12. *Edinburgh*, 1810-11. T

Fauna und Flora des Golfes von Neapel, etc. *See* Zoologische Station zu Neapel. Fauna und Flora.

Fay's Deaf and Dumb American Annals. 3 vols. *Washington*, 1872-80. E

Feuille des Jeunes Naturalistes.
Années 11-18, 20-24. *Paris*, 1880-95. *In progress.* C

Field. V. ls. 40-42, 47-8, 61-2, 64, 67, 68, 70-90. *London*, 1872-97. *In progress.* P

Field Columbian Museum.
Publications. Nos. 1, 8-13. *Chicago*, 1894-96. *In progress.* U

Financial Reform Almanac. *London*, 1877, 1879-84, 1886-91, 1893, 1895-7. *In progress.* P

Financial Review. 1878 and 1889. *New York*, [1878-89]. U

Finanz-Archiv. Bd. 1-6. *Stuttgart*, 1884-89. U

Finska Vetenskaps Societet. (Societas Scientiarum Fennica).
Acta. Vols. 15-18, 20. *Helsingfors*, 1888-95. *In progress.*
Bidrag till Kännedom om Finlands Natur och Folk. Häft. 1-47. *Helsingfors*, 1858-88. (Wanting Häft. 2, 3, and 32). U
Häft. 40-48, 54-56. *Helsingfors*, 1886-91, 1894-5. *In progress.* U
Bidrag till Finlands Naturkännedom, Etnografi och Statistik. 10 Häfte. *Helsingfors*, 1857-64. (Wanting Häft. 5). U
Öfversigt af Förhandlingar. Vols. 27-34, 36-37. *Helsingfors*, 1884-95. *In progress.* C

Fisheries and Fishery Industries of the United States. *See* United States—Commission of Fish and Fisheries.

Fliegende Blaetter aus dem Rauhen Hause zu Horn bei Hamburg.
Serie 1, 2, 4, 7-16, 24, 25, 34, 35. *Hamburg*, 1845-78. U

Florida. School Reports, 1892-94. 1 vol. E

Folk-Lore. Vols. 1-8. *London*, 1890-97. *In progress.* P

Folk-Lore (Espanol). Biblioteca de las Tradiciones Populares Espanolas. Tom. 1-11. *Sevilla*, *Madrid*, 1883-86. P

Fonetic Herald. *Port Hope*, 1885-7. P

Fontes rerum Austriacarum. *See* Kaiserliche Akademie der Wissenschaften. Fontes rerum Austriacarum.

Fonti per la Storia d'Italia. *See* Istituto storico Italiano.

Foreign Quarterly Review. Vol. 12. *Philadelphia*, 1833.   V

Forest and Stream. Vol. 26. *New York*, 1886.   P

Fortnightly Review. Vols. 1-62. *London*, 1865-97. *In progress.*   P
Vols. 52-62   *London* and *New York*, 1889-97. *In progress.*   U

Forum. Vols. 1-23. *New York*, 1886-97. *In progress.*   L.P
Vols. 13 23. *New York*, 1892-97. *In progress.*   U

Foyer Canadien. Vols. 1-4. *Quebec*, 1863-6.   L.P

Foyer Domestique. *Ottawa*, 1877-79.   P

France. Meteorological reports. *See* Observatories : France.

Frank Leslie's Illustrated Paper. Vols. 63, 67. 69-85. *New York*, 1887, 1889, 1890 97. *In progress.*   P

Frankfort-am-Main — Physikalischer Verein. *See* Physikalischer Verein zu Frankfort-am-Main.

Frankfurter Verein fuer Geographie und Statistik.
Beiträge zur Statistik der ('reien) Stadt Frankfort (am Main) 5 Bde. *Frankfurt am-Main*, 1858 90.   U
Neue Folge (Im Auftrage des Magistrats, hrsg. durch das Statistische Amt). Hft. 1-2. *Frankfurt-am-Main*, 1893-95. *In progress.*   U

Franklin Institute of the State of Pennsylvania.
Journal. Vols. 6-132. *Philadelphia*, 1828-90. U
Do. Vols. 1-76, 78-86, 88 93, 99-105. *Philadelphia*, 1826-78.   L
Do. Vols. 51-100, 131-142. *Philadelphia*, 1851-96. *In progress.*   C

Franzoesische Studien. 7 Bde. *Heilbronn*, 1881-89.   U

Fraser's Magazine. Vols. 1-80. *London*, 1830 69. N.S. Vols. 1-26. *London*, 1870 82. L.P

Freemason's Magazine and Masonic Mirror. Vols. 2 6 ; N.S. Vols. 2-4. *London*, 1856-9, 1860-1.   P

Freemason's Quarterly Review. Vols. 1-2, 4-16. *London*, 1834-5, 1837-49.   P

Freies deutsches Hochstift zu Frankfurt-am-Main.
Berichte. Neue Folge. Bd. 2-5. *Frankfurt-am-Main*, 1886 89.   U

Fribourg—Societe des Sciences Naturelles. *See* Société Fribourgeoise des Sciences Naturelles.

Fun. Vols. 1-10. *London*, 1862-69.   L
Vols. 15-38, 45-6, 52, 56, 58. *London*, 1872-83, 1887, 1890, 1892-93.   P

Furniture Gazette. Vols. 21-30. *London*, 1884-93.   P

Garden. Vols. 25-52. *London*, 1884-97. *In progress.*   P

Garden and Forest. Vols. 1-10. *New York*, 1888-97.   P

Gardeners' Chronicle. Vols. 1-33. N.S. Vols. 1-16. *London*, 1841-1881.   P

Gartenlaube. 4 vols. *Leipzig*, 1884-1887. P

Gazette des Architectes et du Batiment. *See* Encyclopédie d'Architecture.

Gazzetta Chimica Italiana. Vols. 15, 21, 22 pt. 2, 24-26. *Palermo*, 1885-1895. *In progress.*   C

Gegenwart. Bd. 1-12. *Leipzig*, 1848-57.   U

General Baptist Repository. *London*, 1833.   Mc

General Magazine. *London*, 1776.   P

Genesee Farmer. Vols. 1-2. *Rochester*, 1831-2.   P

Gentleman's and Citizen's Almanack. *Dublin*, 1786-90, 1808.   P
Continued as :
Treble Almanack. *Dublin*, 1812-13, 1823, 1828-9.

Gentleman's Diary, or The Mathematical Repository. 1833. *London*, [1833].   U

Gentleman's Magazine. Vols. 1-257, 264-282. *London*, 1731-1884, 1888-97. *In progress.* P
Do. Vols. 224-247. *London*, 1868-79.   Mc

Gentlewoman. Vols. 4-6, 10. *London*, 1892-3, 1895.   P

Geographical Journal. *See* Royal Geographical Society. Geographical Journal, etc.

Geographical Society of Australasia.
Proceedings. Vols. 1-4. *Sydney*, 1885-6.
Special volume of the proceedings, 1885.   P

Geographical Society of California.
Bulletin. Vol. 2. *San Francisco*, 1894.   C

Geographical Society of Quebec.
Transactions. Vols. 1-2. *Quebec*, 1880-97. *In progress.*   C

Geographische Abhandlungen. Bd. 1-3. *Wien* and *Olmutz*, 1887-89.   U

Geographische Gesellschaft fuer Thuringen.
Mittheilungen. Bd. 1-9, 11. *Jena*, 1882-'91, 1892.   C

Geographische Gesellschaft in Bern.
Jahresberichte, 7-14. *Bern*, 1884-95.   C

Geographische Gesellschaft in Muenchen.
Jahresberichte, 2-13. *München*, 1872-89.   U
(Wanting No. 3).
Jahresberichte, 12-16. *Munchen*, 1887-96. *In progress.*   C

Geographische Gesellschaft zu Bremen. (Also called Verein für die Deutsche Nordpolarfahrt). Deutsche Geographische Blätter. Bd. 12-19. *Bremen*, 1889-96. *In progress.*   C

Geographische Gesellschaft zu Hannover.
Jahresberichte. *Hannover*, 1879, 1883-92.   C

Geographische Gesellschaft zu Wien. *See* Kaiserlich-Königliche geographische Gesellschaft.

Geographisches Jahrbuch zur Mittheilung aller wichtigern neuen Erforschungen. *See* Physikalischer Atlas. Geographisches Jahrbuch, etc.

Geological and Natural History Survey of Canada.
Reports. 1843-94. *Montreal* and *Ottawa*, 1844-97. *In progress.* P
Do. 1850 94. *Montreal* and *Ottawa*, 1851-97. *In progress.* L
Do. 1843-94. *Montreal* and *Ottawa*, 1844-97. *In progress.* V
Do. 1852-96. *Montreal* and *Ottawa*. *In progress.* U
Do. 1853-6, 1863-6, 1870-94. *Montreal* and *Ottawa*. *In progress.* O
Do. 1858 94. *Ottawa*, 1859 97. *In progress.* E
Do. 1845-57, 1870 94. *Ottawa*, 1846-97. *In progress.* C
Do. 1874-95. Mc.
1881-94. *Ottawa*, 1882-97. *In progress.* S
Maps to reports. C.P
Summary report, 1885-90. *Ottawa*, 1886-91. T
Publications.
Catalogues of Canadian Plants.
Parts 1-6. *Montreal*, 1883-92. T.P
Parts 1, 3-6. " 1883-92. C
Catalogues of (1) Museum, (2) Mineral Exhibits displayed at Centennial Exhibition, Philadelphia ; (3) Exhibits at Cincinnati Exhibition ; (4) at World's Columbian Exposition, Chicago (bound in one vol.). *Ottawa*, 1893. P.C
Comparative Vocabularies of the Indian Tribes of British Columbia. *Montreal*, 1884. P.T
Contributions to Canadian Micro-Palæontology. Parts 1-4. *Ottawa*, 1883-92. C.P.T
Contributions to Canadian Palæontology.
Vol. 1, parts 1-4. *Ottawa*, 1885-92. C.P.T
" 2, part 1. *Ottawa*, 1895. C.P
" 3, part 1. *Ottawa*, 1891. C.P
Figures and Descriptions of Canadian Organic Remains. Decades 1-4. *Montreal*, 1858-65. P
List of Canadian Hepaticæ. *Montreal*, 1890. P.T
" Publications. 1879. P.V
Mesozoic Fossils. Vol. 1 (parts 1-3). 1876-84. C.P
(Wanting part 1, C).
Palæozoic Fossils. Vols. 1, 2 (part 1), Vol. 3 (parts 1-3), 1865-95. C.P

Geological and Polytechnic Society of the West Riding of Yorkshire.
Proceedings. Vol. 2. *Leeds*, 1842 48. C

Geological Magazine, or Monthly Journal of Geology.
New Series. Decade III. Vols. 6-10. *London*, 1889-93.
Decade IV. Vols. 1-3. *London*, 1894-96. *In progress.*

Geological Record. *London*, 1874-76. C

Geological Society of America.
Bulletin. Vols. 1-7. *Washington* and *Rochester*, 1890-96. *In progress.* U

Geological Society of Dublin.
Journal. Vols. 1-6, 8, 10. 1833-59. *Dublin*, 1838-60.
(Vol. 10 contains index to Vols. 1-10).
Continued as :
Royal Geological Society of Ireland.
Journal. Vols. 1-5. 1804-80. *London*, 1867-80. C

Geological Society of Glasgow.
Transactions. Vols. 1-3, 6-9. *Glasgow*, 1863-91. C
Do. Vols. 6-9. *Glasgow*, 1879-91. U

Geological Society of London.
Proceedings. 4 vols. (1826-45). *London*, 1834-46. C.L.U
Continued as :
Quarterly Journal. Vols. 5-52. *London*, 1845-96. *In progress.* U
Do. Vols. 2, 5, 10-28, 29 (pt. 3), 30-53. *London*, 1842-97. *In progress.* C
Do. Vols. 34-53. *London*, 1878-97. *In progress.* P
Transactions. 5 vols. *London*, 1811-21. U
New series. Vols. 1-3. *London*, 1824-35. U

Geologiska Forening i Stockholm.
Förhandlingar. Bde. 10-18. *Stockholm*, 1888-96. *In progress.* C

Geologist, a Popular Magazine of Geology.
Vols. 1-4. *London*, 1858-61. U

Georgia Historical Society.
Collections. Vols. 2-4. *Savannah*, 1841-78. C
Do. Vol. 4. *Savannah*, 1878.

Germania, Vierteljahrsschrift fuer deutsche Alterthumskunde.
37 Bde. *Stuttgart, Wien*, 1856-92. U
Germanistische Studien, Supplement zur Germania. 2 Bde. *Wien*, 1872-75. U

Germanischer National-Museum.
Mittheilungen. *Nürnberg*, 1889-95. *In progress.* C
Anzeiger. *Nürnberg*, 1890-95. *In progress.* C

Germanistische Abhandlungen.
Hft. 1-8. *Breslau*, 1882 91. U

Germanistische Studien. *See* Germania.

Gesellschaft fuer deutsche Philologie.
Jahresbericht über die Erscheinungen auf dem Gebiete der germanischen Philologie. Jahrg. 1-17 (1879 95). *Berlin, Dresden* and *Leipzig*, 1880-96. *In progress.* U

Gesellschaft fuer Erdkunde zu Berlin.
Verhandlungen. Bd. 1-23. *Berlin*, 1873-96. *In progress.* U
Bd. 11-15, 17-19, 21-23. *Berlin*, 1884-8, 1890 92, 1894-6. *In progress.* C
Zeitschrift. Bd. 20-30. *Berlin*, 1885 95. *In progress.* U

Gesellschaft naturforschender Freunde zu Berlin.
Sitzungsberichte. Jahrg. 1874-89. *Berlin*, 1874-89. U

Gesellschaft fuer vaterlaendische Alterthuemer. *See* Antiquarische Gesellschalt n Zürich.

Gewerbehalle. *Stuttgart*, 1885. P

Gifford Lectures. *London*, 1888-96. *In progress.* U

Gilbert's Annalen. *See* Annalen der Physik.

Giornale del Genio Civile. Parte Ufficiale. Vols. 19-27, 29-33. *Roma*, 1881-95. *In progress.* C
Parte Non-Ufficiale. Serie 4. Tom. 1-2, 4-5. Serie 5. Tom. 1-3. *Roma*, 1881-9. C
Disegni. Serie 4. Tom. 1 6. Serie 5. Tom. 1-2. *Roma*, 1881-8. C

Giornale di Filologia Romanza. *See* Rivista di Filologia Romanza.

Giornale Storico della Letteratura Italiana. Vols. 1-28. *Torino*, 1883-96. *In progress.* U

Giurisprudenza Internazionale. Anno I. *Napoli*, 1893. C

Glasgow Colonial Society (for Promoting Improvement of Scottish Settlers in British North America).
Annual Reports. *Glasgow*, 1826-35. 3 vols.
Correspondence and original letters, 1821-43, in MS., 9 vols.
Minutes in MS., 2 vols. K

Glasgow Geological Society. *See* Geological Society of Glasgow.

Glasgow Natural History Society. *See* Natural History Society of Glasgow.

Glasgow Philosophical Society. *See* Philosophical Society of Glasgow.

Globe Annual and Encyclopædia of Useful Information. *Toronto*, 1896-7. *In progress.* P.E

Globus, illustrirte Zeitschrift fuer Laender-und Voelkerkunde. Bd. 1-11. *Hildburghausen, Braunschweig*, 1862-67. U

Goerlitz-Naturforschende Gesellschaft. *See* Naturforschende Gesellschaft zu Görlitz.

Goerres-Gessellschaft zur Pflege der Wissenschaft im katholischen Deutschland.
Festschriften, 2 nos. *Koln*, 1880-85. U
Historisches Jahrbuch. Bd. 7-17. *München*, 1886-96. *In progress.* C
Jahresberichte, 1877-89. *Koln*, 1878-90. U
Philosophisches Jahrbuch. Bd. 1-9. *Fulda*, 1888-96. *In progress.* U
Vereinschriften, 31 nos. *Koln*, 1877-89. U

Goethe-Gesellschaft.
Schriften. Bd. 1-10. *Weimar*, 1885-95. *In progress.* U

Goethe-Jahrbuch. Bd. 1-17. *Frankfurt-am-Main*, 1880-96. U
Gesammtregister. Bd. 1-10.

Goettingen - Georg - Augusts - Universitaet. *See* Königliche Gesellschaft der Wissenschaften zu Göttingen. Nachrichten, etc.

Goettingen-Koenigliche Gesellschaft der Wissenschaften. *See* Königliche Gesellschaft der Wissenschaften zu Göttingen.

Good Words. *London*, 1861-96. *In progress.* L
Do. *London*, 1863-1896. *In progress.* P

Gornozavodskaya. Proizvoditelnost Rossii v 1882 godu. *S. Petersburg*, 1884. U

Gornui Institut.
Gornui Jurnal izdannui Uchenuim Komitetom. God. 1877-8. *S. Petersburg*, 1877-78. U

Gospel Magazine. Vol. 2. *London*, 1767. T

Gospel Tribune. Vols. 1-3. *Toronto*, 1854-57. P.E

Government Year-Book. *London*, 1888-9. P

Grampian Club.
Publications. 22 vols. *Edinburgh* and *London*, 1870-1884. P

Grand Annuaire de Quebec. (1881-82.) *Quebec*, 1881-82. U

Grand Lodge of Ancient Free and Accepted Masons of Canada.
Proceedings. 1856-1896. *Hamilton*, 1874-96. *In progress.* P

Grand Magazine of Magazines.
Vols. 1-2. *London*, 1758-9. P

Grand National Curling Club Annual. *New York*, 1868-9, 1880-1. P

Grand Priory of the United Orders of the Temple and Hospital [Knights Templar, St. John of Jerusalem, Palestine, Rhodes and Malta] for the Dominion of Canada.
Proceedings. *Montreal, Toronto*, 1872-85, 1888-92. P

Graphic. Vols. 1-27, 30-55. *London*, 1869-97. *In progress.* P
Vols. 1-3, 7-38, 40-51. *London*, 1869-95. L

Great Britain (State Papers).
State Papers relative to the war against France.
Vols. 1-10. *London*, 1794-1801. (Wanting Vol. 10, L.) L.P
State Papers. Vols. 1-30. *London*, 1801-23. P
British and Foreign State Papers, 1812-82.
73 vols. *London*, 1841-89. U
Do. 1812-60. L.
Do. 1814-17, 1820-8. P
Bulletins and other State Intelligence, 1813-88.
113 vols. *London*, 1813-88. U
Imperial White Books. Vols. 1-2. *London*, 1886-7. P
Record Commissioners' Publications (various).
62 vols. *London*, 1805-52. U

Parliamentary.
House of Lords. Journals, 1509-1896- *London*, n.d. *In progress.* L
Do. Do. 1691-1767. O
House of Commons. Journals, 1547-1896. *London*, n.d. *In progress.* L
Do. Do. 1547-1802. O
Parliamentary History of England, 1066-1803 (Cobbett). 36 vols. *London*, 1806-20. L.O
Continued as:
Parliamentary Debates, 1803-96 (Hansard).
4 Series. *London*, 1803-96. *In progress.* L.O
Parliamentary or constitutional history of England, 1106-1660. 24 vols. *London*, 1751-62. L
Debates in the House of Commons, 1667-94 (Grey). 10 vols. *London*, 1763. L
Debates in Parliament, 1668-1711 (Torbuck).
21 vols. *London*, 1741-2. L
Parliamentary Register (Debates), 1743-1801. 88 vols. *London*, 1774-1801. L
The Senator, or Clarendon's Parliamentary Chronicle, 1790-94. 10 vols. *London*, 1790-95. L

Mirror of Parliament, 1828-41 (Barrow). 60 vols. *London*, v.d. L
Parliamentary Chronicle (Northcroft). Vols. 1-2. *London*, 1833-34. L

Educational.
Committee of the Council of Education.
Annual report. *London*, 1840-96. *In progress.* E
Minutes. *London*, 1844, 1846-50. T
" " 1851-55. V
Education Enquiry Abstract. 4 vols. *London*, 1819-35. E
International Congress on Education. Proceedings. 4 vols. *London*, 1884. E
National Society. School reports, 2 vols. *London*, 1841-7. E
Report on education, Manchester and Salford. *London*, 1852-3. E
School and College Inquiry, England. 4 vols. *London*, 1862. E
School Inquiry, England. 20 vols. *London*, 1861-9. E
School reports, England. 2 vols. *London*, 1835-51. E
School reports, England and Scotland. *London*, 1846-9. E
School reports, Irish, English and Scotch. *Dublin*, 1832-51. E
Science and Art Department. Examination papers, 2 vols. *London*, 1867-77. E
Reports. *London*, 1853-60. E
Patents.
Specifications of Patents, 1617-1895. *In progress.* P
Plates of specifications, 1852-1863. P
Abridgments, 1588, 1888. *In progress.* P
Abridgment Class and Index Key, 1897. P
Amendments, 1879-1891. *In progress.* P
Indexes.
Subject-matter index, 1617-1872, 1876-92.
Index to fire-arms and projectiles, 1717-1853.
Alphabetical index of patentees, 1617-1864, 1867-9, 1871-2, 1874-88.
Chronological index of patents, 1617-1863, 1867-75.
Reference index of patents, 1617-1852.

Green Bag. Vols. 1-9. *Boston*, 1889-97. *In progress.* L.O.P

Greenock Philosophical Society.
Annual Report. *Greenock*, 1889-96. *In progress.* C

Grinchuckle. Vol. 1. *Montreal*, 1869-70. P

Grip. Vols. 1-42. *Toronto*, 1873-4. L.P
(Wanting Vols. 39-40, L).

Grip Cartoons. Vols. 1-2, 1873. *Toronto*, 1875. P

Grumbler. 2 vols. *Toronto*, 1858-9. P

Guardian of Education. Vols. 1-5. *London*, 1802-6. V

Hakluyt Society.
Publications. Nos. 1-95. *London*, 1848-96. *In progress.* P
Do. Nos. 4, 9, 11, 13-35, 38-95. *London*, 1850-96. *In progress.* U

Half-Yearly Abstract of the Medical Sciences, &c. Vols. 29-48. *London*, 1859-68. U

Haliburton Club.
Proceedings. Nos. 1-2. *Windsor, N.S*, 1889-97. *In progress.* P

Hall's Journal of Health. Vols. 36-38. *New York*, 1889-92. P

Hamburg — Naturwissenschaftlicher Verein. *See* Naturwissenschaftlicher Verein in Hamburg.

Hamburg—Verein fuer naturwissenschaftliche Unterhaltung. *See* Verein für naturwissenschaftliche Unterhaltung zu Hamburg.

Hamburgische wissenschaftliche Anstalten. *See* Jahrbuch der Hamburgischen wissenschaftlichen Anstalten.

Hamilton Association.
Journal and proceedings. Nos. 1-12. *Hamilton*, 1882-96. *In progress.* C.P
(Wanting Nos. 3-5, C).
Do. Nos. 8-12 *Hamilton*, 1892-6. *In progress.* U

Hanau—Wetterauische Gesellschaft, &c. *See* Wetterauische Gesellschaft, &c.

Handbook of Jamaica. 1883-9. *London* and *Jamaica*, 1883-88. U
Do. 1883-5. *London* and *Jamaica*, 1883-4. P

Handbuch der chemischen Technologie. *Brunswick*, 1862-97. *In progress.* S

Hanserd Knollys Society.
Publications. 9 vols. *London*, 1846-49, 1850, 1853-4. Mc

Hansische Geschichtsblaetter. *See* Verein für Hansische Geschichte. Hansische Geschichtsblätter.

Harleian Society. Publications. Vols. 25-39. *London*, 1887-96. *In progress.* U
Visitations. Vols. 8-41. *London*, 1873-97. *In progress.* P
Registers. Vols. 1-13, 15-21, 23. *London*, 1877-87, 1889-95, 1897. *In progress.* P
Registers. Vols. 9-21. *London*, 1884-96. *In progress.*
(Wanting Vol. 15 of Registers). U

Harper's Bazar. Vols. 17, 20-30. *New York*, 1884, 1887-97. *In progress.* P

Harper's Magazine. Vols. 1-94. *New York*, 1850-97. *In progress.* P
Index to Vols. 1-85.
Vols. 2-5, 7-93. *New York*, 1850-96. *In progress.* L

Harper's Weekly. Vols. 1-41. *New York*, 1857-97. *In progress.* P

Hartford. Report on Deaf and Dumb Asylums, 1817-81. 1 vol. E
School Reports. E

Hartford Seminary Record. Vols. 2-8. *Hartford*, 1892-98. *In progress.* P.U

Hart's Army List. *London*, 1864, 1867-69, 1871, 1873-77, 1879, 1881. L
Do. *London*, 1884-98. *In progress.* P

Harvard Law Review. Vols. 6-10. *Cambridge*, 1893-96. *In progress.* U

Harvard Magazine. Vols. 1-2. *Cambridge*, 1854-56. E

Harvard Museum of Comparative Zoology. *See* Museum of Comparative Zoology at Harvard College in Cambridge.

Harvard Studies in Classical Philology. Vol. 1. *Boston*, 1890. U

Harvard University Publications.
Harvard Historical monographs. Nos. 1-2. *Boston*, 1890-91.   P

Harvard Historical Studies.
Vols. 1-5. *New York*, 1896 8. *In progress.*   P

Hazell's Annual. *London*, 1889, 1891-03.   L

Hebraica, a quarterly journal in the interests of Semitic Study.
Vols. 3-6, 8, 11.   *New Haven, Chicago,*
1886-94.   Mc
Vols. 3-11. *New Haven, Chicago.* 1886-94.
(Wanting Vol. 4).   U
Continued as :
American Journal of Semitic Languages.
Vols. 12-13. *Chicago*, 1895-6. *In progress.* T.U

Helios.   Gesammtgebiete d. Wissenschaften.
Abhandlungen und monatl. Mittheilungen.
Vols. 10-13. *Berlin*, 1892-96. *In progress.* C

Herald of Peace. *London*, 1861-1881.   Mc

Hermathena, a Series of Papers on Literature, Science and Philosophy, by Members of Trinity College, Dublin. Vols. 1-9. *Dublin*, 1873-96. *In progress.*   U

Hermes, Zeitschrift für classische Philologie.
Jahrg. 1-31. *Berlin*, 1866-96. *In progress.* U
General-Register, Bd. 1-25.   (Wanting Bd. 26).

Herrig's Archiv. *See* Archiv für das Studium der neueren Sprachen und Literaturen.

Hibbert Lectures. 1878-80, 1882-9, 1891-4.
London, 1879-95. *In progress.*   K
1878 94. *London*, 1879-95. *In progress.*   P
1879-86 and 1891-94. *London*, 1880 (1884-95). U

Highland (and Agricultural) Society of Scotland.
Journal. *Edinburgh*, 1854-5.   C
Transactions.   4th Series.   Vols. 4-5, 8-20.
Edinburgh, 1872-88.   L
4th Series. Vols. 9 18, 20.   *Edinburgh*,
1877-1888.   P
5th Series. Vols. 1-5. *Edinburgh*, 1889-93. L

Historic Society of Lancashire and Cheshire.
Proceedings and Papers. (after Vol. 6 : Transactions). Vols. 3-31. *Liverpool*, 1851-79.
(Wanting Vols. 22-24).   U

Historical and Archæological Society of Ireland. *See* Kilkenny Archæological Society.

Historical and Philosophical Society of Ohio.
Annual Reports. *Cincinnati*, 1889-92, 1894, 1896. *In progress.*   C

Historical and Scientific Society of Manitoba.
Annual Reports. *Winnipeg*, 1880-96. *In progress.*   P
Do. *Winnipeg*, 1889, 1893-6. *In progress.* U
Do. *Winnipeg*, 1882-96. *In progress.*   C
Transactions. Nos. 1-50. *Winnipeg*, 1879-97. *In progress.*   P
Do. Nos. 35-38, 43, 45-50. *Winnipeg*, 1889-97. *In progress.*   U
Do. Nos. 1-3, 5 - 33, 35 - date   C

Historical Collections of Louisiana.
Parts 1-2, 5.   *New York* and *Philadelphia*, 1846-50, 1853.   P
Continued as :
Historical Collections of Louisiana and Florida.
New series. *New York*, 1869.   P

Historical Magazine.   Vol. 1.   *London*, 1789.   T

Historical Magazine.
1st Series. Vols. 1-7, 9. *Boston* and *Morrisania*, 1857-63, 1865.   P
2nd Series. Vols. 1-9. *Morrisania*, 1867-71.
C.L.P
3rd Series. Vols. 1-2.   *Morrisania*, 1872-3.
C.L.P

Historical Manuscripts Commission.
Reports 1-7. *London*, 1870-79.   U

Historical Register, 1716-37.   22 vols.
London, 1717 [38].   L

Historical Register. Vols. 1-3.   *Washington*, 1812-14.   T

Historical Society of Pennsylvania.
Memoirs. Vols. 1-4. *Philadelphia*, 1826-50. P
Vols. 5-12. *Philadelphia*, 1855-76.   U
Vols. 5-7, 10-13. *Philadelphia*, 1858 91.   C
Pennsylvania Magazine of History and Biography.
Vols. 1-13. *Philadelphia*, 1877-89.   U
Vols. 1-21. *Philadelphia*, 1877-97. *In progress.* (Wanting Vol. 13, 9).   C.P

Historische Gesellschaft des Kuenstlerverein (zu Bremen). *See* Künstlerverein.

Historische Gesellschaft fuer die Provinz Posen. Zeitschrift. Jahrg. 9-19.
Posen, 1894-97. *In progress.*   C

Historische Zeitschrift.
Bd. 51-52 and 70-77. *München* and *Leipzig*, 1884-96. *In progress.* Register, Bd. 1-56. U

Historischer Verein fuer Niedersachsen. Zeitschrift. *Hannover*, 1885-96. *In progress.*   C

Historischer Verein fuer Steiermark.
Mittheilungen. Hefte 36 44. *Graz*, 1888-96. *In progress.*   C

Historisches Taschenbuch.
10 Jahrg. *Leipzig*, 1830-39.
Neue Folge. 10 Jahrg. *Leipzig*, 1840-49.
3te   "   10   "   "   1850-59.
4te   "   10   "   "   1860-69.
5te   "   10   "   "   1871-80.
6te   "   Jahrg. 1-9.   "   1882-90. U

History of the Year.
Toronto, 1891, 1893-4.   P

Hollandsche Maatschappij der Wetenschappen. 3de Verz. Deel II. Nos. 3, 5-6. *Harlem*, 1874-7.   C

Home (The).   4 vols.   *New York* and *Buffalo*, 1857-59.   E

Home and Foreign Record of the Canada Presbyterian Church. *See* Presbyterian Church.

Home and School.   Vols. 4-5.   *Louisville*, 1875-76.   E

Homiletic Quarterly.   Vols. 1-8.   *London*, 1877-82.   E

Homiletic Review. Vols. 9-24. *New York*, 1879-94. V

Homilist. 1st Series. Vols. 1-7. *London*, 1852-8. V
 2nd Series. Vols. 1-4. *London*, 1859-62. V
 3rd " Vols. 1-10. *London*, 1863-67. V
 4th " Vols. 1-4. *London*, 1868-9. V
 Editor's Series. Vols. 1-12. *London*, 1870-75. V
 Editor's Enlarged Series. Vols. 1 6. *London*, 1876-78. P
 Do. Vol. 4. *London*, 1877. V
 Excelsior Series. Vols. 1-7. *London*, 1879-82. V

Hong Kong. Blue Book. *Victoria, Hong Kong*, 1889-96. *In progress.* C
 Sessional Papers, 1887-96. C

Horen (Die). (hrsg. von Schiller). Jahrg. 1795-97. *Tubingen.* U

Horticultural Society.
 Transactions. 1st Series. Vols. 1-7. *London*, 1815-1830. Mc
 Do. 2nd Series. Vols. 1-2. *London*, 1835 42. C

Household Words. (ed. by Charles Dickens). Vols. 1-18. *London*, 1850-58. U
 Vols. 5-19. *London*, 1852-9. P
 New Series (with which is incorporated All the Year Round). Vols. 29 32. *London*, 1895 7. *In progress.* P
 Household Narrative of Current Events, being a monthly supplement to Household Words. 1850-51. *London*, 1850-51. U

Howitt's Journal of Literature and Popular Progress. Vols. 1-3. *London*, 1847-8. P

Hulsean Lectures. *London*, 1826. T
 Do. *Cambridge, London* and *Edinburgh*, 1820-93. K
 (Wanting years 1826, 1835, 1847-8, 1864 7, 1873, 1884-5).
 Do. *London*, 1859, 1883-4, 1893-4. P

Humanitarian. Vols. 1-2. *New York*, 1892-3. P

Hunt's Merchant's Magazine and Commercial Review.
 Vols. 1-54. *New York*, 1839 66. L
 Vols. 16-21, 33-35, 37-39, 41-42, 44 45. *New York*, 1847-1861. P
 Vols. 27-44, 52 (Part 2), 54-59, 61 (Part 1), 62 (Part 2). *New York*, 1852-61. C
 Vols. 36-61. *New York*, 1857-69. E

Ibis. 5th Series. 6 vols. *London*, 1883-8. P
 6th Series. 6 vols. *London*, 1889-94. P
 7th Series. Vols. 1-3. *London*, 1895-97. *In progress.* P

Illinois. Reports to General Assembly, 1877-81. L
 Natural History Survey. Ornithology. Vol. 1. *Springfield*, 1889.
 State Board of Health. Reports. *Springfield*, 1883-4. P
 State Laboratory of Natural History. Bulletin. Vol. 2, 4-5. *Champaign, Springfield*, 1884-95. C
 School Reports, annual, 1857-80, 1883-88. E

Illinois State Agricultural Society. Transactions, with Notices and Proceedings of County Societies and Kindred Associations. Vols. 2-4. *Springfield*, 1857 60. C

Illinois Teacher. 14 vols. *Peoria, Ill.*, 1858-70. E

Illustrated Archæologist. Vols. 1-2. *London*, 1893-4. P

Illustrated Canadian Almanac. *Toronto*, 1889. P

Illustrated Carpenter and Builder. Vols. 14-15, 17-40. *London*, 1883-97. *In progress.* P

Illustrated London News.
 Vols. 1-110. *London*, 1842-97. *In progress.* P
 Vols. 2-41. *London*, 1843 62. Mc
 Vo's. 12-83. *London*, 1848-83. U

Illustrated Times. Vols. 1-14. *London*, 1855 62; N.S. Vols. 1-13. *London*, 1862-71. P

Imperatorskoye Sanktpeterburgskoye Mineralogieskoye Obshchestvo (or Russisch-kaiserliche mineralogische Gesellschaft zu St. Petersburg).
 Materialui dlya Geologii Rossii. Tom. 1-7. *Sanktpeterburg*, 1869-77.
 Zapiski. Chast. 1-6. *Sanktpeterburg*, 1866-71. U

Imperial and Asiatic Quarterly Review. Vols. 9-10. *Woking, Eng.*, 1895. L

Imperial Federation. Vols. 1-4. *London*, 1886-89. U
 Vois. 3, 8. *London*, 1888, 1893. U

Imperial Institute Year Book. *London*, 1892, 1894, supplement 1895. P

Imperial University of Japan. College of Science, Journal. Vols. 4-8. *Tokyo*, 1891-5. *In progress.* C

Independent Whig. *London*, 1814. L

Index Society. Publications. Vols. 1-11, 13. *London*, 1879 82. P

India.
 Geological Survey of India.
 Annual Reports. *Calcutta*, 1859-67. C
 Memoirs. Vols. 1-24. *Calcutta*, 1856-91. C
 Index to Vols. 1-20.
 Memoirs. Palæontologia Indica.
 Series 1. Series 9. Vol. 1.
 " 2. Vol. 1. " 10. Vols. 1-3.
 " 4. Vol. 1. " 11. Vol. 2.
 " 5. Vol. 2. " 12. Vol. 3.
 " 6. Vol. 3. " 13. Vols. 1-2.
 " 7. Vol. 1. " 14, 15. Vol. 2.
 " 8. Vol. 4. *In progress.* C
 Records. *Calcutta*, 1861-95. Vols. 1-28. *Calcutta*, 1868-95.
 Name index to Vols. 1-20.
 Subject index to Vols. 1-20.
 Survey of India Department.
 General Report of Operations. *Calcutta*, 1884-94. C
 Great Trignometrical Survey of India. Account. Vols. 4, 10-15 (explorations for years 1872-92). *Dehras Dun*, 1836 93. C
 Government Central Museum. Catalogues. *Madras*, 1888-94. C
 Meteorological reports. *See* Observatories : India.
 Reports on the Administration of the Meteorological Department of the Government of India. 1881-88. (Wanting Reports for 1884-85). U

Indian. Vol. 1. *Hagersville, Ont.*, 1885-6. P

Indian Antiquary. Vols. 15, 18-24. *Bombay*, 1886 95. *In progress.* C

Indian Engineering. Vols. 1-4. *Calcutta,* 1887-8. U

Indian Evangelical Review. *Madras,* 1883, 1885, 1887, 1890-92. Mc

Indiana. School Reports, annual, 1852-80. (Wanting 1865, 1871-74, 1877-78.) E

Indiana Academy of Science. Proceedings, 1891-93. *Brookville,* 1892-94. C.U

Indiana School Journal. Vol. 2. *Indianapolis.* 1857. E

Industries : A Journal of Engineering, Electricity and Chemistry for the Mechanical and Manufacturing Trades. Vols 1-5 and 7 (imperfect). *London* and *Manchester,* 1886-89. U

Inland Architect and News Record. Vols. 15-18, 21-28. *Chicago,* 1890-92, 1893-97. *In progress.* P
Do. Vols. 21-28. *Chicago,* 1893-97. *In progress.* S

Insect Life. *See* United States : Department of Agriculture, Entomology.

Institut ; Journal des Académies et Sociétés scientifiques de la France et de l'Étranger. Tom. 4 6. *Paris,* 1836-38. U

Institut Archeologique Liegeois. Bulletin. Tom. 24-25. *Liège,* 1894-5. *In progress.* C

Institut Canadien de Quebec. Annuaire. Nos. 1-13. *Quebec,* 1874 89. P
Do. Nos. 1,3-5,7,12-13. *Quebec,* 1874-89. C

Institut de Droit International. Annuaire. Années 1, 2, 8 and 9. *Gand,* 1877-88. U

Institut de France. *See* Académie des Inscriptions et Belles-Lettres, *and* Académie (Royale) des Sciences.

Institut Egyptien. Bulletin. 2me Série. Nos. 9-10.
3me Série. Nos. 1-6. *Caire,* 1888-95. C.Mc
Comité de Conservation des Monuments de l'Art Arabe. Procès Verbal et Rapport. *Caire,* 1890-94. C

Institut fuer Oesterreichische Geschichtsforschung. Mittheilungen. Vols. 11-17. *Innsbruck,* 1890-96. *In progress.* C

Institut International de Statistique. Bul etin. Tom. 1-9. *Rome,* 1886-96. *In progress.* U

Institut National Genevois. Bulletin. Tom. 29-33. *Genève,* 1889-95. C
Mémoires. Tom. 17. *Genèva,* 1886-89. C

Institut Royal Grand-Ducal de Luxembourg. Publications. [Section des Sciences Naturelles et Mathématiques] Tom. 21-24. 1891-96. *In progress.* C

Institute of Actuaries. Journal, and Assurance Magazine. Vols. 1-25. *London,* 1851 1886. P
Index to Vols. 1-20.

Institute of Bankers. Journal Vols. 1-15. *London,* 1879-94. *In progress* P
General index to vols. 1-15.

Institute of Jamaica. Journal. Vols 1-2. *Kingston, Jamaica,* 1891-96. *In progress.* C
Special Publications. No. 1. 1891. C

Institution of Civil Engineers. Proceedings. Vols. 1-126. *London,* 1837-96. *In progress.* P
Do. Vols 59-126. *London,* 1879-96. *In progress.* U
Do. Vols. 31-126. *London,* 1870.96. *In progress.* C
Name index to vols. 1-58. C.P
Subject index to vols. 1-126. P
Do. Vols. 59-118. U
Transactions. Vols. 1-3. *London,* 1836 42. C

Institution of Civil Engineers of Dublin. Transactions. Vols. 15, 17, 19, 23-25. *Dublin,* 1883-96. *In progress.* C

Institution of Engineers and Shipbuilders in Scotland. Transactions. *Glasgow,* 1885-96. *In progress.* C

Institution of Mechanical Engineers. Proceedings. 1847-94. *Birmingham, Westminster,* [1847-94] *In progress.* U
Do. 1877-96. *Birmingham, Westminster. In prog ess* S
General index, 1847-73. S

Instituto Fisico-Geografico. Anales. Nos. 2-6. *San Jose,* 1889-93. M

Instituto Geografico Argentino. Boletin. Vols. 11-14, 16-17. *Buenos Aires,* 1890-96. *In progress.* C

Instituto Historico, Geographico, e Ethnographico de Brazil. Revista Trimensal. Tom. 46, 49-50, 52-58. *Rio de Janeiro,* 1883-96. *In progress.* C

Instructor and Select Weekly Advertiser. *London,* 1814. V

Insurance Society and Fireman's Review. Vols. 1-5.
Continued as :
Insurance and Finance Chronicle. Vols. 6-16. *Montreal,* 1881-96. *In progress.* C

Insurance Year-Book. *New York,* 1888. P

International Journal of Ethics. *See* Ethical Record.

International Magazine. Vol. 2. *New York,* 1852. E

International Sanitary Conference. 1881. *Washington,* 1881. U

International Standard. *Cleveland,* 1884-5, 1887. P

Internationale Monatsschrift fuer Anatomie und Histologie. (After Bd. 3: Internationale Monatsschrift für Anatomie und Physiologie). Bd. 1-13. *Paris, Leipzig, London,* 1884-96. *In progress.* U
General Register, Bd. 1-10.

Internationale Polarforschung, 1882-83.
Beobachtungs Ergebnisse der österreichischen
Polars'ation Jan Mayen. Bd. 1-3. *Wien,* 1886.
Beobachtungs-Ergebnisse d r deutschen Sta-
tionen. Bd. 1 and 2. *Berlin,* 1886.　U

**Internationale Zeitschrift fuer allge-
meine Sprachwissenschaft.**
Bd. 5. *Heilbronn,* 1890.　U

**Internationaler statistischer Con-
gress in Berlin.** 5te Sitzungsperiode.
Berichte über die Verhandlungen. 2 Bde.
Berlin, 1865.　U

**Inventor's Advocate and Patentees'
Recorder.** Vols. 1-5. *London,* 1839-41.　P

Investor's Review. Vols. 7-8. *London,*
1896.　L

Iowa.
Documents, 1874-1878.
Journals of the Senate, 1874-1878.
Journals of the House, 1872-1878.　L
School Reports, annual, 1848-89.　E

Iowa Historical Records. Vols. 1-12.
Iowa, 1885-96. *In progress.*　U

Iowa School Journal. 4 vols. 1862-71.
De Moines.　E

Iowa State University.
Bulletin from the laboratories of Natural History.
Vol. 3. *Iowa,* 1894-96. *In progress.*　P

Ireland.
Census 1857, 6 vols. *Dublin.*　E
House of Commons Journals. Vols. 1-22, 24-
31. 1613-1794　L
Meteorological reports. *See* Observatories:
Ireland.
Reports Respecting the Public Records. Vols.
11-15, 1821-1825.　L
Reports of the Commissioners of National Edu-
cation in Ireland.
Vols. 1-5 (1834-50). *Dublin,* 1851.　U
Do. 1834-54. *Dublin.* (Wanting 1852).　V
Do. 1834-76, 1886. *Dublin.*　E
School Inquiry, 1868. 6 vols. *Dublin.*　E
Science and Art, Commissioners' Report, 1868.
London.　E
See also Great Britain.

Irish Archæological Society.
Tracts relating to Ireland. Vols. 1-15. *Dublin,*
1841-51.　L
Publications. *Dublin,* 1841-6, 1848-51.　L
(United in 1853 with Celtic Society).　P
Continued as :
Irish Archæological and Celtic Society. Publi-
cations. *Dublin,* 1857, 1860, 1862, 1864,
1868-80.　P

Irish Congregational Magazine.
Vols. 1-5, 7-9. *Dublin,* 1862-1875.　Mc

Irish Record Publications. 11 vols.
Dublin, 1861-95. (Wanting one vol. of the series).
In progress.　U

Iron. *See* Mechanics' Magazine.

Iron and Steel Institute.
Journal. *London,* 1872, 1886 (pt. 2), 1887-96.
In progress.　C
Index, 1869-84.

"Isis." *See* Naturwissenschaftliche Gesellschaft
"Isis."

Isis Moderne. Vol 1. *Paris,* 1896-7. *In
progress.*　P

**Istituto Fisico-Geografico y Museo
Nacional.**
Tom. 3-4. *Costa Rica,* 1892-3.　C

Istituto Storico Italiano.
Fonti per la Storia d'Italia. 15 vols. *Roma,*
1887-93. *In progress.*　U

Italy. Meteorological reports. *See* Observatories :
Italy.

Jahrbuch (hrsg. von Schumacher). *Stuttgart*
and *Tübingen.* 1838-41.　U

Jahrbuch der Chemie. Jahrg. 1-6 (1891-93).
Braunschweig, 1892-97. *In progress.*　U

**Jahrbuch der Hamburgischen wis-
senschaftlichen Anstalten.**
Jahrg. 1-11. *Hamburg,* 1882-92.　U
Jahrg. 7-13. *Hamburg,* 1889-95. *In progress.* C
Beiheft zum Jahrg. 10-13, Hefte 1-4, 1892-5.　C

Jahrbuch fuer Bremische Statistik.
See Bureau für Bremische Statistik. Jahrbuch.

**Jahrbuch fuer Gesetzgebung, Verwal-
tung und Rechtspflege des deutschen Reichs.** 4 Jahrg. *Leipzig,* 1871-76.
Continued as :
Jahrbuch für Gesetzgebung Verwaltung und
Volkswirthschaft im deutschen Reich. Jahrg.
1-20. *Leipzig,* 1877-96. *In progress.*　U

**Jahrbuch fuer romanische und en-
glische Sprache und Literatur.**
Bd. 2-12. *Berlin, Leipzig,* 1859-73.
Neue Folge. Bd. 1-3. *Leipzig,* 1874-76.　U

Jahrbuecher fuer deutsche Theologie.
Stuttgart, Gotha, 1856-71.　Mc

**Jahrbuecher fuer Nationaloekonomie
und Statistik.** 34 Bde. Neue Folge, 21
Bde. 3 te Folge, Bd. 3-12. *Jena,* 1863-96. *In
progress.*
Register Bd. 1-50.

**Jahrbuecher fuer wissenschaftliche
Botanik.** Bd. 1-29. *Berlin, Leipzig,* 1858-96.
In progress.　E

**Jahresbericht des Ausschusses fuer
Beobachtungsstationen der Voegel
Deutschlands.** *See* Allgemeine deutsche
ornithologische Gesellschaft zu Berlin. Journal für
Ornithologie, &c.

**Jahresbericht ueber die Erscheinun-
gen auf dem Gebiete der germanischen Philologie.** *See* Gesellschaft für
deutsche Philologie.

**Jahresbericht ueber die Fortschritte
der Anatomie und Physiologie.**
20 Bde. *Leipzig,* 1873-91　U

**Jahresbericht ueber die Fortschritte
der classischen Alterthumswissen-
schaft** (hrsg. von Bursian). Bd. 1-65. *Berlin,*
1873-90.　U
See also Biographisches Jahrbuch für Alterthumskunde.

**Jahresbericht ueber die Fortschritte
der Physiologie.** Bd. 1-4 (1892-95). *Bonn,*
1894-96. *In progress.*　U

Jahresbericht ueber die Fortschritte der (reinen pharmaceutischen, und technischen) Chemie, &c., 1847-89. *Giessen,* 1849-95. *In progress.* U
Register, 1847-76, in 3 vols.

Jahresbericht ueber die Fortschritte der Thierchemie. Bd. 1-24. *Wiesbaden,* 1873-97. *In progress.* S

Jahresbericht ueber die Fortschritte in der Lehre von den pathogenen Mikroorganismen. Jahrg. 1-10 (1885-94). *Braunschweig,* 1886-96. *In progress.* U
Namen-und Sach-Register, Jahrg. 1-5.

Jahresbericht ueber die Leistungen der chemischen Technologie. *Leipzig,* 1892-97. *In progress.* S

Jahresbericht ueber die Leistungen und Fortschritte in der gesammten Medicin. Jahrg. 7-8 (1872-73). *Berlin,* 1873-74. U

Jahresberichte der Geschichtswissenschaft. Jahrg. 9 (1886). *Berlin,* 1889. U

Jahresberichte fuer neuere deutsche Litteraturgeschichte. Bd. 1-5 (1890 94). *Stuttgart, Leipzig,* 1892-96. *In progress.* U

Jamaica. Reports on Education, annual. *Kingston,* 1887-95. *In progress.* E

Jamaica Society of Arts.
Transactions. Vols. 1-2. *Kingston,* 1854-6. C

Japan.
Meteorological reports. *See* Observatories : Japan.
School Reports, annual. *Tokyo,* 1887-92, 1894. *In progress.* E

Jefferson County Historical Society.
Transactions. Vols. 1-4. *Watertown, N. Y.,* 1886-96. *In progress.* P

Java. Meteorological reports. *See* Observatories : Java.

Jenaische Zeitschrift. *See* Medizinisch-naturwis-enschaftliche Gesellschaft zu Jena. Jena-ische Zeitschrift. etc

Jewish Quarterly Review. Vol. 1. *London,* 1889. U

Johns Hopkins Hospital.
Reports. Vol. 2. *Baltimore,* 1890. U
Bullet n. Vols. 1-7. *Baltimore,* 1889-96. *In progress.* U

Johns Hopkins University.
Circulars. Vols. 5-10, 12, 14-15. *Baltimore,* 1885-96. *In progress.* C
Studies in Historical and Political Science. Vols. 1-14. *Baltimore,* 1883 96. *In progress.* O.P.U
Do. Extra Vols. 1-16. *Baltimore,* 1886-97. *In progress.* P

Journal d' Hygiene. Vols. 10, 12-16. *Paris,* 1885-91. L

Journal de l'Anatomie et de la Physiologie normales et pathologiques de l'homme et des animaux.
Années 1-32. *Paris,* 1864-96. *In progress.* U

Journal de L'Instruction Publique.
Vols. 1-22. *Montreal,* 1858 78.
N.S. Vols. 1 3, 5, 8 12. *Montreal,* 1881-94. E

Journal de Mathematiques Elementaires et speciales. 1 re Série. 5 tom.; 2 me Série. 5 tom.; 3 me Série. 5 tom.; 4 me Série. 5 tom. *Paris,* 1877-96. *In progress.* U

Journal de Mathematiques pures et appliques. 1 re Série. 20 tom.; 2 me Série. 19 tom.; 3 me Série. 10 tom.; 4 me Série. 10 tom.; 5 me Série. Tom. 1-2. *Paris,* 1836-96. *In progress.* U

Journal de Micrographie. Tom. 1-10. *Paris,* 1877-87. (Wanting Tom. 7). U

Journal de Physique, theorique et appliquee. 1 re Série. 10 tom.; 2 me Série. 10 tom.; 3 me Série. Tom. 1-4. *Paris,* 1872-95. *In progress.* U

Journal de Zoologie. 6 tom. *Paris,* 1872-77. U

Journal des Economistes. Tom. 31-37. *Paris,* 1852-53.
2 me Série. 48 tom. *Paris,* 1854-65.
3 me " Tom. 1-10. *Paris,* 1866-68.
5 me " Tom. 13-26. *Paris,* 1893-96. *In progress.* U

Journal des Mines. 38 tom. *Paris,* 1795-1815.
Continued as :
Annales des Mines. 13 tom. *Paris,* 1816-26.
2 me Série. 8 tom. *Paris,* 1827-31.
3 me " 20 " " 1832-41.
4 me " 20 " " 1842-51.
5 me " 20 " and Recueil de lois, etc.
10 tom. *Paris,* 1852-61.
6 me Série. 20 tom., and Recueil de lois, etc.
10 tom. *Paris,* 1862-71.
7 me Série. 20 tom., and Recueil de lois, etc.
10 tom. *Paris,* 1872-81.
8 me Série. 20 tom., and Recueil de lois, etc.
10 tom. *Paris,* 1882-91.
9 me Série. Tom. 1-10. and Recueil de lois, etc. Tom. 1-4. *Paris,* 1892-96. *In progress.* U
(Wanting Tom. 8 of Recueil de lois of 8me Série, and Tom. 2 of Recueil de lois of 9me Série).
Tables, 1795-1871, in 7 vols.
Do. 5 me Série. Tom. 7-20, and Recueil de lois, Tom. 4-8. *Paris,* 1854-60. (Tom. 5-6 incomplete).
6 me Série. Tom. 1-9, 11-17, 20, and Recueil de lois, Tom. 2-4, 6-8. *Paris,* 1862-71. (Tom. 10 incomplete).
7 me Série. Tom. 2-3, 5, 8-11, 13-20, and Recueil de lois, Tom. 5 and 7. *Paris,* 1872-81. (Tom. 1, 4, 6-7, 12 incomplete).
8 me Série. Tom. 1-19, 22, and Recueil de lois, Tom. 2-10. *Paris,* 1882-91.
9 me Série. Tom. 1-10, and Recueil de lois, Tom. 1-2. *Paris,* 1892-96. *In progress.* C

Journal des Savants. *Paris,* 1855-7. E
Do. *Paris,* 1893-6. *In progress.* U

Journal des Societes Scientifiques. Anneé 3. *Paris,* 1887.

Journal fuer die reine und angewandte Mathematik. Bd. 1-115. *Berlin,* 1826-96. *In progress.* U

Journal fuer praktische Chemie.
Bd. 1-161. *Leipzig,* 1834-96. *In progress.* U
Register, Bd. 1-158, in 4 vols.

Journal of American Ethnology and Archæology. Vols. 1-4. *Boston* and *New York*, 1891-4. P

Do. Vols. 1-3. *Boston* and *New York*, 1891-2. C

Journal of American Folk-Lore. Vols. 1-10. *Boston* and *New York*, 1888-97. *In progress.* C.P

Journal of Anatomy and Physiology. Vols. 1-30. *London* and *Cambridge*, 1866-96. *In progress.* Index, Vols. 1-20. (Wanting Vols. 19, 20 and 25). U

Journal of Classical and Sacred Philology. 4 vols. *Cambridge*, 1854-59. U
Vols. 1-3. *Cambridge*, 1854-6. T

Journal of Commerce. Vols. 11, 12, 14-19, 26-29, 34. *Montreal*, 1881-92. L

Journal of Comparative Medicine and Surgery. Vols. 1-10. *New York*, 1880-89. C

Journal of Comparative Neurology. Vols. 1-6. *Cincinnati, Granville (Ohio)*, 1891-96. *In progress.* C.U

Journal of Decorative Art. Vols. 4-17. *London* and *Manchester*, 1884-97. *In progress.* P

Journal of Education. Vols. 15-19. *London*, 1893-7. *In progress.* E

Journal of Education and Agriculture. *Halifax*, 1858-60. E

Journal of Education for Iowa. Vol. 1. *Dubuque*, 1853. E

Journal of Education for Lower Canada. Vols. 1-21. *Montreal*, 1857-77. E

Journal of Education for New England. Vols. 1-42. *Boston*, 1875-95. *In progress.* E

Journal of Education for Upper Canada. Vols. 1-30. *Toronto*, 1848-77. E

Do. Vols. 2-30. *Toronto*, 1849-77. L

Do. Vols. 1-10, 13-14, 18, 20-22, 25-29. *Toronto*, 1848-76.

Journal of Hellenic Studies. *See* Society for the Promotion of Hellenic Studies. Journal, etc.

Journal of Mental Science. *See* Asylum Journal of Mental Science.

Journal of Morphology. Vols. 1-10. *Boston*, 1887-96. (Wanting Vol. 4). *In progress.* U

Journal of Nervous and Mental Disease. N.S. Vols. 18-23. *New York*, 1893-96. *In progress.* U

Journal of Pathology and Bacteriology. Vols. 1-4. *Edinburgh* and *London*, 1892-96. *In progress.* U

Journal of Philology. Vols. 1-25. *London* and *Cambridge*, 1868-97. *In progress.* U
Vols. 14-25. *London*, 1885-97. *In progress.* T

Journal of Physiology. Vols. 1-19. *London* and *Cambridge*, 1878-96. *In progress.* U

Journal of Politics. *See* American Journal of Politics.

Journal of Sacred Literature. Vols. 1-14. *London*, 1855-61. Mc

Journal of Speculative Philosophy. Vols. 1-22. *St. Louis, New York*, 1867-88. *In progress.* (Wanting Vols. 6, 11 and 17). U
Do. Vols. 10-22. *St. Louis* and *New York*, 1876-88. C

Journal of the Board of Arts and Manufactures for Upper Canada. Vols. 1-7. *Toronto*, 1861-7. L.P (Wanting Vol. 2, P).

Judge. *New York*, 1888-92. L

Judy. Vol. 2. *London*, 1868. L
Do. Vols. 35, 38-61. *London*, 1884, 1886-97. *In progress.* P

Jugoslavenska Akademija Znanosti i Umjetnosti. Ljetapsis. Tom. 6-10 ; N.S. Vol. 1. *Agram*, 1891-6. *In progress.* C
Rad. Tom. 11-13, 15-20, 22. *Agram*, 1891-6. *In progress.* C
Division of Mathematical and Natural Science. Vols. 104, 106-7, 111, 113, 117, 120, 122-3, 126, 128, 130. *Agram*, 1891-7. *In progress.* C

Just's Botanischer Jahresbericht. *See* Botanischer Jahresbericht.

Justus Liebig's Annalen der Chemie. *See* Annalen der Chemie und Pharmacie.

Kaiserlich-Koenigliche Naturhistorische Hofmuseum. Annalen. Bd. 1-9. *Wien*, 1886-94. *In progress.* C

Kaiserlich-Koenigliche Geographische Gesellschaft. Mittheilungen. Jahrg. 1-4, 6-9, 16-38. *Wien*, 1857-65, 1873-95. *In progress.* C

Kaiserlich-Koenigliche Geologische Reichsanstalt. Jahrbuch. Bd. 27-45. *Wien*, 1877-95. *In progress.* C
Verhandlungen. Jahrg. 1832, 1886-88, 1890-96. *Wien*. C
General Register, 1860-70.

Kaiserlich-koenigliche Gesellschaft der Aerzte zu Wien. Anzeiger. 1871-87. *Wien*, 1881-87. U
Medizinische Jahrbücher. Jahrg. 17-44. *Wien*, 1861-88. U
Wochenblatt der Zeitschrift. 1855-57, 1861-70. *Wien*, 1855-70. U
Zeitschrift. Jahrg. 7-16. *Wien*, 1851-60. U

Kaiserlich-koenigliche zoologisch-botanische Gesellschaft in Wien. *See* Zoologisch-Botanischer Verein.

Kaiserlich-koenigliches allgemeines Krankenhaus. Aerztlicher Bericht. 1883-85, 1888. *Wien*, 1884-90. U

Kaiserliche Akademie der Wissenschaften.

Archiv für Kunde österreichischer Geschichts-Quellen. Bd. 1-14. *Wien*, 1848-55. (Wanting Bd. 7 and 8.) U

Monumenta Habsburgica, Sammlung von Actenstücken und Briefen zur Geschichte des Hauses Habsburg, etc. Abth. 1, Bd. 1 and 2. Abth. 2, Bd. 1. *Wien*, 1853-55 U

Sitzungsberichte. Bd. 1. *Wien*, 1848. U
(This volume contains reports of both classes of the Academy.)
Continued in divisions :
(1) Sitzungsberichte. Philosophisch-historische Classe. Bd. 2-135. *Wien*, 1849 96. *In progress.* U
Register, Bd. 1-130.
(2) Sitzungsberichte. Mathematisch-naturwissenschaftliche Classe. Bd. 2-105. *Wien*, 1849 96. *In progress.* U
Register, Bd. 1-60.

Fontes Rerum Austriacarum, Oesterreichische Geschichtsquellen.
Abth. 1, Bd. 1-8. *Wien*, 1855-75.
Abth. 2, Bd. 1-47. *Wien*, 1849-92. U

Kansas. School Reports, annual. *Topeka*, 1863-9, 1871-6, 1878, 1880-90. E

Kansas Academy of Science.
Transactions. Vols. 8-13. *Topeka*, 1883 93. U
(Wanting Vol. 12)
Do. Vols. 9-14. *Topeka*, 1883-94. C

Kansas City Review. *See* Western Review of Science and Industry.

Kansas State Historical Society.
Biennial Reports. Nos. 6-9. *Topeka*, 1887-94. C
Transactions. Vols. 1-2, 4. *Topeka*, 1875-90. C

Kansas University Quarterly. *Cū. Bull*
Vols 1-4. *Lawrence*, 1892-6. *In progress.* C

Kennel Club Stud Book. 1859-74, 1876-82, 1884 91. *London*, 1874-91. P

Kennel Gazette. Vols. 12, 15. *London*, 1891-95. P

Kentucky. School reports, annual 1855-9, 1861-3, 1865-8. E

Kermesse (La). *Quebec*, 1892-93. P

Kilkenny Archaeological Society.
Transactions. Vols. 1-3. 1849-55. *Dublin*, 1853-56.
Continued as :
(Royal) Historical and Archæological Society of Ireland. Journal. New Series. Vols. 1-6. 1856-67. *Dublin*, 1858-71.
Do. 3rd Series. Vol. 1. 1868-9. *Dublin*, 1873.
Do. 4th Series. Vols. 1-4. 1870-78. *Dublin*, 1878-9. P

Kindergarten. Vols. 1-7. *Toronto*, 1885-95. *In progress.* E

King's College Hospital.
Reports. Vols. 1 and 2. (1893-96). *London*, 1895-96. *In progress.* U

Knowledge. Vols. 5-20. *London*, 1884-97. *In progress.* P

Knox College Monthly. Vols 6-20. *Toronto*, 1887-96. P
Do. Vols. 1-14, 16-19. *Toronto*, 1887-95. K

Koeniglich-saechsische Gesellschaft der Wissenschaften.
Abhandlungen der mathematisch - physischen Classe. Bd. 1-15. *Leipzig*, 1852 90. U
Abhandlungen der philologisch - historischen Classe. Bd. 1-11. *Leipzig*, 1850-90. U
Berichte über die Verhandlungen. Bd. 2 (1848). *Leipzig*, 1849. U
Berichte, etc. Mathematisch physische Classe. Bd. 1-41. *Leipzig*, 1849-89. U
Bd. 1-47. *Leipzig*, 1849 95. *In progress.* C
Berichte, etc. Philologisch-historische Classe. Bd. 1-41. *Leipzig*, 1849-89. U
Register, 1846-85.

Koenigliche (or Churfuerstlich)(Baierische) Akademie der Wissenschaften.
Abhandlungen. 10 Bde. *München*, 1763-76 U
Abhandlungen der historischen Classe. Bd. 1-20. *München*, 1833-93. U
Abhandlungen der mathematisch-physikalischen Classe. Bd. 1-17 (1829 92). *München*, 1832-92. U
Abhandlungen der naturwissenschaftlich-technischen Commission. 2 Bde. *München*, 1857 58. U
Abhandlungen der philosophisch philologischen Classe. Bd. 1 19. *München*, 1839-92. U
Almanach. *München*, 1878, 1884, 1896. C
Denkschriften. 9 Bde. (1808-24). *München*, Sulzbach, 1809-25. U
Fest u. Gedachtniss-Reden. *München*, 1888 92. U
Gelehrte Anzeigen. 50 Bde. *München*, 1835-60. C
Historische Abhandlungen. 5 Bde. *München*, 1807-23. U
Neue philosophische Abhandlungen. Bd. 1 5, *München*, 1778-89. U
Sitzungsberichte. Jahrg. 1860 70. *München*, 1860 70. U
Sitzungsberichte der mathematisch-physikalischen Classe. Bd. 1-12. *München*, 1871-82 U
Do. Bd. 7-16, 18-25. *München*, 1877-95 C
Sitzungsberichte der philosophisch philologischen und historischen Classe. Bd. 1-4. *München*, 1871-74. U
Do. Bd. 8-25. *München*, 1878-95. C

Koenigliche (preussische) Akademie der Wissenschaften zu Berlin.
Abhandlungen. 1865 89. *Berlin*, 1866 90. U
Do. 1890 96. *Berlin*, 1891-6. *In progress.*
Astronomisches Jahrbuch. 1829 and 1830. *Berlin*, 1826-27. U
Monatsberichte. 1857-81. *Berlin*, 1857-81. U
Register, 1859-73
Sitzungsberichte. 1882 95. *Berlin*, 1882-95. U
(Wanting 1894).

Koenigliche Boehmische Gesellschaft der Wissenschaften im Prag. Jahresbericht. *Prag*, 1878-96. *In progress.* . C
Mathematisch - Naturwissenschaftliche Classe. Sitzungsberichte. *Prag*, 1878-95. *In progress.* C

Koenigliche Gesellschaft der Wissenschaften zu Goettingen.
Geschäftliche Mittheilungen. *Göttingen*, 1895-6.
In progress. C
Nachrichten von der königlichen Gesellschaft, etc. und der Georg-Augusts Universität. Jahrg. 1884-89. *Göttingen*, 1884 89. U
Do. 1877-81, 1883-93. *In progress.* C

Koenigliches (preussisches) Geodaetisches Institut.
Publicationen. 16 parts. *Berlin*, 1871-90. U

Koenigliches zoologisches (und anthropologisch-ethnographisches) Museum zu Dresden.
Abhandlungen und Berichte. 1886-87. *Dresden*, 1887. U
Mittheilungen. Heft. 1-3. *Dresden*, 1877-78. U

Koenigsberg-Physikalisch-oekonomische Gesellschaft. *See* Physikalisch-ökonomische Gesellschaft zu Königsberg.

Kommission zur wissenschaftlichen Untersuchung der deutschen Meere.
Jahresberichte. Nos. 4-19. *Kiel*, 1878-93. C
Ergebnisse der Beobachtungsstationen an den deutschen Küsten. *Berlin*, 1873-92. C

Kongeligt Dansk videnskabernes Selskab.
Oversigt over Forhandlinger. *Kjobenhavn*, 1877-95. *In progress.* C
Skrifter, 5 te Raekke.
Historisk og philosophisk Afdeling. Bd. 1-5. *Kjobenhavn*, 1852-92. *In progress.* U
(Wanting parts 1-3 of Bd. 5).
Naturvidenskabelig og Mathematisk Afdeling. Bd. 1-12. *Kjobenhavn*, 1852-92. U

Kongeligt Nordisk Oldskrift-Selskab.
(Société Royale des Antiquaires du Nord.)
Aarböger for Nordisk Oldkyndighed og Historie.
Kjobenhaven. 1866-69, 1876, 1879-81. C
Mémoires, 1840-44. *Copenhagn*, 1852-54. P
Do. 1845-60. *Copenhague*, 1852-61. U
Do. Nouv. Sér. 1866-93. *Copenhague* (1866-93). U

Kongeligt Norsk Frederiks Universitet.
Aarsberetning. *Christiania*, 1856-58, 1863 70, 1872-3. C

Kongeligt Norsk Videnskabers Selskab.
Skrifter. *Throndhjem*, 1886-94. C.M

Kongliga Svenska Vetenskaps Akademi.
Abhandlungen, aus dem Schwedischen überselzt. 20 Bde. (1739-58). *Hamburg*, 1749-59. U
Arsberättelse. *Stockholm*, 1821-56. U
Handlingar. 40 vol. (1739-79) and Register. *Stockholm*, 1741 80. U
Nya Handlingar. 33 tom. *Stockho'm*, 1780-1812. U
Handlingar. 1813 54. *Stockholm*, 1813-56. U
(Wanting 1823.)
Do Ny Földj. Bl. 1-12, 22-24. *Stockholm*, 1858-91. U
Do. Bd. 6-27. *Stockholm*, 1864-96. *In progress.* C

Bihang till Handlingar. Bd. 1-18, 20-21. *Stockholm*, 1872-93, 1895-6. *In progress.* C
Ofversigt af Förhandlingar. Arg. 1-32. *Stockholm*, 1845-76. U
Do. Arg. 22-52. *Stockholm*, 1865-95. C

Kongliga Vitterhets, Historie och Antiqvitets Akademi.
Handlingar. Del. 21-32. *Stockholm* (1853)-95. *In progress.* U
Manadsblad. Argang 11-20 (1882-91). *Stockho'm*, 1883-93. *In progress.* U
Antiqvarisk Tidskrift för Sverige. Del. 2-16. *Stockholm*, 1869-95. *In progress.* U

Koninklijk Instituut voor de Taal-Land-en Volkenkunde van Nederlandsch, Indie.
Bijdragen. Deel 39-46. *s'Gravenhage*, 1890-96. *In progress.* C
De Garebög's te ngajogyakarta door J. Groneman. *s'Gravenhage*, 1895. C

Koninklijk Nederlandsch Aardrijkskundig Genootschap.
Tijdschrift. Tweede Serie. Deel 6-13. *Leiden*, 1889-96. *In progress.* C

Koninklijk Zoologisch Genootschap.
Bijdragen tot de Dierkunde.
15e Aflevering. Deel 1-2. Feest-Nummer. *Amsterdam*, 1888. C

Koninklijke Akademie van Wetenschappen.
Jaarboek. *Amsterdam*, 1876 90, 1892,1895. *In progress.* C
Verhandelingen Deel 17-29 ; 2 Sectie. Deel 1-4. *Amsterdam*, 1877-1896. *In progress.* C
Verslagen en mededeelingen. 2 de Reeks, Deel 11-20. 3 de Reeks, Deel 1-9. *Amsterdam*, 1877-92. C
Verslagen van de Zittingen der Wis-en Natuurkundige Afdeeling. Deel 4. 1896. C

Kosmos. *See* V.P. Journal.

Kritische Zeitschrift fuer Chemie (Physik und Mathematik). Jahrg. 1-14. *Erlangen, Heidelberg, Göttingen, Leipzig*, 1858-71.

Kuenstlerverein. Abtheilung fuer Bremische Geschichte und Alterthuemer (later : Historische Gesellschaft des Künstlervereins).
Bremisches Jahrbuch. 15 Bde. *Bremen*, 1864-88. 2 te Serie. Bd. 1. *Bremen*, 1885. U

Ladies' Diary, or Woman's Almanack. 1758-76. *London*, 1758 76. U

Ladies' Diary, or Complete Almanac. 1831-40. *London*, 1831-42. U

Lady's and Gentleman's Diary. 1841-72. *London* (1841 72). U

Lady's Newspaper. Vols. 3-5, 7, 9 13. *London*, 1848-9, 1850, 1851-53. P

Lady's Pictorial. Vols. 15-16, 19-30, 33. *London*, 1888-97. *In progress.* P

Lake Magazine. Vol. 1. *Toronto*, 1892-3. P

Lambeth Conferences. 1867, 1878, 1888. *London*. T

Lamp (The), a Theosophical Monthly. Vols.1-2. *Toronto*, 1894-96 *In progress.* P

Lancashire and Cheshire Historic Society. *See* Historic Society of Lancashire and Cheshire.

Lancet. 1858, 1860-72. *London*, 1858-72. (Wanting Vol. 1 of 1858, and Vol. 2 of 1872). U Do. 1884-97. *London*, 1884-97. *In progress.* P

Lanterne. *Montreal*, 1884. L. P

Law Quarterly Review. Vols. 1-12. *London*, 1885-96. *In progress.* U

Laws of Life. Vols. 25-6, 28 9. *Dansville, N. Y.*, 1882-3, 1885-6. P Do. Vols. 27, 32 34 *Dansville, N. Y.*, 1884-91. L

League. Vols. 1-3. *London*, 1843-46. L. P

Leeds Philosophical and Literary Society.
Annual Reports. *Leeds*, 1824-26, 1830-96. *In progress.* C

Legitimist Kalendar. *London*, 1895. P

Leipzig—Koeniglich-saechsische Gesellschaft der Wissenschaften. *See* Königlich-sächsische Gesellschaft, etc.

Leipzig — Naturforschende Gesellschaft. *See* Naturforschende Gesellschaft zu Leipzig.

Leipzig—Societas Philologa. *See* Societas Philologa Lipsiensis.

Leipzig—Verein fuer Erdkunde. *See* Verein von Freunden der Erdkunde zu Leipzig.

Leisure Hour. *London*, 1852-97. *In progress.* P. U

Leopoldinisch · Carolinische Akademie. *See* Academia Caesarea (Leopoldino-Carolina Germanica) Naturæ Curiosorum.

Library (The). Vols. 1-9. *London*, 1889-97. *In progress.* P. U

Library Chronicle. Vols. 1-5. *London*, 1884-88. P

Library Journal. Vols. 1-22. *New York*, 1876 97. *In progress.* P

Lille, Facultes de. *See* Université de France. Travaux et mémoires des Facultés de Lille.

Linnean Society.
Journal (of the Proceedings); Botany. Vols. 1-29. *London*, 1857-93. *In progress.* C. U
(Wanting Vol. 8, U. ; Wanting Vols. 21-23 and 26 C).
Index, Vols. 1-20. U
Journal (of the Proceedings); Zoology. Vols. 1-24. *London*, 1857-93. *In progress.* C. U
Index, Vols. 1-20. C
Transactions. 30 vols. *London*, 1791-1875. (Wanting Vol. 10). U
Transactions ; Botany. Vols. 1-5. *London*, 1876-96. *In progress.* U
Transactions ; Zoology. Vols. 1-7. *London*, 1876-96. *In progress.* U

Linnean Society of New South Wales.
Proceedings. Series 1. Vols. 9 10 ; Series 2. Vols. 1-10. *Sydney*, 1884 95. *In progress.* C
Index of Authors to Series 1. Vols. 1-10.

Linnean Society of New York.
Abstracts from Proceedings. *New York*, 1889-96. *In progress.* C
Transactions. Vols. 1-2. *New York*, 1882-84. C

Liouville's Journal de Mathematiques. *See* Journal de Mathématiques pures et appliquées.

Lippincott's Magazine. Vols. 1-6, 33-59. *Philadelphia*, 1868-70, 1884 97. *In progress.* P

Literarischer Verein in Stuttgart. Bibliothek. Bd. 4-207. *Stuttgart*, 1849-96. *In progress.* U
(Wanting various early volumes.)

Literarisches Centralblatt fuer Deutschland. Jahrg. 1852-96. *Leipzig*, 1852-96. *In progress.* U
(First year of publication, 1851.)

Literarium (The). Vol. 3. *London*, 1856-7. E

Literary and Educational Year Book. *London*, 1860. P

Literary and Historical Society of Quebec.
Historical Documents. Series 1-5. *Quebec*, 1840-1877. L. P
Transactions. 1st Series, 5 vols. *Quebec*, 1829-62. P
Do. 2nd Series. Nos. 1-21. *Quebec*, 1863-92.

Literary and Philosophical Society of Leicester. Transactions. New Quarterly Series. Vol. 3. *Leicester*, 1892-3. C

Literary and Philosophical Society of Liverpool.
Proceedings. Nos. 14-18, 20-40. *Liverpool*, 1859 86.
No. 26 contains index to Vols 1-25.
" 40 " first report on Fauna of Liverpool Bay. C

Literary and Statistical Magazine for Scotland. Vols. 1-4. *Edinburgh*, 1817-1820. T

Literary Annual Register, or Records of Literature, Domestic and Foreign. 2 vols. *London*, 1807-8. U

Literary Digest. Vols. 1-13. *New York*, 1890-96. *In progress.* V

Literary Garland. Vols. 1-4. N.S, Vols. 1-9. *Montreal*, 1838-51. · L. P

Literary Gazette. 6 vols. *London*, 1853-61. E

Literary Journal. 2nd Series, 2 vols. *London*, 1806. E

Literary Opinion. Vol. 7. *London*, 1891. P

Literary World. *London*, 1839-40. P

Literary World. Vols. 8-21. *Boston*, 1878-90. V

Literary World. Vols. 4-6, 12-13. *New York*, 1849-53. E

Literary Year-Book. *London*, 1897. *In progress.* P

Literaturblatt fuer germanische und romanische Philologie. Bd. 1-17. *Heilbronn*, 1880-96. *In progress.* U

Literature. Vols. 1-2. *London*, 1897-8. *In progress.* P. U. V

Littell's Living Age. Vols. 1-215. *Boston*, 1844-97. *In progress.* P

Liverpool Biological Society. Proceedings and Transactions, Vols. 3-9. *Liverpool*, 1888-95. *In progress* C

Liverpool Geographical Society. Annual Reports. Nos. 2-3. *Liverpool*, 1893-4. C

Liverpool Literary and Philosophical Society. *See* Literary and Philosophical Society of Liverpool.

Liverpool Polytechnic Society. Journal of Sessions 50-53, 55. *Liverpool*, 1857-92. C

London. School Board: Minutes and Proceedings, annual. *London*, 1872-95. *In progress.* E Appendix to Report of the School Management Committee, Annual. *London*, 1887-95. *In progress.* E

London Chemical Society. *See* Chemical Society.

London, Edinburgh (and Dublin) Philosophical Magazine. *See* Philosophical Magazine.

London Magazine, or Gentleman's Monthly Intelligencer (between 1735 and 1746 : London Magazine and Monthly Chronologer), for the years 1732, 1736-40, 1744, 1779, and 1780. *London*, 1732-80. U

London Mathematical Society. Proceedings. Vols. 1-20. *London*, 1865-89. U Do. Vols. 14-26. *London*, 1882-96. *In progress.* C

London Medical Press and Circular, 1866-72. *London*, 1866-72. U

London Post Office Directory. *London*, 1866, 1884, 1887, 1890, 1894, 1898. *In progress.* P

London Quarterly Review. Vols. 1-2, 14, 16-29, 78. *London*, 1853-4, 1860-68, 1892. *In progress.* V Do. Vols. 1-29, 38-43, 51-54, 56. *London*, 1853-80. L

London Society. Vols. 1-72. *London*, 1862-97. *In progress.* P

Longman's Magazine. Vols. 1-30. *London*, 1882-97. *In progress.* P

Louisiana. School reports, annual, 1874. E

Louisville. School reports, annual, 1859-65. E

Lowell, Mass. School reports, 1839-70. E

Lower Canada Jurist. Vols. 1-18. (Wanting Vols. 12 and 14). *Montreal*, 1857-74. E

Loyalist. *See* U. E. Loyalist.

Loyalist and Conservative Advocate. 1st Series. Vols. 3-4 ; N.S. Vol. 1. *Fredericton, N.B.*, 1844-5, 1852. P

Lucifer, a Theosophical Magazine. Vols. 1-20. *London*, 1887-97. *In progress.* P

Lunds Universitet. Acta Universitatis Lundensis. Tom. 1-2, 5, 7, 9-17, 19, 22-25, 27-31. *Lund*, 1864-95. C Index to Tom. 1-30.

Lundy's Lane Historical Society. Publications. *Welland* and *Niagara Falls*, 1891-97. *In progress.* P

Luxembourg. Meteorological reports. *See* Observatories : Luxembourg.

Lyceum of Natural History (afterwards : New York Academy of Natural Sciences, q.v.). Annals. Vols. 1-11. *New York*, 1824-76. C

McMaster University Monthly. Vols. 1-6. *Toronto*, 1892-7. *In progress.* Mc.P

Macmillan's Magazine. Vols. 1-76. *London*, 1859-97. (Wanting Vols. 29-34, L). *In progress.* L.P

Madagascar. Meteorological reports. *See* Observatories : Madagascar.

Magasin du Bas Canada. *See* Bibliothèque Canadienne.

Magazin de Zoologie. 8 Années. *Paris*, 1831-38. Continued as : Magazin de Zoologie, d'Anatomie comparée, et de Paléontologie. 2me Série. Année 1-7. *Paris*, 1839-45. (For continuation, *see* Revue et Magazin de Zoologie). U

Magazin fuer die gesammte Heilkunde. Bd. 1-38. *Berlin*, 1816-32. U (Wanting Bd. 20).

Magazin fuer die neue Historie und Geographie. Th. 1-22. *Hamburg, Halle*, 1767-88. U

Magazin fuer Literatur. Jahrg. 61-64. *Berlin*, 1892-96. *In progress.* U

Magazine of American History. Vols. 2-30. *New York*, 1878-93. P Vols. 15-22. *New York*, 1886-89. C Vols. 4-6. *New York*, 1880-81. U

Magazine of Art. Vols. 1-20. *London*, 1878-97. *In progress.* P Do. Vols. 5-13. *London*, 1882-90. U

Magazine of Christian Literature. Vol. 12. *New York*, 1889-90. Mc

Magazine of Natural History and Journal of Zoology, Botany, Mineralogy, Geology, and Meteorology (conducted by J. Loudon, &c.). 9 vols. *London*, 1829-36. New Series (conducted by E. Charlesworth). 4 vols. *London*, 1837-40. U (The Annals and Magazine of Natural History was intended as a continuation).

Magazine of Poetry. Vols. 1-8. *London*, 1889-96. P

Magazine of Popular Science and Journal of the Useful Arts. 4 vols. *London*, 1836-7. U

Magazine of Western History. Vols. 1-14. *Cleveland* and *New York*, 1886-91. Continued as : National Magazine. Vols. 15-19. *New York*, 1891-94. P

Maine. School reports, annual, 1848-52, 1854, 1881, 1885-88, 1890-92. E

Maine Historical Society. Collections. 1st Series. Vols. 1-9. *Portland*, 1865-87. P Do. 2nd Series. Vols. 1-5. *Portland*, 1869-97. *In progress.* P Index to 1st Series. Vols. 1-9.

Maine Journal of Education. 3 vols. *Portland*, 1871-74. E

Maine Teacher. 2 vols. *Portland*, 1858-63.
　　　　　　　　　　　　　　　　　　　　E

Maitland Club.
Publications. Nos. 1-75. *Edinburgh*, 1829-59. P

Maitre Phonetique. Années 4-11. *Paris*,
1889-96. *In progress.*　　　　　　　　U

**Manchester Association of Employ-
ers, Foremen and Draughtsmen.**
Papers, etc. *Manchester*, 1883-86　　　C

Manchester Association of Engineers.
Papers and Reports for 1887-90.
Transactions for 1891. *Manchester.*　　C

Manchester Geographical Society.
Journal. Vols. 4-10. *Manchester*, 1888-94. C

Manchester Geological Society.
Transactions. Vols. 15-19, 21, 24. *Manchester*,
1878-96. *In progress.*　　　　　　　C

**Manchester Literary and Philosophi-
cal Society.**
Memoirs. Series 1, Vol. 4 (Part 2). Vol. 5
(Part 1). *Manchester*, 1796-98.
　Series 2. Vols. 2-15. *London* and *Manchester*
　1813-60.
　Series 3. Vols. 1, 8, 10. *London*, 1862-87.
　Series 4. Vols. 1-5. *London*, 1888-92.　C
Proceedings. Vols. 2-26. *Manchester*, 1860-
87.　　　　　　　　　　　　　　　C
　　Continued as :
Memoirs and Proceedings. Series 4. Vols.
8-10. *London,* 1893-96. *In progress.*　C
A centenary of science in Manchester in a series
of notes. *London*, 1883.　　　　　　C

Manhattan Magazine. Vol. 3. *New York*,
1884.　　　　　　　　　　　　　　P

Manitoba.
Journals of Legislative Assembly. 1871-97. *In
progress.*　　　　　　　　　　　L.O
Gazette. Vol. 26. 1896. *In progress.*　　O
Report of the Department of Education of Man-
itoba, 1891-95.　　　　　　　　　V

**Manitoba Historical and Scientific
Society.** *See* Historical and Scientific Society
of Manitoba.

Manitoban (The). Vols. 1-2. *Winnipeg*,
1892-3.　　　　　　　　　　　　P

**Manual of the Railroads of the
United States** (ed. by H. V. Poor). 1872-3,
1876-78, 1881-87. *New York*, 1872-87.

Manufacturer and Builder.
Vols. 1 and 2. *New York*, 1869-70.　　U
　Vol. 3. *New York*, 1871.　　　　　P

Manx Society.
Publications. Vols. 1-31. *Douglas (Isle of Man)*,
1859-82.　　　　　　　　　　　P

Maple Leaf. Vols. 1-4. *Montreal*, 1852-54. L.P

**Marine Biological Association of the
United Kingdom.** Journal. New Series.
Vol. 1-3. *London*, 1890-96. *In progress.*

Maryland. School Reports, annual. 1865-82.
(Wanting 1869, 1888-9, 1891.)　　　E

Masonic Review. Vols. 23-25. *Cincinnati*,
1860-1.　　　　　　　　　　　　P

Massachusetts.
Public Documents. 1866-95　　　　　L
Report on Labor Statistics. 1871-79, 1881-92. L
School Reports, annual. 1840-95. (Wanting
1849, 1859.) *In progress.*　　　　E
State Entomologist's Reports. Nos. 12, 14, 17.
Springfield, 1883-91.　　　　　　C

**Massachusetts Common School Jour-
nal.** 13 vols. *Boston*, 1839-50.　　E

Massachusetts Historical Society.
Collections.
　1st Series. 10 vols. *Boston*, 1792-1809.
　2nd " Vols. 1 6,8,10. " 1814-5, 1826, 1843.
　3rd " " 3-8. *Boston* and *Cambridge*, 1833-43.
　4th " " 2-10. *Boston*, 1854-71.
　5th " 10 vols. " 1871-88.
　6th " Vols. 1-8. " 1886 96. *In progress.*　　　　　　　　　　　P
　General indexes to Series 4-5.
Proceedings. 1st Series, 20 vols. *Boston*, 1791-
1883. 2nd Series. Vols. 1-11. *Boston*, 1884-
97. *In progress.*　　　　　　　　P
　Index to 1st Series.

**Massachusetts Institute of Technol-
ogy.**
Technology Quarterly. Vols. 5-10. *Boston*,
1892-96. *In progress.*　　　　　　S

Massachusetts Missionary Magazine.
Vols. 2-5. *Salem*, 1804-7.　　　　Mc

Massachusetts Teacher. 13 vols. *Boston*,
1848-67.　　　　　　　　　　　E

Massey's Magazine. Vols. 1-3. *Toronto*,
1896-7.　　　　　　　　　　E.P

Materialui dlya Geologii Rossii. *See*
Imperatorskoye Sanktpeterburgskoye Mineralogi-
cheskoye Obshchesto. Materialui, etc.

**Materiaux et Documents d'Architec-
ture et de Sculpture.** Vols. 1-24. *Paris*,
1872 96. *In progress.*　　　　　　S

**Mathematical and Physical Society
of the University of Toronto.**
Papers. *Toronto*, 1892.　　　　　　T

Mathematical Monthly. Vols. 1-3. *Cambridge, Mass.*, 1858-61.　　　　　U

**Mathematical Questions and Solu-
tions from the "Educational Times."**
Vols. 1-64. *London*, 1863 (1886)-96. *In progress.*
　　　　　　　　　　　　　　　U

Mathematical Repository. N S. Vols.
2-4. *London*, 1809-19　　　　　　U

Mathematische Annalen. Bd. 1-47. *Leipzig*, 1869-96. *In progress.*　　　　U

**Mathematische und naturwissen-
schaftliche Berichte aus Ungarn.**
Bd. 1-5. *Berlin*, 1882-87.　　　　U

Mauritius. Meteorological Reports. *See* Observatories : Mauritius.

Mechanical News. Vols. 15, 19-22. *New
York*, 1885 93.　　　　　　　　P

Mechanics' Magazine. N.S. Vols. 8-28.
London, 1862-72.
　　Continued as :
Iron, the Journal of Science, Metals and Manu-
factures. Vols. 1-23, 26-41. *London*, 1873-
93.　　　　　　　　　　　　　P

Mechanics' Magazine and Engineers' Journal. (Appleton.) Vol. 1. *New York*, 1851.   C

(Royal) Medical and Chirurgical Society of London.
Medico-Chirurgical Transactions. Vols. 1-72.
London, 1809-89. (Wanting Vol. 32)   U
General Index. Vols. 1-53.

Medical and Physical Society of Bombay.
Transactions. Vols. 1-9. *Bombay*, 1838-49 U

Medical Association Journal. *See* American Medical Assoc ation Journal.

Medical Bulletin. Vols. 9-14. *Philadelphia*, 1887-92.   L

Medical Chronicle. Vol. 5. *Montreal*, 1857-8.   P

Medical Circular and General Medical Advertiser. Vols. 17-27. *London*, 1860 65.   U

Medical News. Vols. 50-51. *Philadelphia*, 1887.   P

Medical Record. Vols. 31-2. *New York*, 1887.   P

Medical Times and Gazette. *London*, 1860-72. (Wanting Vol. 1 of 1860, and Vol. 2 of 1872.)   U

Medico-Chirurgical Society of Edinburgh.
Transactions. Vols. 1-3. *Edinburgh*, 1821-29. C

Medico-Chirurgical Transactions. *See* Medical and Chirurgical Society of London. Medico-Chirurgical Transactions.

Medico-Legal Journal. Vols. 2-15. *New York*, 1885-97. *In progress.*   O

Medizinisch - naturwissenschaftliche Gesellschaft zu Jena.
Jenaische Zeitschrift für (Medicin und) Naturwissenschaft. Bd. 1-31. *Leipzig, Jena*, 1864-96. *In progress.*
Sitzungsberichte. 1885-6. *Jena*, 1879-86. U

Medizinische National-Zeitung für Deutschland. Jahrg. 2. *Altenburg*, 1799. Continued as :
Allgemeine medizinische Annalen. 1800 1806. *Altenburg*, 1800-1806.   U

Meehan's Monthly. Vols. 1-7. *Philadelphia*, 1891-97. *In progress.*   P

Melanges biologiques. *See* Academia Scientiarum Imperialis Petropolitana. Mélanges biologiques tirés du Bulletin physico-mathématique.

Melanges d'Archeologie et d'Histoire. *See* École française de Rome. Mélanges d'Archéologie, etc.

Melanges mathematiques et astronomiques. *See* Academia Scientiarum Imperialis Petropolitana. Mélanges mathématiques et astronomiques tirés du Bulletin physico-mathématique.

Meliora. Vols. 1-9. *London*, 1859-66.   P

Merchants' and Bankers' Almanac. *New York*, 1865, 1868.   P
Do. *New York*, 1870 73.   U

Merchants' Magazine. *See* Hunt's Merchants' Magazine.

Meriden Scientific Association.
Transactions. Vols. 1-5, 7. *Meriden, Conn.*, 1884-95. *In progress.*   C

Messenger of Mathematics. *See* Oxford, Cambridge and Dublin Messenger of Mathematics.

Messenger of the Sacred Heart. Vol. 1. *Montreal*, 1891.   P

Metal Worker. Vols. 21-48. *New York*, 1884 97. *In progress.*   P

Metaphysical Magazine. Vols. 1-6. *New York*, 1895-97. *In progress.*   P

Meteorologisch Jaarboek. *See* Observatories : Netherlands. Meteorologische Waarnemingen.

Meteorologische Waarnemingen in Nederland. *See* Observatories : Netherlands.

Meteorologisk Aarbog. *See* Observatories : Denmark. Meteorologisk Aarbog.

Methodist Church.
Minutes of the Methodist Conferences annually held in America ; from 1773 to 1813. *New York*, 1813.   P
Minutes of Annual Conferences of Wesleyan Methodist Church in Canada, from 1824 to 1845. Vol. 1. *Toronto*, 1846.
Do. Vol. 2, 1846 to 1857. *Toronto*, 1863. O, P
Memorials of Quebec Conference. *Quebec*, 1863.   P

Methodist Magazine. Vols. 1-11. *New York*, 1818-28.
Continued as :
Methodist Magazine and Quarterly Review.
New Series. Vols. 1-11. *New York*, 1830-40.
Continued as :
Methodist Quarterly Review.
3rd Series. Vols. 1-8. *New York*, 1841-48.
4th Series. Vols. 1-31, 33-35. *New York*, 1849-83.
5th Series. Vols. 1-2. *New York*, 1885-6. Mc

Methodist Magazine and Wesleyan Methodist Magazine. *See* Arminian Magazine.

Methodist (Quarterly) Review. Vols. 40, 42-3, 45-50, 52-3, 55-57, 59 61, 65, 67-69,72, 75. *New York*, 1858 94. *In progress.* V

Metropolitan. Vol. 5. *Baltimore*, 1857.   E

Mexico.
Secretaria de Fomento.
Anales. Tom. 8. *Mexico*, 1887.   C
Boletin de Agricultura, mineria e industrias. Tom. 5. *Mexico*, 1895-6.   C
Memoria. Tom. 2-4. *Mexico*, 1883 5.   C

Michigan. Joint Documents, 1894.
Senate Journal, 1893-95.
House Journal, 1893 95.
Board of Agriculture. Reports. *Lansing*, 1862-90.
Index General to Reports, including Transactions of State Agricultural Society, 1849 -59,
Board of Health. Reports. *Lansing*, 1874-76, 1882-94.   M
Geological Survey of Michigan. Report, 1849.   C
First Biennial Report of Progress of Geological Survey of Michigan. *Lansing*, 1860.   C
School Reports, annual, 1844-50, 1855-88, 1891. (Wanting 1873).   E

Michigan Journal of Education.
4 vols. *Detroit*, 1856-59.   E

Michigan Pioneer and Historical Society. Collections. Vols. 1-27. *Lansing*, 1874-97. *In progress.*   L.P

Michigan Teacher. Vols. 8 and 10. *Kalamazoo*, 1872, 1875.   E

Microscopical Society of London. Transactions. N.S. Vols. 3, 9 16. *London*, 1855 68. (Bound with volumes of the Quarterly Journal of Microscopical Science for corresponding years). ·   U

Midland Institute of Mining, Civil and Mechanical Engineers. Transactions. Vol. 11, 13. *Bormley*, 1887-89, 1891-93. *suffield*   C

Midland Naturalist. *See* Midland Union of Natural History Societies, etc. Journal.

Midland Union of Natural History Societies, and Birmingham Natural History and Microscopical Society. Journal (known as The Midland Naturalist.) Vols. 7-16. *London* and *Birmingham*, 1887-93. C

Mind, a Quarterly Review of Psychology and Philosophy. Vols. 1-16. *London*, 1876-91.   U
Do. Vols. 8-16. *London*, 1883-91.   T
Do. Vols. 15-16. *London*, 1890 91.   V
Do. New Series. Vols. 1-6. *London*, 1891-97. (Wanting Vol. 1, U). *In progress.* T.U.V

Mineral Industry (Edited by R. P. Rothwell). Vols. 1-5, 1892-96. *New York*, 1893-97. *In progress.*   P.S

Mineral Resources of the U. S. *See* United States Department of Interior : Surveys.

Mineralogische und petrographische Mitthe lungen. Neue Folge. Bd. 1-16. *Wien*, 1878-96. *In progress.*   U

Minerva. Jahrbuch der gelehrten Welt. Jahrg. 2-7. 1892-98. *Strassburg*, 1892 98. *In progress.* U

Mining, Iron and Steel Manual. *See* Canadian Mining Manual.

Mining Journal, Railway and Commercial Gazette. Vols. 24-32. *London*, 1854 62.   C
Do. Vols. 37-59. *London*, 1867-89.   U

Mining Society of Nova Scotia. Transactions. Vol. 3. *Halifax*, 1894-5.   C

Mining World and Engineering Record. Vols. 31-52. *Lonaon*, 1886-97. *In progress.*   P

Minneapolis. Annual Reports of City Officers. 1889, 1892-6.   P

Minnesota.
Executive Documents, 1894. 4 vols. *St. Paul, Minn.*, 1895.   L.P
Geological Survey. Annual Reports. Vols. 1-7, 13-23. *St. Paul*, 1872 94.   C
Do. Bulletins 1-8, 10. *St. Paul* and *Minneapolis*, 1885-94.   C
School Reports, annual, 1861-80.   E

Minnesota Historical Society. Collections. Vols. 1-7. *St. Paul*, 1873-93. *In progress.*   P.U

Mirror of Literature, Amusement and Instruction. Vols. 1-38; N.S. Vols. 1-4. *London*, 1822-43.   L

Mirror of Parliament. *See* Great Britain : Parliamentary.

Mission Field. *See* Society for the Propagation of the Gospel at Home and Abroad. Mission Field.

Missionary Herald. *Boston*, 1843-85.   Mc

Missionary Magazine. Vols. 4-6. *Edinburgh*, 1799-1801.   T

Missionary Magazine and Chronicle. *London*, 1846 66.
Continued as :
Chronicle of the London Missionary Society. *London*, 1867 86.   Mc

Missionary Register. 1813-29. *London*, 1813-29. (Wanting vol. for 1820).   U

Missionary Review of the World. 1st Series. Vol. 9. *New York*, 1886.   Mc
Do. 2nd Series. Vols. 1-10. *New York*, 1888-97. *In progress.*   V
Do. Vols. 1-5, 8-10. *New York*, 1888-97. *In progress.*   Mc

Mississippi. School Reports, annual. 1889-93.   E

Missouri.
Geological Survey ; Biennial Report of the State Geologist. 1891-93.   C
Bulletins. Nos. 3-5. *Jefferson City*, 1890-92.   C
Preliminary Report on Coal Deposits of Missouri, made from field work of 1890-91.   C
School Reports, annual. 1872-3, 1878-9.   E

Missouri Botanical Garden. Report. *St. Louis*, 1890-96. *In progress.*   C

Missouri Educator. Vol. 1. *Jefferson City*, 1858-9.   E

Missouri Historical Society. Publications. Nos. 1 7, 12. *St. Louis*, 1880 96. *In progress.*   C

Mittheilungen aus dem gesammten Gebiete der englischen Sprache und Litteratur. Beiblatt zur "Anglia." *See* Anglia.

(Dr. A. Petermann's) Mittheilungen aus Justus Perthes' Geographischer Anstalt. Bd. 1-3, 6, 7, 16, 35-37, and Ergänzungsbänder 1, 20, 21. *Gotha*, 1855 91.   U

Mnemosyne, Tijdschrift voor Classicke Litteratuur (after Deel 5 (1856): Mnemosyne, Bibliotheca Philologica Batava). Vols. 1-11. *Leyden, Amstelodami*, 1852-62. N.S. Vols. 1-18. *Lugduni Batavorum*, 1873 90. (The publication was discontinued during the years 1863-72.)

Modern Language Notes. Vols. 1-11. *Baltimore*, 1886-96. *In progress.*   U

Modern Review. Vols. 8-12. *Baltimore*, 1893-97. *In progress.*   V
Vols. 1-5. *London*, 1880 84.   Mc.P. (Wanting vol. 3, P.)

Moderne Kunst. Vols. 6-11. *Berlin*, 1891-97. *In progress.*   P

Moleschott's Untersuchungen. *See* Untersuchungen zur Naturlehre des Menschen und Thiere.

Molieriste. 10 Années. *Paris*, 1879 89. U

Monatliche Mittheilungen aus dem Gesammtgebiete der Naturwissenschaften. *See* Naturwissenschaftlicher Verein des Regierungsbezirks Frankfurt. Monatliche Mittheilungen, etc.

Monatsblatt fuer oeffentliche Gesundheitspflege. *See* Verein für öffentliche Gesundheitspflege im Herzogthum Braunschweig.

Monatshefte fuer Chemie, &c. Bd. 1-16. *Wien*, 1881-95. *In progress.* U General-Regis er, Bd. 1-10.

Monatsschrift fuer Geburtskunde und Frauenkrankheiten. Bd. 11-26. *Berlin*, 1858-65. U

Mondes (Les), Revue hebdomadaire des Sciences et de leurs applications aux Arts et a l'Industrie. Tom. 1-17. *Paris*, 1863 68. (Wanting Tom. 5 and 9 11). U

Monetary Times. *Toronto*, 1881-87. L Do. *Toronto*, 1885-97. *In progress.* P

Monist. Vols. 1-6. *Chicago*, 1890-96. *In progress.* U.V

Monthly Illustrator. *See* Quarterly Illustrator:

Monthly Magazine or British Register. Vols. 16-60. *London*, 1800-30. New Series. Vols. 1-5. *London*, 1831-33. T

Monthly Repository. *London*, 1807-8, 1810, 1813-14, 1816, 1818-23, 1825-6. Mc

Monthly Review. Vol. 1. *Montreal*, 1841. P

Monthly Review and Literary Miscellany of the United States. Vol. 1. *Charleston*, 1806. T

Monthly Review (or Literary Journal). 1st Series. 81 vols. *London*, 1749 [1809]-89. U 2nd Series. 108 vols. *London*, 1790-1825. (Wanting Vols. 107 and 108). U Do. Vols. 40-108. *London*, 1803-1825. (Wanting Vols. 49-51). T 3rd Series. Vols. 1-8. *London*, 1826-28. U Do. Vols. 1-18. *London*, 1826-37. T General Index to 1st Series, in 3 vols.

Monthly Visitor. Vol. 1. *Norfolk, Va.*, 1871. E

Montreal. Municipal Reports, annual, 1865, 1874-93. L Do. 1880-94. P

Montreal City Directory. *Montreal*, 1842-3. P

Montreal Medical Journal. Vols. 17-23. *Montreal*, 1888 95. *In progress.* C

Montreal Register, 1842-4, 1845-7, 1848, 1849. Mc

Montreal Natural History Society. *See* Natural History Society of Montreal.

Montreal True Witness. Vols. 1-26. *Montreal*, 1850 76. P

Montreal Witness. 12 vols. *Montreal*, 1846-51, 1859-60. K

Monumenta Habsburgica. *See* Kaiserliche Akademie der Wissenschaften. Monumenta Habsburgica.

Moonshine. *London*, 1885, 1887-92, 1896. *In progress.* P

Morgan's Dominion Annual Register. *See* Dominion Annual Register.

Morning Watch. Vols. 1-7. *London*, 1830-33. T

Morphologisches Jahrbuch. Bd. 1-21. *Leipzig*, 1876-96. *In progress.* (Wanting Bd. 17). Register, Bd. 1-20. U

Moscow—Societe imperiale des Naturalistes. *See* Société impériale des Naturalistes de Moscou.

Mother's Magazine. Vol. 8. *New York*, 1840. E

Munich—Royal Bavarian Academy of Science. *See* Königliche Baierische Akademie der Wissenschaften.

Munsey's Magazine. Vols. 10, 11, 13-17. *New York*, 1894-97. *In progress.* L

Murray's Magazine. Vols. 1-10. *London*, 1887-91. P

Musee Guimet. Annales. Tom. 1-25. *Paris*, 1881-94. C Annales Bibliothèques d'Études. Tom. 1-5. *Paris*, 1892-95. C Annales, Revue de l'Histoire des Religions. Tom. 1-5, 27-32. *Paris*, 1880-95. C

Musee Royal d'Histoire Naturelle de Belgique. Bulletin. Vols. 1-4. *Bruxelles*, 1882 86. C

Musee Teyler. Archives. Series 2. Tom. 1, 3-4. *Haarlem, Paris, Leipzig*, 1881-93. X

Musen-Almanach (hrsg. von Schiller). 1796-1800. *Neustrelitz, Tübingen* (1795 99). U

Museo Civico di Storia Naturale. Atti. Tom. 7-9. *Trieste*, 1884-90, 1895. C

Museo de La Plata. Anales. *La Plata*, 1890-1. C Palaeontologia Argentina 2-3, 1893-4. C Revista. Tom. 1 2, 5. *La Plata*, 1890-1, 1894. C

Museo Nacional. Annales. Tom. 1. *Costa Rica*, 1887. C Informe. *Costa Rica*, 1895 6. *In progress.* C

Museo Nacional de Buenos Aires. Annles. Tom. 4. *Buenos Aires*, 1895. C

Museo Nacional de Mexico. Anales. Vols. 1-4. (1 and 4 incomplete.) 1878-87. P

Museo Nacional de Montevideo. Anales. Nos. 1-5, 7. *Montevideo*, 1894-6. *In progress.* C

Museo Nacional de Rio de Janeiro. Archivos. Vols. 1-8. *Rio de Janeiro*, 1876-92. P Do. Vols. 1, 6 8. *Rio de Janeiro*, 1876, 1885 92. C

Museum; or, Literary and Historical Register. Vols. 1-3. *London*, 1746-7. P

Museum Criticum, or Cambridge Classical Researches. 2 vols. *Cambridge*, 1814 (1826)-26. U

Museum d'Histoire Naturelle de Paris. Nouvelles Archives.
1st Series, 10 vols. *Paris*, 1865-74.
2nd '' 7 vols, '' 1878-84. · U

Museum fuer Voelkerkunde.
Berichte, 20-23. *Leipzig*, 1892-95. C

Museum of Comparative Zoology at Harvard College in Cambridge.
Annual Reports. *Cambridge, Mass.*, 1877-81, 1894-96. *In progress.* C
Bulletin. Vols. 1-27, 29. *Cambridge, Mass.*, 1863-96. *In progress.* C
Do. Vols. 1-23, 25-27, 30. *Cambridge, Mass.*, 1863-97 U
Memoirs. Vols. 1, 2, 5-19. *Cambridge, Mass.*, 1864-96. U

Musical Journal. Vols. 1-2. *Toronto*, 1887-8. P.T.

Musical World. Vols. 62, 64-66. *London*, 1884, 1886-8. P

Narragansett Club.
Publications. Nos. 1-6. *Providence, (R.I.)*, 1867, 1871-74. Mc.

Nassauischer Verein fuer Naturkunde.
Jahrbücher. *Wiesbaden*, 1862-3, 1885-94, 1896. C
Do. Jahrg. 41 and 42. *Wiesbaden*, 1888-9.

Nation. Vols. 1, 2, 5-11. *New York*, 1865-70. U
Do. Vols. 8, 10-13, 15-19, 38-65. *New York*, 1869-97. *In progress.* P
Do. Vols. 58-65. *New York*, 1894-97. *In progress.*

Nation. Vols. 1-2. *Toronto*, 1874-5. P

National Academy of Sciences.
Memoirs. Vols. 3-7. *Washington*, 1884-95. *In progress.* U

National Almanac and Annual Record. 1863. *Philadelphia*, 1863. P.U

National Association for the Promotion of Social Science.
Transactions. 1856-80. *London*, 1857-81. E
Do. 1856-83. *London*, 1857-1884. L
Do. 1859-84. *London*, 1860-85. U
(Wanting Vol. for 1883.)
Do. 1857-84. *London*, 1858-85. P
(Wanting Vols. for 1872, 1883.)
Report on Trades' Societies. *London*, 1860. P

National Church. New Series. Vols. 6-12. *London*, 1877-83. Mc
Do. Vol. 20. *London*, 1892. T

National Conference of Charities and Correction. *See* Conference of Charities.

National Magazine. Vols. 1-3, 5. *New York*, 1852-54. V
Do. Vol. 6. *New York*, 1855. E

National Magazine. *See* Magazine of Western History.

National Repository. N.S. Vols. 1-3, 6-8. *Cincinnati*, 1877-80. V

National Review. Vols. 1-28. *London*, 1883-97. *In progress.* P

National Society. Monthly Paper. 8 vols. *London*, 1857-66. E

National Teacher's Monthly. Vols. 2-3. *New York* and *Chicago*, 1876-7. E

Naturae Novitates. Bibliographie neuer Erscheinungen aller Länder auf dem Gebiete der Naturgeschichte und der exacten Wissenschaften 1879-89, 1893-96. *Berlin*, 1879-96. *In progress.* U

Natural History Review and Quarterly Journal of Science. Vols. 7, 10-12. *London*, 1860-64. C

Natural History Society of Dublin. Proceedings. Vol. 3. *Dublin*, 1859-62. C

Natural History Society of Glasgow. Proceedings. 5 vols. *Glasgow*, 1868-82. U
Do. N.S. Vols. 1-2. *Glasgow*, 1885-88. U
Do. Do. Vols. 1-3. *Glasgow*, 1885-92. C

Natural History Society of Montreal. Annual Reports, 25, 27, 28. *Montreal*, 1853-6. C
Canadian Naturalist and Geologist. Vols. 1-8. *Montreal*, 1856-63. C.P
(Wanting Vol. 8, P.).
Do. New Series. Vols. 1-10. *Montreal*, 1864-83. C.P
Continued as :
Canadian Record of Science. Vols. 1-5. *Montreal*, 1884-92. *In progress.*

Natural History Society of New Brunswick.
Annual Report, 1880. C
Bulletin. Nos. 1-15. *St. John, N.B.*, 1882-97. *In progress.* C.P
Do. Nos. 10-15. *St. John, N.B.*, 1892-97. *In progress.* U

Natural Science. Vols. 1-5. *London*, 1892-94. P

Naturalist. 8 vols. *London*, 1851-58. U

Naturaliste Canadien.
Vols. 1-16. *Quebec*, 1868-86. P
Vols. 15-19, 23. *Cap-Rouge, Chicoutimi, Quebec*, 1885-96. *In progress.* C

Nature. Vols. 1-56. *London*, 1869-97. *In progress.*
Do. Vols. 1-51. *London*, 1869-95. L
Do. Vols. 29-56. *London*, 1884-97. *In progress.* P.T
Do. Vols. 51-56. *London* and *New York*, 1894-97. *In progress.* E
Do. Vols. 15-56. *London* and *New York*, 1876-97. *In progress.* S

Naturforschende Gesellschaft in Bern.
Mittheilungen. *Bern*, 1874-89. U
Do. *Bern*, 1880-94. C

Naturforschende Gesellschaft in Dantzig.
Schriften. Neue Folge. Bd. 3-7. *Dantzig*, 1873-91. U
Do. Bd. 7-8. *Dantzig*, 1887-94. C

Naturforschende Gesellschaft in Emden.
Jahresberichte, 56-74. *Emden*, 1871-90. U
Do. 56-75. '' 1871-91. M
Kleine Schriften, 4-18. '' 1856-79. C

Naturforschende Gesellschaft in Zuerich.
Vierteljahrsschrift. Bd. 30, 32, 37-40. *Zürich,*
1885-95. C

Naturforschende Gesellschaft zu Freiburg im Breisgau.
Berichte. Bd. 1-9. *Freiburg i. B.*, 1886-95. *In progress.* C

Naturforschende Gesellschaft zu Goerlitz.
Abhandlungen. Bd. 2-6, 12-19. *Görlitz,* 1836-81. U

Naturforschende Gesellschaft zu Leipzig.
Sitzungsberichte. Jahrg. 1-18. *Leipzig,* 1875-92. U
Do. Jahrg. 8-13, 18-21. *Leipzig,* 1882-87, 1892-94. C

Naturhistorisch-Medicinischer Verein zu Heidelberg.
Verhandlungen. Neue Folge. Bd. 4. *Heidelberg,* 1887-92. C

Naturhistorische Gesellschaft zu Hannover.
Jahresberichte. *Hannover,* 1883-93. C

Naturhistorische Gesellschaft zu Nuernberg.
Abhandlungen und Jahresberichte. Bd. 8-9. *Nürnberg,* 1884-91. C

Naturhistorischer Verein der preussischen Rheinlande und Westphalens.
Verhandlungen. Jahrg. 22-46. *Bonn,* 1865-89. U
Do. Jahrg. 34-38, 41, 44, 47-52. *Bonn,* 1877-95. C

Naturhistorisches Museum zu Hamburg.
Berichte. *Hamburg,* 1884, 1887. C
Mittheilungen. Bd. 6, 13. *Hamburg,* 1888-95. *In progress.* C

Naturhistorisk Tidskrift. 3e Raekke.
14 Bind. *Kjobenhaven,* 1861-84. U

Naturwissenschaftlich-astronomisches Jahrbuch. *See* Astronomisches Jahrbuch für physische und naturhistorische Himmelsforscher, etc.

Naturwissenschaftliche Gesellschaft "Isis."
Sitzungsberichte. Jahrg. 1861-89. *Dresden,* 1862-90. U
Do. Jahrg. 1868-83, 1885-89, 1891-95. *Dresden,* 1869-96. *In progress.* C

Naturwissenschaftliche Wochenschrift. Bd. 2-5 (imperfect). *Berlin,* 1888-9. U

Naturwissenschaftlicher Verein des Regierungsbezirks Frankfurt.
Monatliche Mittheilungen aus dem Gesammtgebiete der Naturwissenschaften. Bd. 4-7. *Berlin,* 1887-90. C

Naturwissenschaftlicher Verein fuer Sachsen und Thueringen.
Zeitschrift für (die gesammte) Naturwissenschaften. 55 Bde. *Halle,* 1853-82. U

Naturwissenschaftlicher Verein in Hamburg.
Abhandlungen aus dem Gebiete der Naturwissenschaften. Bd. 1-11. *Hamburg,* 1846-89. U

Naturwissenschaftlicher Verein zu Bremen.
Abhandlungen. Bd. 1-11. *Bremen,* 1868-90. U
Do. Bd. 3-14. " 1872-96. C
Jahresberichte, 1866, 1870, 1877-8, 1880. *Bremen.* C

Naturwissenschaftlicher Verein fuer Schleswig-Holstein.
Schriften. Bd. 3-10. *Kiel,* 1878-95. C

Naturwissenschaftlicher Verein zu Hamburg-Altona.
Verhandlungen. *Hamburg,* 1875-1881. C

Naturkundig Tijdschrift voor Nederlandsch Indie. *See* Natuurkundig Vereeniging in Nederlandsch Indië. Natuurkundig Tijdschrift, &c.

Naturkundig Vereeniging in Nederlandsch Indie.
Natuurkundig Tijdschrift voor Nederlandsch Indië. Deel. 2-46 (imperfect). *Batavia,* 1851-87. U

Nautical Almanac and Astronomical Ephemeris. 1836, 1842, 1854, 1855, 1857, 1859-73, 1890, 1893, 1895, 1899. *London,* 1834-97. *In progress.* U
Do. 1881-88 *London,* 1876-1884. L
Do. 1842, 1844-5, 1858-9. *London,* 1834-1855. T
Do. 1884-97. *London,* 1880-94. *In progress.* P

Nautical Magazine. Vol. 49. *London,* 1880. L

Naval and Military Magazine.
Vols. 1-8. *London,* 1884-88. L

Navy and Army Illustrated. Vols. 1-3. *London,* 1895-7. *In progress.* L

Navy Annual. Vols. 1-2. *Portsmouth,* 1896-7. *In progress.* P

Navy Records Society.
Publications. Vols. 1-10. *London,* 1895-97. *In progress.* C

Nebraska State Historical Society.
Proceedings and Collections. Series 2. Vol. 1. *Lincoln,* 1894-5. C
Transactions and Reports. Vols. 1-4. *Lincoln,* 1885-91. C

Nederlandisch Meteorologisch Jaarboek. *See* Observatories : Netherlands.

Nederlandsch-Indische Maatschappij van Nijverheid en Landbouw.
Tijdschrift. Deel 37, 38, 40, 41. *Batavia,* 1880-90. C

Nederlandsche Botanische Vereeniging.
Kruidkundig Archief. Tweede Serie. Deel 4-6. *Nijmegen,* 1883-92. C

Nederlandsche Dierkundige Vereeniging.
Tijdschrift. Deel 1-6. *Leiden,* 1872-85.
Supplement to Deel 1. *Leiden,* 1883-4.
Serie 2. Deel 1-4. *Leiden,* 1885-93. C

Netherlands. Meteorological reports. *See* Observatories : Netherlands.

Neue deutsche Schule. Jahrg. 1 and 2.
Hamburg, 1889 90. U
Neue Jahrbuecher fuer Philologie und Paedagogik. Bd. 127. *Leipzig*, 1883. U
Neue Thalia (hr-g. von Schiller). 4 Bde. *Leipzig*, 1792-3. (Continuation of Thalia). U
Neue Zeitschrift fuer Ruebenzucker-Industrie. Bd. 1-24. *Berlin*, 1878-90. U
Register, B.1. 1-20.
Neueren Sprachen (Die). *See* Phonetische Studien.
Neues Jahrbuch fuer Mineralogie, Geologie und Palaeontologie. Jahrg. 1889-96 ; and Beiträge-Bd. 6-10. *Stuttgart*, 1889-96. *In progress.* U
✗ **Neues Lausitzisches Magazin.** Bd. 65-72. *Görlitz*, 1889 96. *In progress.* C
Neuphilologisches Centralblatt. Jahrg. 1-9. *Hannover*, 1887-96. *In progress.* U
Neurological Society of London. *See* Brain, a Journal of Neurology.
New Bedford. City documents, 1893 4. P
New Brunswick.
Journals of the Legislative Assembly, and Sessional Papers. 1867-96. *In progress.* O.L
Royal Gazette. Vols. 53, 54. 1895-6. *Fredericton. In progress.* O
Educational Report. *Fredericton*, 1852-95. *In progress.* E
New Brunswick Educational Review. Vols. 1-8. *St. John*, 1887-95. *In progress.* E
New Brunswick Natural History Society. *See* Natural History Society of New Brunswick.
New Dominion Monthly. Vols. 1-25. *Montreal*, 1867-78. P.L
New England Magazine. *See* Bay State Monthly.
New Englander. Vols. 2-36. *New Haven, Connecticut*, 1844-77.
New Series. Vols. 1-17. (After Vol. 8 : New Englander and Yale Review). *New Haven*, 1878-90. (Wanting 1st Series. Vols. 9, 14, 15, 20 and 26). U
New Hampshire.
Journals of the Senate, 1873-93. L
Journals of the House, 1873-93. L
Reports, 1874-1895. L
School Reports, annual. 1856-60, 1863-69, 1873-78, 1883, 1885, 1887, 1889 and 1891. E
New Hampshire Historical Society. Collections. Vols. 1-10. *Concord* and *Manchester*, 1824-93. P
New Hampshire Journal of Education. 3 vols. *Concord*, 1860 62. E
New Haven. School Reports, annual. 1850-81. (Wanting 1871.) E
New Jersey.
Adjutant-General's Report. 1890-1. *Trenton.* C
Archives. Documents relating to Colonial History of the State of New Jersey from 1631-1776. Series 1. Vols. 1-10, 15-16. *Newark*, and *Trenton.* C
Agriculture, Board of. Annual Reports. 1890 1. *Trenton.* C

Agricultural Station. Annual Report, 1890. *Trenton.* C
Assessors, Board of. Annual Reports. 1890-1. *Trenton.* C
Charities. Annual Report. 1890. *Trenton.* C
Dairy Commissioners. Annual Report. 1890-1. *Trenton.* C
Dentistry, Board of Registration in. Annual Report. 1891. C
Factories and Workshops, Inspector of. Reports. 1890-1. *Trenton.* C
Geological Annual Report. 1890-1. *Trenton.* C
Industrial School for Girls. Annual Report. *Trenton*, 1890-1. C
Insurance Reports (Pts. 1-2.) 1890. *Trenton.* C
Journal of 47th Senate. *Trenton*, 1891. C
Librarian. Annual Report. 1891. *Trenton.* C
Medical Examiners, Board of. Report. 1891. *Trenton.* C
Pharmacy, Board of. Report. 1891. C
Pilotage, Commissioners of. Reports. 1890-1. *Trenton.* C
Prison Department. Report. *Trenton*, 1890-1. C
Prison Report. 1891. *Trenton.* C
Quarter-Master General's Report. 1890-1. *Trenton.* C
Railroads and Canals. Annual Statements. *Trenton*, 1891. C
Riparian Commissioners. 1890-1. *Trenton.* C
School Reports. *Trenton*, 1849-79. E
Sinking Fund, Commissioners of. Report. 1890. *Trenton.* C
Statistics, Bureau of. 13th, 14th, 15th Annual Reports. *Trenton*, 1890-92. C
Taxation, Board of. First Annual Report. 1891. *Trenton.* C
Treasurer's Accounts, Committee on. Annual Reports. 1890-1. *Trenton.* C
Treasury, Comptroller of the. Annual Report. 1890-1. *Trenton.* C
New Jersey Historical Society.
Proceedings. Series 1. Vols. 1, 4, 6-10. *Newark*, 1845-66. C
Do. Series 2. Vols. 1-9, 10 (Parts 1, 3), Vol. 11 (Parts 3-4). *Newark*, 1867-91. C
New Jersey Washington Association. Annual Report. *Trenton*, 1891. C
New Monthly Magazine and Universal Register. 14 vols. *London*, 1814-20. U
Continued as :
New Monthly Magazine and Literary Journal.
Vols. 1-22. *London*, 1821-28. U
Vols. 1-101. *London*, 1821-54. U
New Popular Educator. Vols. 1-2. *London*. n.d. P
New Princeton Review. *See* Princeton Review.
New Review. Vols. 1-17. *London*, 1889-97. (Wanting Vol. 9, 1893, L). L.P
New Shakespeare Society.
Publications.
Series 1 (Transactions), pts. 1-13. U
Do. Do. " 1-10. P
" 2 (Plays), pts. 1, 2, 5-11, and 15. U
" 1-11, 15. P
" 3 (Originals), pt. 1. P.U

" 4 (Allusion Books), pts. 1-3.   P.U
" 6 (Shakspere's England), pts. 1 8, 12
    and 14.   U
Do.   Do.   pts. 1-8, 12.   P
" 7 (Mysteries), pt. 1.   P.U
" 8 (Miscellanies), pts. 1-4.   U
            " 1-3.   P
    London, 1874-92. *In progress.*

New South Wales.
Department of Mines and Agriculture. Annual
reports, 1875-81, 1885-95. *Sydney.*   C
Publications. Mineral Products of New South
Wales. By John Mackenzie, F.G.S.,
Examiner of Coal Fields. *Sydney*, 1887. C
Mineral Products of New South Wales, and
Notes on Geology. *Sydney*, 1882.   C
Mineral Statistics and Notes on Geological
Collection. *Sydney*, 1875.   C
Geological Survey of New South Wales :
Memoirs. No. 5. *Sydney*, 1894.   C
Memoirs (Palæontology). Nos. 1-5, 7-9.
Sydney, 1888-95.   C
Records. Vols. 1-2, 4. *Sydney*, 1889-92,
1894-5.   C
Geology of Vegetable Creek. Tin-mining
Field, New South Wales. *Sydney*, 1887. C
Historical Records. By Lieut. James Cook.
Vols. 1-3. 1762-1799. *Sydney*, 1893.   C
Legislative Assembly. Report on Technical
Education. 1885, 1887. *Sydney.*   C
Report on Museums for Technology, Science
and Art ; and upon Scientific, Professional and
Technical Instruction. 1880.   C
Railways of New South Wales. Reports on
Construction and Working. *Sydney*, 1872-76.
                                         C
Reports on Education, annual. 1867-78, 1880-
82, 1884-5, 1887-95. *In progress. Sydney.* E
Statistics. 1874-81.   L

New South Wales Philosophical Society.
Transactions. *Sydney*, 1862-65.   C

New South Wales Statistical Register.
For the year 1894 and previous years.
Sydney, 1896. *In progress.*   U

New Sydenham Society.
Publications. 43 vols. *London*, 1859-96. *In progress.*   U
(Complete only from 1892.)

New World.
Vols. 1-6. *Boston*, 1892 97. *In progress.* (Wanting Vol. 1, Mc.)   Mc.V

New York.
Assembly Documents, 1851-2. 11 vols. *Albany.*
                                         T
Do. 1866-96. *Albany.*   L
Assembly Journal, 1866-96.   L
Journal of the Legislative Council. 1691-1775. L
Provincial Congress, Journal. 1775-77. Vols.
1-2. *Albany*, 1842.   T
Senate Documents, 1851-2. 6 vols. *Albany.* T
            1866-96.   "   L
" Journal, 1866-95.   "   L
Archives, etc.
State Archives. Vol. 1. 1887 (being Vol. 15 of
the Colonial History).   C.P.L
Documents relating to the Colonial History of
New York State. Vols. 1-15. *Albany*, 1856-
1887. (Wanting Vol. 11, C.)   C.L.P.U

Documentary History of New York. Vols. 1-4.
Albany, 1850-1.   C.E.L.P.T
School Reports. *Albany*, 1843-75, 1878-9, 1881-95.
In progress.   E
State Geologist. Annual reports. Nos. 5-6, 8-
13. *Albany*, 1886-93.   C

New York (City).
School Reports, annual.
1848-77, 1879-89.   E

New York Academy of Sciences.
Annals. Vols. 1-9. *New York*, 1880-96. *In progress.* (Wanting Vol. 6.)   U
Memoirs. No. 1. *New York*, 1895. *In progress.*   U
Transactions. Vols. 1-14. *New York*, 1881-96.
In progress. (Wanting Vols. 10 and 11.) U
Do. Vols. 1-3, 12-14. *New York*, 1881-96.
Annals. *In progress.*   C

New York Chamber of Commerce.
Annual Reports. *New York*, 1874-5, 1882-97.
In progress.   P

New York Daily Graphic.
Vols. 1-25.
New York, 1873-81.   L

New York Historical Society.
Collections. 1st Series. Vols. 1-5. *New York*, 1809-30.
Do. 2nd Series. Vols. 1-3. *New York*, 1841-57.   P
Do. Publication Fund Series. Vols. 1-23.
New York, 1868-91. *In progress.*   U
Do. Vols. 1-6, 8-23. *New York*, 1868-90.
In progress.   P
Proceedings. *New York*, 1843-49.   P.U

New York Literary and Philosophical Society.
Transactions. *New York*, 1815.   T

New York Mathematical Society.
Bulletin. 3 vols. *New York*, 1892-94. U
(For continuation, *see* American Mathematical Society.)

New York Medical Journal.
Vols. 41-56.
New York, 1885 92.   L

New York Microscopical Society.
Journal. Vols. 1-12. *New York*, 1885-96. *In progress.*   C
Do. Vols. 1-5. *New York*, 1885-89.   U

New York Produce Exchange.
Annual Reports. *New York*, 1872-86.   P

New York School Journal.
7 vols. *New York*, 1871-83.   E

New York State Agricultural Society.
Transactions. *Albany*, 1843, 1850-1.   T
Do. 1853.   V
Do. 1883-86. *Albany*, 1889.   P

New York State Educational Journal.
Vol. 1. *Albany*, 1882-3.   E

New York State Museum (of Natural History).
Annual Report. Nos. 13, 24, 26, 33-35, 38-9,
41-47. *Albany*, 1860-93.   C
Bulletin. Vols. 1-3 (Nos. 1-15). *Albany*, 1892-
95. *In progress.*   U

New York Teacher.
17 vols. *Albany*, 1853-69.   E

New Zealand.

Journals and Appendix, House of Representatives. 1880 95. (Imperfect).   L
Journals of the Legislative Council, with Appendix. 1881-95. (Imperfect).   L
Parliamentary Debates. 1854 96 (imperfect). L
Reports on Education. *Wellington*, 1877-96. *In progress.*   E
Colonial Museum and Geological Survey of New Zealand.
Annual Reports of Colonial Museum and Laboratory. Nos. 8-14. *Wellington*, 1872-83.   C
Publications.
Fishes of New Zealand. Catalogue with diagnosis of species. *Wellington*, 1872. C
Manual of Indigenous Grasses of New Zealand. *Wellington*, 1880.   C
Manual of New Zealand Coleoptera. Parts 1-2. *Wellington*, 1880-1.   C
Manual of New Zealand Mollusca. *Wellington*, 1880.   C
New Zealand Diptera, Orthoptera, Hymenoptera. Catalogue with descriptions of the species. *Wellington*, 1881.   C
Paleontology of New Zealand. Part 4 : Corals and Brizozoa of Neozoic Period. *Wellington*, 1880.   C
Studies in Biology for New Zealand Students. Nos. 1-2. *Wellington*, 1881.   C
Tertiary Mollusca and Echinodermata of New Zealand in the Museum Collection, Catalogue. *Wellington*, 1873.   C
Handbook of New Zealand. 1883.   C
Reports of Geological Explorations. 1879-84. *Wellington.*   C

New Zealand Institute.

Transactions and Proceedings. Vols. 1, 5-7, 9-19, 21-28. *Wellington*, 1868-95. *In progress.* C
Index to Vols. 1-8.

Newcastle-upon-Tyne Society of Antiquaries.

Archæologia Æliana, or Miscellaneous Tracts Relating to Antiquity. 4 vols. *Newcastle-upon-Tyne*, 1822-55.   P
Do. New Series. Vols. 1-18. *Newcastle-upon-Tyne*, 1857-96. *In progress.*   P

Newfoundland.

Gazette. Vols. 88-89. *St. John's*, 1895-6. *In progress.*   O
Journals of the Legislative Council, 1876.   L
Journals of the House of Assembly, 1869, 1875, 1892-94.   L
Fisheries Commission. Annual Report for 1889. *St. John's.*
Report on the Public Schools in Newfoundland under Methodist Boards. 1890   V

Newgate Monthly Magazine.

Vols. 1-2. *London*, 1824 6.   P

Newport Natural History Society.

Proceedings. *Newport*, 1883-87; 1888-90. C

News of the Churches. *Edinburgh*, 1857-62.   V

Newspaper Companion. *See* Companion to the Newspaper.

Newspaper Press Directory for the United Kingdom. *London*, 1887; 1893. P

Niederdeutsche Denkmaeler. *See* Verein für niederdeutsche Sprachforschung.

Niederlaendisches Archiv fuer Zoologie. Bd. 1-5. *Leipzig, Leiden*, 1871-79. U

Niederrheinische Gesellschaft fuer Natur und Heilkunde.

Sitzungsberichte. *Bonn*, 1895.   C

Niles' Weekly Register. 52 vols. *Baltimore*, 1816-37.   P
Continued as :
Niles' National Register. Vols. 53-63. *Baltimore*, 1837-43.   P

Nineteenth Century. Vols. 1-42. *London* and *New York*, 1877-97. *In progress.* L.Mc.P.U
Vols. 31-42. *London*, 1892-97. *In progress.* E
Vols. 1, 27, 29, 32-42. *London*, 1879-97. *In progress.*   V

Nord und Sued. Bd. 50 63. *Breslau*, 1889-92.   U

Nordisk Tidskrift for Filologi og Pædagogik.

Række 2. Bd. 9-10.
"   3. Bd. 1-4. *Kjobenhavn*, 1885-96. *In progress.*

Norske Gradenaalings-kommission.

Udgivet af Vandstandsobservationen. Hefte 1-5. *Christiania*, 1882 93.   C

North American. Vol. 1. *Toronto*, 1850-52. P

North American Review. Vols. 1-112, 120-135, 138-165. *New York*, 1815-97. *In progress.*   L
Vols. 10-165. *Boston* and *New York*, 1820-97. *In progress.*   P
Vols. 154-165. *New York*, 1892-97. *In progress.*   U
Vols. 158-165. *Boston*, 1861 97. *In progress.*   E

North British Review. Vols. 1-53. *London*, 1844-71.   L.P
(Wanting Vols. 1-5, 26-7, 38-9, 46, 49, P).

North of England Institute of Mining and Mechanical Engineers.

Transactions. Vols. 1-2, 7-20, 22-42, 44, 45. *Newcastle-upon-Tyne*, 1852-96. *In progress.* C
General Index of Vols. 1-25.
Report of Proceedings of Flameless-explosives Committee. Parts 1-3. *Newcastle-on-Tyne*, 1894-96. *In progress.*   C

North-West Territories.

Journals of the Legislative Assembly. 1877-96. *In progress.*   O.L
Do. 1877-87.
Gazette. Vols. 1-13. *Regina*, 1884-96. *In progress.*   O

Norton's Literary Guide. Vol. 1. *New York*, 1854.   E

Norway. Meteorological reports. *See* Observatories : Norway.

Norwegische Commission der Europaeischen Gradmessung.

Publicationen (Geodätische Arbeiten). Hefte
1-7. *Christiania,* 1880-90. C
Astronomische Beobachtungen. *Christiania,* 1895.
Resultate d. im-Sommer-1894-ausgeführten Pendelbeobachtungen. C

Notes and Queries.

1st Series.	12 vols.	*London.*	1850-55.	L.O.P
2nd "	12 "	*London,*	1856-61.	O.P
3rd "	12 "	*London,*	1862 68.	O.P
4th "	12 "	*London,*	1868 73.	P
5th "	12 "	*London,*	1874-79.	P
6th "	12 "	*London,*	1880-85.	P
7th "	12 "	*London,*	1886 91.	L.P
8th "	12 "	*London,*	1892-97.	

In progress. Indexes to Series 1 8. P

Nouvelles Annales de Mathematiques.

20 tom. *Paris,* 1842-61.
2me Série. 20 tom. *Paris,* 1862 81.
3me " Tom. 1-15. *Paris,* 1882-96. *In progress.* U

Nova Scotia.

House of Assembly Journals and Proceedings, with Appendices. 1825, 1830, 1836, 1838 96. *In progress.* O
Do. 1867-96. *In progress.* L
Index, 1758-1830.
Legislative Council Journals and Proceedings. 1839, 1841-50, 1852-54, 1856-65, 1868, 1870-74, 1876-78, 1881. O
Do. 1867-96. *In progress.* L
Annual Report of the Superintendent of Education. *Halifax.* 1870-96. *In progress.* E

Nova Scotia Historical Society.

Collections. Vols. 2-9. *Halifax,* 1879 95. C✗
Do. Vols. 2, 3, and 9. *Halifax,* 1881-96. *In progress.* U
Do. Vols. 1-9. *Halifax,* 1884 6. *In progress.* P

Nova Scotian Institute of (Natural) Science.

Proceedings and Transactions. Vols. 2-9 (1867-95). *Halifax,* 1870-96. *In progress.* (Wanting Vol. 3 and Vol. 4, Pts. 1-2). U
Do. Vols. 3-8. (1871-94). *Halifax,* 1874-95. *In progress.* P
Do. Vols. 2, 8-9 (1867-95). *Halifax,* 1870-96. *In progress.* C✗

Nuova Antologia di Scienze, Lettere ed Arte.

3ta (-4ta) Serie. Vols. 21-66. *Roma,* 1889-96 *In progress.* (Wanting Vols. 22, 24). U

Nuttall Ornithological Club.

Bulletin. Vols. 1-8. *Cambridge* and *Boston,* 1876-83.
Continued as :
The Auk. Vols. 1-14. *Boston* and *New York,* 1884-97. *In progress.* P

Nyt Magazin for Naturvidenskaberne.

Vols. 13-20. *Christiania,* 1864-74.
Anden raekke. 6 vols. *Christiania,* 1875-81. ✗
Tredie " Vol. 3. *Christiania,* 1886

Oberhessische Gesellschaft fuer Natur-und Heilkunde.

Berichte. 14-29. *Giessen,* 1873-93. (Wanting No. 28). U
Do. 21-34. *Giessen,* 1882-95. C✗

Observateur (L').
See Bibliothèque Canadienne.

Observatories.

International Meteorological Committee (Comité météorologique international).
Reports. Meetings. *London,* 1872-96. *In progress.* M
Reports. Meetings, 1-4. *London,* 1880-88. U
(Also in French, published at Paris).
International Meteorological Congress at Vienna.
Reports of the Permanent Committee. 1873, 1874, 1876, and 1878. *London,* 1874-79. U
Do. 1873-4, 1876, 1878, 1888. *London,* 1874-9. M
International Meteorological Observations. Bulletin. January, February, March, May, and July, 1876. U

AFRICA.

Cape of Good Hope. Meteorological Commission. Reports for the years 1882-3, 1886. *Cape Town,* 1883-7. M
Reports for the years 1880-1 and 1884-88. *Cape Town,* 1881-89. U
Results of Astronomical Observations made during the years 1834-38 at the Cape of Good Hope by Sir J. F. W. Herschel. *London,* 1847. U
Royal Observatory. Observations. Vol. 1 (1841-46). *London,* 1851. U

Guinea.
Observationes meteorologicæ per annos 1829 34 and 1836-42 in Guinea factæ. *Hauniæ,* 1845. U

AUSTRALIA AND NEW ZEALAND.

New South Wales. Meteorological Service. Daily Weather Charts of Australia and New Zealand. *Sydney,* 1891-96. *In progress.* M
Meteorological Observations. *Sydney.* 1865-77, 1880 84. M
Results of Rain and River Observations. Annual. *Sydney,* 1873-96. *In progress.* M
New Zealand. Meteorological Reports. *Wellington,* 1873-83. C

Queensland.
Daily Weather Reports (v.d.). *Brisbane.* M
Annual Report. *Brisbane,* 1887-91. M
Reports of the Government Meteorological Observer, Supplement to Queensland Gazette (Rainfall Reports). *Brisbane,* 1891-97. *In progress.* M

South Australia.
Meteorological Observations made at the Adelaide Observatory and other places in South Australia and the Northern Territory. 1876-78. *Adelaide,* 1877-79. M
Do. 1878, 1880-82. *Adelaide,* 1879-83. U
Observations (Rainfall). *Adelaide,* 1887, 1894. M

Tasmania. Magnetical and Meteorological Observatory at Hobart Town.
Observations made at the . . . Observatory at Hobarton in Van Diemen's Island, and by the Antarctic Naval Expedition. Vols. 1-3 (1841-48). *London,* 1850-53. U

Observatories.

Tasmania.
Result of 25 years' Meteorological Observations for Hobart Town, etc. *Hobart Town,* 1866.   U

Victoria.
Results of the Meteorological Observations taken in the Colony of Victoria. 1859-62. *Melbourne,* 1864.   U
Results of Observations on Meteorology, Terrestrial Magnetism, etc. Vols. 1-5 (1872-76). *Melbourne* (1873-77).   U

Western Australia.
Meteorological Reports.   *Perth,* 1879-87, 1891-93.   M

AUSTRIA-HUNGARY.
Budapest. Königl. und Reichs-Anstalt für Meteorologie und Erdmagnetismus. Jahrbücher. Bd. 1-22, 24.   *Budapest,* 1871-92, 1894.   *In progress.*   M
Prag.   Kaiserlich-königliche Sternwarte zu Prag.
Magnetische und meteorologische Beobachtungen. Jahrg. 1-28 (1839-67).   *Prag,* 1841-68.   U
Do. Jahrg. 5-10, 12-13, 15-36, 38-57 (1843-95). *Prag,* 1844-96. *In progress.* C
Do. Jahrg. 48-57. *Prag,* 1887-96. *In progress.*   M
Trieste.   Osservatorio marittimo di Trieste.
Rapporti annuali.   Vols. 1-3 (1884-86). *Trieste,* 1886-89.   U
Do. Vols. 1-11 (1884-94).   *Trieste,*1886-96. *In progress.*   M
Wien.   Kaiserlich-königliche Central-Anstalt für Meterologie und Erdmagnetismus. Jahrbücher.   Bd. 4-8 (1852-56). *Wien,* 1856-61.
Do. Neue Folge.   Bd. 1-4 (1864-67), 20-22 (1883-85) and 24 (1887). *Wien,* 1866-88.   U
Do. Bd. 3-33. *Wien,* 1866-96.   M
Do. Bd. 20-28, 30. *Wien,* 1883-93.   C
Wien.   Kaiserlich - königliche Universitäts-Sternwarte.
Annalen. Bd. 2-6 (1882-86). *Wien,* 1884-88.   U
Astronomischer Kalender, 1887-90. *Wien.* U
Wein.   Kaiserlich-königliches Gradmessungs-Bureau.
Astronomische Arbeiten.   Bd. 1 and 3. *Wien,* 1889-91.   U
Do. Bd. 1. *Wien,* 1889.   C
Verhandlungen. Protokolle. *Wien,* 1891, 1894-96. *In progress.*   C
Osterreichischen Gradmessungs-Commission.

BELGIUM.
Observatoire (royal) de Bruxelles.
Annales. Tom. 1-19. *Bruxelles,* 1834-69.   U
Do. Tom. 25, and N.S. Tom. 1-4. *Bruxelles,* 1876-95.   M
Annuaires. *Bruxelles,* Annee 45-64. 1878-97.   M

CANADA.
Magnetic (and Meteorological) Observatory, Toronto.
Annual Reports. *Toronto* and *Ottawa,*1841-80.   L

Annual Reports.   *Toronto* and *Ottawa,* 1872-9, 1881-4, 1886-9.   C
Do. *Toronto,* 1869-90, 1895.   M
Do. *Toronto,* 1866-71.   E
Meteorological Register.   *Toronto,* 1861-97. *In progress.*   M
Do. *Toronto,* 1883, 1886-7, 1889, 1893. 1895-6. *In progress.*   C
Observations. Vols. 1-3 (1840-48). *London,* 1845-57.   U
Abstracts of Meteorological Observations. 1854-59. *Toronto,* 1864.   M.U
Do. 1853-62. *Toronto.*   C
Abstracts of Magnetical Observations. 1856-62. *Toronto,* 1862.   P.U
Results of Meteorological Observations. 1860-62. *Toronto,* 1864.   P.U
Abstracts and Results of Magnetical and Meteorological Observations. 1841-71. *Toronto,* 1875.   M.U
Monthly Weather Review. *Ottawa* and *Toronto,* 1878, 1880-83, 1885-95. *In progress.*   M
Do. 1890-93. *Toronto,* 1890-94.   U
Do. 1879-97. *Toronto,* 1880-97. *In progress.*   M
Daily Maps of North America. 1872-97. *In progress.*   M
Monthly Maps, January, 1895-97. *In progress.*   M

CENTRAL AMERICA.
Observatorio Astron. y Meteor. de San Salvador.   Anales. *San Salvador,* 1895. C

CEYLON.
Colombo. Report on the Meteorology of Ceylon (Ceylon Administration Report). 1882-95(1882 gives average results from 1869) *In progress.*   M

CHILI.
Observatorio Astronomico de Santiago. Annals. *Santiago de Chile,* 1873-81 (incomplete).   M
Observaciones meteorologicas.   1882-84. *Santiago de Chile,* 1885.   U

CHINA.
Hong-Kong Observatory.
Observations. 1884-87. *Hong-Kong,* 1885-88.   U
Do. 1884-95, *Hong-Kong.* 1885-96. *In progress.*   M
China Coast Meteorological Register. *Hong-Kong,* 1896. *In progress.*   M
Shanghai.   Observatoire de Zi-Ka-Wei. Bulletin Mensuel, 1877-95. *In progress.* M
Reports on the Typhoons of 1892-3, 1896. M
Shanghai. Meteorological Society.   Annual Report. 1893-95. *In progress.*   M

CUBA.
Observaciones Magneticas y Meteorologicas. *Habana,* 1874-76, 1885-95. *In progress.* M

DENMARK.
Dansk Meteorologisk Institut.
Meteorologisk Aarbog.   1880, 1881 and 1883. *Kjobenhavn,* 1881-84.   U
Do. 1874-95. *Kjöbenhavn,* 1875-96. *In progress.*   M
Observatoire Magnétique.   Annales. *Copenhague,* 1892-4.   M
Bulletin Meteorologique du Nord. *Copenhague,* 1874-96. *In progress.*   M

Observatories.

ENGLAND.

Cambridge University Observatory.
Astronomical Observations. Vols. 1-22
(1828-69). *Cambridge*, 1829-90. U
Greenwich Royal Observatory.
Astronomical Observations. Vols. 1-4 (1765-1810). *London*, 1776-1811. M
Do. (1811-22, 1825, 1829-40). *London*, 1815-42. U
(The vols. for 1839 and 1840 bear the title "Astronomical, Magnetical and Meteorological Observations ").
Continued in two divisions :
Astronomical Observations. 1841-47. *London*, 1843-49. U
Do. 1836-46. *London*, 1837-48. M
Magnetical and Meteorological Observations. 1840-47. *London*, 1843-49. M, U
Continued as :
Astronomical and Magnetical and Meteorological Observations. 1848-68. *London*, 1850-70. U
Do. 1848-94. *London*, 1850-97. M
Reductions of the Observations of Planets from 1750 to 1830. *London*, 1845. M.U
Reductions of the Observations of the Moon from 1750 to 1851. 3 vols. *London*, 1848-59. U
Do. Vol. 1; 1750-1830. *London*, 1848. M
Report of Her Majesty's Astronomers, 1879-96. *In progress*. M
Results of the Astronomical Observations (extracted from the Greenwich Observations). 1848-68. [*London*, 1850-70]. U
Do. 1849-83. [*London*, 1851-85]. M
Results of the Magnetical and Meteorological Observations (extracted from the Greenwich Observations). 1849-68. [*London*, 1850-70]. U
Meteorological reductions. 1847-73. *London*, 1878. M
Spectroscopic and Photographic Results. 1882-91. *London*, 1884-93. M
London Board of Trade.
Meteorological Papers of the Meteorological Department. Nos. 2, 6, 9, 10 and 11. *London*, 1861-2. M
Do. Report, 1862-64. M
London Meteorological Office.
Daily Weather Report. Jan., 1872-74, 1876-97. *In progress*. M
Hourly Means. 1874 93. *In progress*. M
Monthly Weather Report. 1884-87, 1890-97. *In progress*. M
Observations on days of Unusual Magnetic Disturbance, made at the British Colonial Magnetic Observatories. Vol. 1 (1840-44). *London*, 1851. U
Quarterly Summary of Weekly Reports. 1869-80, 1892-96. *In progress*. M
Quarterly Weather Reports. 1867-79. *London*, 1870-87. U
Report of the Meteorological Council. 1867-71, 1873-75, 1877-84, 1886, 1888-96. *In progress*. M
Weekly Weather Report. 1878-82, 1884-97. *In progress*. M

Oxford University—Radcliffe Observatory.
Meteorological Observations. 1857. *Oxford*, [1857]. U
Results of Astronomical Observations made in the year 1866. *Oxford*, 1868. U
Results of Astronomical and Meteorological Observations. Vols. 4-46 (1843-89). *Oxford*, 1845-96. *In progress*. M
Results of Meteorological Observations. 1858-85. *Oxford*, 1861-89. M

FINLAND.

Helsingfors. Institut Météorologique Central. Observations. Liv. 1. Vols. 1-13. *Helsingfors*, 1882-94. *In progress*. C
Kuopio. Société des Sciences de Finland. Observations météorologiques. *Kuopio*, 1881-91. C

FRANCE.

Lyons. Observatoire. Données pour l'année Météorologique. 1879, 1879-1880, 1880-81. *Lyons*, 1880-82. M
Lyons. Commission Départmentale de météorologie du Rhone. 1880-82. *Lyons*, 1881-85. M
Marseille. Commission météorologique du Département des Bouches-du-Rhone. Bulletin annuel. 1882-96. *Marseille*, 1883-97. M
Paris Bureau Central Météorologique de France.
Annales. *Paris*, 1878-97. *In progress*. M
Paris Bureau des Longitudes.
Annales du Bureau des Longitudes et de l'Observatoire astronomique de Montsouris. Tom. 1. *Paris*, 1877. U
Annuaire. 1830-49, 1880 and 1884. *Paris*, 1829-83. U
Do. 1838-9, 1880-82, 1890-91. *Paris*, 1837-90. M
Connaissance des Temps ou des Mouvements Célestes. 1883 and 1886. *Paris*, 1881-84. U
Paris Observatoire.
Bulletin Astronomique. Tom. 1-6. *Paris*, 1884-89. U
Perpignan. Bulletin Météorologique Pyrenees-Orientales. 1890-93, 1895. *Perpignon*, 1891-6. *In progress*. M

GERMANY.

Berlin.
Deutsche Polar-Kommission.
Internationale Polarforschung. 1882-3. Bd. 1-2. *Berlin*, 1886. M
Jahresbericht über die Beobachtungs-Ergebnisse der von den fortlichen Versuchsanstalten des Königreichs Preussen, des Herzogthums Braunschweig, der Reichslande und dem Landesdirectorium der Provinz Hannover. 1875-95. *Berlin*, 1877-97. *In progress*. M
Berlin. Königliche Sternwarte.
Astronomische Beobachtungen. Bd. 1-4. *Berlin*, 1840-57. U
Berlin. Königliches Preussisches Meteorologisches Institut.
Abhandlungen. Band I. (Nos. 1-5). *Berlin*, 1890-92. M
Bericht über die Thätigkeit. 1891-6. *Berlin*, 1893-97. *In progress*. M

Observatories.

GERMANY.

Berlin.
Ergebnisse der Beobachtungen an dem Stationen II. und III. Ordnung im Jahres 1886-8, 1889-93 (Hefte 1-3), 1894-5 (Hefte 1-2), 1896 (Heft 2). *Berlin*, 1888-97 *In progress.*   M
Ergebnisse der Gewitter-Beobachtungen 1891-4. *Berlin*, 1895 97. *In progress.* M
Ergebnisse der Magnetischen Beobachtungen in Potsdam. 1890-91, 1893, 1894-5 (Hefte 1-2). *Berlin*, 1894-97. *In progress.* M
Ergebnisse der Niederschlags-Beobachtungen. 1891 94. *Berlin*, 1893-97. *In progress.* M
Preussische Statistik. 1879-85. *Berlin*, 1880-87. (Afterwards called Ergebnisse der Beobachtungen as above).   M
Bonn. Sternwarte der Königlichen Rheinischen Friedrich-Wilhelms Universität.
Astronomische Beobachtungen. Bd. 1-8. *Bonn*, 1846-86   U
Bremen. Deutsches Meteorologisches Jahrbuch, Meteorologische Station. I. Ordnung in Bremen. 1891-94. *Bremen*, 1892-95. *In progress.*   M
Do. 1894. *Bremen*, 1895. *In progress.* C
Chemnitz. Königl. Sächsisches Meteorologisches Institut.
Jährbuch, 1885 95. *Chemnitz*, 1886-96. *In progress.*   M
Göttingen. Königliche Sternwarte.
Astronomische Mittheilungen. Theil. 4. *Göttingen*, 1895.   M
Hamburg.
Deutsche Seewarte.
Aus dem Archiv. Jahrg. 8-11 (1885-88). *Hamburg*, 1886-89.   U
Do. Jahrg. 1-19 (1878-96). *Hamburg*, 1879-97. *In progress.*   M
Cartes Synoptiques Journalières du Temps pour le Nord de l'Atlantique, et une partie des Continents Avoisinants. Publiées par l'Institut Météorologique Danois et le Deutsche Seewarte. 1875-6, 1881-91. *Copenhague et Hamburg*,1879-97. *In progress.* M
Meteorologische Beobachtungen in Deutschland. Jahrg. 1876-7. *Leipzig*, 1878-79. M
Do. Jahrg. 1-9 (1878-86). *Hamburg*, 1880-88.   M.U
Ergebnisse der meteorologischen Beobachtungen. 1887 and 1888. *Hamburg*, 1889-90.   U
Do. 1887-95. *Hamburg*, 1889-97. *In progress.*   M
Deutsche überseeische meteorologische Beobachtungen. Heft. 1-3 (1883-89). [*Hamburg*, 1886-89].   U
Do. Heft. 1-7. (1883-93). [*Hamburg*, 1887-96].   M
Monatliche Uebersicht der Witterung. Jahrg. 1-14. *Hamburg*, 1876-89. (Wanting Jahrg. 3).   U
Do. Jahrg. 1-10. (1876-85). *Hamburg*, 1878-87.   M
Continued as :
Monatsbericht.
Jahrg. 11-16 (1886-91). *Hamburg*, 1888-93.   M

Vierteljahrs-Wetter-Rundschau an der Hand der täglichen synoptischen Wetterkarten für Nordatlantischen Ocean des Danischen Meteorologischen Instituts und der Deutschen Seewarte. Bd. 1-8, 1883 91. *Berlin*, 1888-96. *In progress.*   M
Hanover. Ergebnisse der Witterungs-Beobachtungen. (1864-73). *Hanover*, 1876.   M
Innsbruck. K. K. Universität.
Meteorologische Beobachtungen. 1891-93. *Innsbruck*, 1892-96. *In progress.*   M
Karlsruhe.
Beiträge zur Hydographie des Grossherzogthums Baden. Heft 2. 1885. *Karlsruhe*, 1885.   M
Niederschlagsbeobachtungen der Meteorologischen Stationen in Grossherzogthum Baden, 1888-96. *Karlsruhe*, 1892-97. *In progress.*   M
Karlsruhe. Meteorologische Central Station Karlsruhe.
Jahresbericht. *Karlsruhe*, 1869-76, 1878-86.   M
Leipzig.
Meteorologische Bericht für Wetterprognosen im Königreich Sachsen. 1880. *Leipzig*, 1881.   M
Ergebnisse der Niederschlags-Beobachtungen in Leipzig,~ 1864-81. *Leipzig*, 1882.   M
Königl. Sächsische Meteorologische Institut in Leipzig. Jahrbuch. 1883-4. *Leipzig*, 1883-85.   M
Monatliche Berichte über die Resultate aus den Meteorologischen Beobachtungen Angestellt an den Königlich Sächsischen Stationen, 1873-79. *Dresden* and *Leipzig*, 1873-79.   M
Resultate aus dem Meteorologischen Beobachtungen, 1864-75, 1875-85. *Dresden* and *Leipzig*, 1866-87.   M
Magdeburg. Wetterwarte der Magdeburgischen Zeitung. Jahrbuch der Meteorologischen Beobachtungen, 1881-95. *Magdeburg*, 1882-96. *In progress.*   M
Mannheim. Discussion of the Meteorological and Magnetical Observations made . . . during the years 1858-63. *Mannheim*, 1867.
Metz. Académie de Metz.
Observations Météorologiques faites à Metz. 1877, 1879-83, 1885. *Metz*, 1879 89.   M
München. Königliche Sternwarte.
Jahrbuch. 1838-41. *München*, (1838-41). U
Meteorologische und Magnetische Beobachtungen, 1876-82. *München*.   C
Neue Annalen. Bd. 1-2. *München*, 1890-91.   C
München. Beobachtungen der Meteorologischen Stationen im Königreich Bayern. Jahrg. 4-10 (1882-1888). *München* [1882-88].   U
Do. Jahrg. 1-18 (1879-96). *München* [1879-97]. *In progress.*   M
Monatliche Uebersichten über die Witterungs —Verhaltnisse im Königreich Bayern. *München*, 1881, 1887.   M
Strassburg. Deutsches Meteorologisches Jahrbuch. Beobachtungs system von Elsass-Lothringen. *Strassburg*, 1890-94.   M

Observatories.

Strassburg. Kaiserliche Sternwarte.
Annalen. Bd. 1. 1882-86. *Karlsruhe*, 1896
M
Stuttgart. Meteorologische Centralstation.
Mittheilungen, 1876-86. *Stuttgart*, 1878-
87. M
Ergebnisse der Meteorologische Beobacht-
ungen in Württemberg, 1887-96. *Stuttgart*,
1888-97. *In progress.* M
Resultate vom 1887. *Stuttgart*, 1888. M
Zehnjährige Resultate der an der Württemb.
Meteorologischen Stationen in der Zeit
1866 bis 1875. Angestellten Böobach-
tungen. M

INDIA.
Bengal Daily Weather Report. 1868-74.
Calcutta, 1869-75. M
Bombay. Magnetical and Meteorological
Observatory (afterwards called Government
Observatory). Observations, 1845-64. *Bom-
bay*, 1862-67. C
Do. 1843 and 1845-48. *Bombay*, 1843-
51. U
Magnetical and Meteorological Observations.
1879-82 and 1886. *Bombay*, 1883-88. U
Calcutta. Meteorological Department of
India.
Cyclone Memoirs. Parts 1, 3-5. *Calcutta*,
1888 93. M
Daily Weather Report. 1880-97. *Calcutta*,
1880-97. *In progress.* M
Indian Meteorological Memoirs. Vols. 1-9.
1876-97. *Calcutta*, 1876-98. *In progress.*
M
Monthly Weather Report. 1891-97. *Cal-
cutta*, 1891-98. *In progress.* M
Rainfall Data. 1891-95. *In progress.* M
Reports on the administration of the Meteor-
ological Department of the Government of
India. 1875-97. *Calcutta*, 1876 98. *In
progress.* M
Do. 1877, 1880, 1884-88. *Calcutta*,
1879-89. U
Madras. (Honourable East India Company's
Observatory). Astronomical Observations.
1843-47. *Madras*, 1848. C
Meteorological Observations. 1841-45.
n.p., n.d. U
Do. 1841, 1844-50. n.p., n.d. C
Results of Observations of the Fixed Stars.
1862-67. *Madras*, 1867-88. U
Meteorological Bungalow, Dodavetta. Ob-
servations. *Dodavetta*, 1847-50. C
Simla. Monsoon Area, Daily Report. 1893-
97. *Simla*, 1893-97. *In progress.* M
Singapore. (Honourable East India Com-
pany's Magnetical Observatory).
Meteorological Observations. 1841-45.
Madras, 1850. C.U

IRELAND.
Armagh Observatory. Places of 5,345 stars
observed from 1825 to 1854. *Dublin*, 1859.
M
Dublin.
Trinity College Observatory.
Astronomical Observations and Researches
made at Dunsink. Parts 1-2. *Dublin*,
1870 73. M

Do. Parts 2, 4-6. *Dublin*, 1873-87. U
Observations made at the Magnetical and
Meteorological Observatory. Vols. 1-2
(1840-50). *Dublin*, 1865-69. M.U

ITALY.
Genova. Regia Universita di Genova.
Stato Meteorologico e Magnetico di Genova.
Anno 57-59 (1889-91). *Genova*, 1890-92. M
Variazioni Ordinarie e Straordinarie del
Magnete di declinazione diurna osservate
in Genova. 1872-84. *Genova*, 1885. M
Milano. Real Osservatorio di Brera.
Osservazioni Meteorologiche Essquite.
1882-96. *Milan*, 1883-97 *In progress.* M
Publicazioni. Vols. 7 (Part 2), 15, 17-18,
23-24, 26-30, 32-38. 1845-93. *Milan*,
1880-93. M
Modena. Reale Osservatorio di Modena.
Osservazioni Meteorologiche ed cliofanome-
triche. 1882-95. *Modena*, 1893-6. *In
progress.* M
Napoli. Real Osservatorio Astronomico.
Bulletino Meteorologico. 1881-85. *Napoli*,
1882-87. M
Real Osservatorio di Capodimonte, Rias-
sunti decadici e mensili delle Osservazioni
Meteoriche. 1883-84. *Napoli*, 1884-87.
M
Roma. Ufficio Centrale Meteorologico e
Geodinamico Italiano.
Annali. Vol. 6-16 (1894-91). (Imperfect).
Roma, 1886-96. *In progress.* M
Torino. Società Meteorologica Italiana.
Annuario Meteorologico Italiano. Anno 1-6.
(1886-91). *Torino*, 1886-91. M
Bulletino Decadico. 1880-85. *Torino*, 1881-
85. M
Bulletino Mensuale. 1880-82, 1886-97.
Torino, 1881-97. *In progress.* M
Bulletino Meteorologico. Anno 9-21.
Torino, 1874-86. C
Materiali per l'altimetria Italiana. Fascicolo
1-2. *Torino*, 1882-4. M
Reale Accademia delle Scienze di Torino. Ob-
servazioni Meteorologiche. *Torino*, 1893-
95. C

JAPAN.
Tokio. Imperial Central Meteorological Ob-
servatory.
Annual Reports. 1892-3. *Tokio*, 1893-97.
In progress. M
Monthly Reports of Meteorological Stations.
1883 86. *Tokio*, 1884-87. M
Monthly Reports of the Central Meteoro-
logical Observatory. 1892-96. *Tokio*,
1892-98. *In progress.* M
Monthly Summaries. 1883-85, 1887-90.
Tokio, 1884-92. M

JAVA.
Batavia Observatorium.
Observations. 1884-96. *Batavia*, 1885-97.
In progress. M
Do. Vols. 1-3 (1866-75). *Batavia*, 1871-
78. U
Regenwaarnemingen in Nederlandsch Indie.
1879-96. *Batavia*, 1880-97. *In progress.*
M

Observatories.

LUXEMBOURG.

Observations Météorologiques faites à Luxembourg, 1844-88, 1890.   C

MADAGASCAR.

Observatoire Royale de Madagascar.   Observations. *Tananarive*, 1892.   M

MAURITIUS.

Port Louis, Royal Alfred Observatory.
Annual Reports.   1876, 1886-94.   M
Results of Meteorological Observations taken at Port Louis.   1876, 1885-95.   M
Do.   1884-85.   U

MEXICO.

Mexico.   Observatorio Meteorologico-magnetico central de Mexico.
Boletin Mensual. *Mexico*, 1889.   C
Tacubaya.   Observatorio Astronomico Nacional.
Annuario.   Tom. 8-9, 11-17.   *Tacubaya*, 1888-97.   *In progress.*   M
Do.   Tom. 11-17.   *Tacubaya*, 1891-97.   *In progress.*   C
Boletin Mensual.   *Tacubaya*, 1888-90, 1895-97.   *In progress.*   M
Do.   *Tacubaya*, 1890-96. *In progress.*   C
Vera Cruz.   Observatorio Central d. Estado de Vera Cruz Llave.   Meteorologico y Agricola.
Boletin Mensual.   *Xalapa-Enriquez*, 1896.   *In progress.*   C
Do.   *Xalapa-Enriquez*, 1895-97.   *In progress.*   M
Registro de Observaciones Meteorologicas, 1894.   *Xalapa-Enriquez*, 1894.   M

NETHERLANDS.

Koninklijk Nederlandsch Meteorologisch Instituut.
Meteorologische Waarnemingen in Nederland en Zijne Bezittingen.   (After 1864 : (Nederlandsch) Meteorologisch Jaarboek).   1857-60, 1864-67.   *Utrecht*, 1857-68.   U
Do.   1856-57, 1862-69, 1881-2, 1888.   *Utrecht*, 1857-89.   C
Do.   1871, 1874, 1878-95.   *Utrecht*, 1871-97.   *In progress.*   M

NORWAY.

Norwegisches Meteorologisches Institut.
Jahrbuch.   1874-96.   *Christiania*, 1875-97.   *In progress.*   M
Do.   1882-4, 1887.   *Christiania*, 1883-89. U

PHILIPPINE ISLANDS.

Manilla.   Observatorio Meteorologico.
Boletin Mensuel.   *Manilla*, 1895-6.   *In progress.*   M
Observaciones.   *Manilla*, 1878-83, 1890-94.   *In progress.*   M

PORTUGAL.

Coimbra.   Observatorio Meteorologico.
Observacoes Meteorologicas e Magneticas.   *Coimbra*, 1875-95.   *In progress.*   M
Lisboa.   Observatorio do Infante D. Luiz.
Annaes.   Vols. 1-5, 8 and 11 (imperfect). (1856-73).   *Lisboa*, 1864-73.   U
Postos meteorologicos.   1874-76.   *Lisboa*, 1875-77.   U

ROUMANIA.

Bucharest.   Institutul Meteorologic.
Analele.   Tom. 1-11.   *Bucharest*, 1885-95.   *In progress.*   C.M
Buletinul Observatiunilor Meteorologice din Romania.   Anul. 1-5.   *Bucharest*, 1892-96.   *In progress.*   M
Do.   Anul. 3-5.   *Bucharest*, 1894-6.   *In progress.*   C
Résumé des Observations Météorologiques de Bucarest, pour l'année 1890 et pour la périod 1885 à 1890. *Bucuresti*, 1893.   M
Colectiunea Studiilor, Notitelor si Observatiunilor Meteorologice relative la Romania.   No. 1-7.   Stefan C. Hepites.   M

RUSSIA.

Charkow.   Universitäts-Sternwarte.
Publicationen.   Heft. No. 2-3.   *Charkow*, 1893-95.   *In progress.*   M
Dorpat.   Kaiserliche Livlandische gemein-ützige und ökonomische Sozietät.
Bericht über die Ergebnisse der Beobachtungen an dem Regenstationen.   1885-96.   *Dorpat*, 1886-97.   *In progress.*   M
Dorpat.   Kaiserliche Universitäts-Sternwarte.
Observationes Astronomicæ.   Vols. 1-15 (1814-49).   *Dorpat*, 1817-59.   U
Meteorologische Beobachtungen angestellt in Dorpat.   Jahrg. 5-18 (1866-83).   *Dorpat*, 1868-84.   U
Do.   Jahrg. 14-34 (1877-94).   *Dorpat*, 1884-97.   *In progress.*   U
Kazan.   Université de Kazan.
Observatoire Magnétique.
Observations.   1894-96.   *Kazan*, 1895-6.   *In progress.*   C
Nijne-Taguilsk.   Observations météorologiques faites à Nijne-Taguilsk. 1846-63.   *Paris*, 1848-64.   M
Odessa.   Université Impériale.
Revue Méténrologique.   Travaux du réseau Météorologique du Sud-Ouest de la Russie.   1886-95.   *Odessa*, 1896.
Do.   Extra series.   Vols. 3-6.   *Odessa*, 1892-3.   *In progress.*   M
St. Petersburg.   Kaiserlich Russischen Geographischen Gesellschaft.
Russischen Polarstation an der Lenamundung.   1882-84, 3 parts.   *St. Petersburg*, 1886-95.   M
Kaiserlichen Academie der Wissenschaften.
Repertorium für Meteorologie.   *St. Petersburg*, 1875-94.   *In progress.*   M
Observatoire Physique Central.
Jahresbericht, 1894.   *St. Petersburg*, 1895.   M
Meteorologische Beobachtungen.   Angestellt auf Schiffen der russischen Flotte.   Bd. 1.   *St. Petersburg*, 1883.   M
Tiflis.   Physikalisches Observatorium.
Beobachtungen.   1879-80, 1886-7, 1890.   *Tiflis*, 1880-91.   M
Beobachtungen der Temperatur des Erbodens.   1881-90.   *Tiflis*, 1886-95.   V.M
Materialien zu einer Klimatologie des Kaukasus.   1871-79.   *Tiflis*, 1872-80.   M
Magnetische Beobachtungen.   1880-83. *Tiflis*, 1881-85.   U

Observatories.

RUSSIA.

Tiflis.
Meteorologische Beobachtungen. 1879-90.
Tiflis, 1880-91. M
Meteorologische u. Magnetische Beobachtungen. 1880-91, 1893-4. *Tiflis*, 1881-95. *In progress* C
Do. 1890-94. *Tiflis*, 1891-95. *In progress*. M

ST. HELENA.
Magnetical and Meteorological Observatory at St. Helena.
Observations. Vols. 1-2 (1840-49). *London*, 1847-60. C.T.U

SCOTLAND.
Dun Echt Observatory.
Publications. Vols. I-III. *Dun Echt*, 1876-85. M
Edinburgh. Royal Observatory.
Astronomical Observations. Vols. 1-14 (1834-77). *Edinburgh*, 1838-77. (Wanting Vol. 13). U
Do. Vol. 15 (1877-86). *Edinburgh*, 1886. C
Do. Vols. 13-15 (1860-86). *Edinburgh*, 1871-87. M
Edinburgh. Markerstoun Observatory.
Observations of Magnetism and Meteorology. 1841-46. *Edinburgh*, 1845-50. M

SOUTH AMERICA.
Argentine Republic. Oficina Meteorologica Argentina. Anales. Tom. 1-11. *Buenos Aires*, 1878-97. *In progress*. M
Brazil. Observatorio do Rio de Janeiro.
Anuario. *Rio de Janeiro*, 1888-96. *In progress*. M
Do. *Rio de Janeiro*, 1889-92. C
Revista. Vols. 5-6. *Rio de Janeiro*, 1890-91. C
Uruguay. Observatorio Meteorologico del Colegio pio de Villa Colon.
Boletin Mensual. *Montevideo*, 1888-96. *In progress*. M

SPAIN.

Observatorio de Madrid.
Anuario. 1873, 1876-80. *Madrid*, 1872, 1875-9. M
Do. 1868-73, 1876-79. C
Exposicion y resumen de las Observaciones, efectuadas, 1860-1889. *Madrid*, 1893. M
Observaciones Meteorologicas. *Madrid*, 1865-75. C
Do. *Madrid*, 1871-95. *In progress*. M
Ona. Observaciones Meteorologicas en Ona, 1894-5. *Bilbao*, 1895-97. *In progress*. M
Vilafranca del Panadés. Estacion meteorologica. Observaciones Meteorologicas efectuadas, 1890-92. *Vilafranca*, 1891-3. M

SWEDEN.

Stockholm. Kongl. Svenska Vetenskaps-Akademien. Meteorologiska Iakttagilser I Sverige, 1864-92. *Stockholm*, 1866-97 *In progress*. U
Upsala. Observatoire Météorologique de l'Université. Bulletin Mensuel. *Upsala*, 1879-96. *In progress*. M

SWITZERLAND.
Mont Blanc. Observatoire.
Annales. Tom. 1-2. *Paris*, 1893-6. *In progress*. M

TURKEY.
Observatoire Impérial.
Bulletin Météorologique et Seismique. *Constantinople*, 1895-6. *In progress*. M
Annual Bulletin. *Constantinople*, 1893-94. *In progress*. M

UNITED STATES.

Department of Agriculture.
Weather Bureau (formerly Signal Service).
Annual Report. 1871-93. *Washington*, 1871-94. *In progress*. M
Bulletins. Nos. 1-19. *Washington*, 1892-97. *In progress*. C.M
Monthly Weather Review. 1882-85, 1887-88. *Washington*, 1883-89. U
Tri-Daily Meteorological Record. 1878. *Washington*, 1884. U
Naval Observatory.
Meteorological Reports to the United States Navy. Nos. 1-4. *Washington*, 1843-57. C
Do. Nos. 2, 4. *Washington*, 1849-1857. P
Astronomical (Magnetic and Meteorological) Observations. 1845-52, 1861-67, 1869, 1871, 1872, 1874-90. *Washington*, 1846-95. *In progress*. U
Do. 1848-90. *Washington*, 1856-95. (imperfect). *In progress*. M
Report of Superintendent. *Washington*, 1889, 1891, 1893. C
Solar Eclipse of 1869 and 1870. *Washington*, 1870. P
Patent Office and Smithsonian Institution. Results of Meteorological Observations, 1854-59, Vols. 1-2. *Washington*. E.M.T
Do. Vol. 1, parts 1-2. *Washington*, 1861. C
War Department.
Army Meteorological Register, 1843-54. *Washington*, 1885. C
Daily Bulletin of the Signal Service. *Washington*, 1872-77. M
Professional Papers of the Signal Service. 1871-84. *Washington*, 1881-85. M
California. Lick Observatory of University of California.
Publications. Vols. 2-3. *Sacramento*. C
Massachusetts. Harvard College.
Astronomical Observations.
Annals. Vol. 1, parts 1-2. Vol. 34. *Cambridge*, 1846-53, 1895. C
Do. Vols. 19-50. 1840-88, 1887-95. *Cambridge*, 1889-96. M
Reports. *Cambridge*, 1863, 1895-6. C
Do. *Cambridge*, 1895-6. C
New Jersey. Bureau of Weather Service.
Annual Reports 1-2. *Trenton*, 1890-91. C
New York. Meteorological Observations made in the State of New York, 1826-63. *Albany*. C
Dudley Observatory. Annals. Vols. 1-2. *Albany*, 1866-71. U
Pennsylvania. Girard College. Magnetic and Meteorological Observations. 3 vols. *Philadelphia*, 1840-45. M.T

Observatory (The). A monthly review of astronomy. Vols. 13-19. *London*, 1890-1897. *In progress.*   S
   Do. Vols. 1-19. (1877-97). *London*, 18789-8. *In progress.*   M

Obstetrical Society of London. Transactions. Vols. 2-31. *London*, 1861-89. U

Oesterreichische Gradmessungs-Commission. Verhandlungen : Protokolle über die Sitzungen, 1889-93. *Wien*, 1889-93.   U
   Do. 1885-97. *Wien*, 1885-97. *In progress.* C

Oesterreichischer Ingenieur.-und Architekten-Verein. Wochenschrift. Jahrg. 15-16, *Wien*, 1890-91. Zeitschrift. Jahrg. 39-41, 46, *Wien*, 1887-96. *In progress.*   C

Offenbacher Verein fuer Naturkunde. Berichte 2-28. *Offenbach am Main*, 1861-88. (Wanting Nos. 3 and 4.)   U
   Do. 11, 59-36. *Offenbach am Main*, 1869-70, 1887-95. *In progress.*   C

Ohio. Executive Documents 1867-1887. Senate Journal 1867-1887. House Journal 1867-1887.   L
   Geological Survey. Vols. 1-5, 1873-1884. L
   Do. Vol. 6. *Columbus*, 1888. C
   School Reports, annual, 1851-91. (Wanting 1875, 1883, 1885, 1890.)   E

Ohio Journal of Education and Ohio Educational Monthly. 17 vols. *Columbus*, 1846-69.   E

Ohio School Journal. *Cleveland*, 1846. E

Old South Leaflets. Nos. 1-50. *Boston.* n.d.   P

Old Testament Student. Vols. 3-4. *Chicago*, 1883-4.   V
   Do. Vols. 3-5, 7. *Chicago*, 1883-8. Mc
   Continued as :
   Old and New Testament. Vols. 9-14. *Hartford*, 1889-92.   V
   Continued as :
   Biblical World. Vols. 3-8. *Chicago*, 1894-96. *In progress.*   V

Oliver and Boyd's New Edinburgh Almanac. *Edinburgh*, 1838, 1840, 1842, 1845, 1846, 1848, 1849, 1851, 1854-1857, 1859, 1860, 1865-1867, 1869, 1870, 1872, 1877, 1879, 1880.
   Do. *Edinburgh*, 1884-8.   P

Once a Week. Vols. 1-19. *London*, 1858-68.   P

Oneida Historical Society. Transactions with Annual Report. *Utica*, 1881, 1885-92.   C

Ontario. Journals of the Legislative Assembly, 1867-97. *In progress.*   E.L.O.P.V
   Index, 1867-83, 2 vols.   P
   Index to Debates of Legislative Assembly, 1867-77. By S. J. Watson.   P
   Sessional Papers, 1867-97. *In progress.*   E L.O.P.V
   Index to Journals and Sessional Papers, 1867-88, By A. H. Sydere.   P
   The Sessional Papers contain the annual reports of the following departments as well as

all important returns and statements presented to the Legislature :
Education.
Provincial Public Account.
Crown Lands.
Immigration.
Division Courts.
Public Works.
Insurance and Friendly Societies.
Lunatic and Idiot Asylums.
Gaols, Prisons and Reformatories.
Blind, Deaf and Dumb.
Children's Protection.
Agricultural College.
Entomological Society.
Fruit Growers' Association.
Bee Keepers' Association.
Poultry Association.
Dairymen and Creameries' Association.
Farmers' Institute.
Road Making.
Live Stock Association.
Inspection of Factories.
Births, Deaths and Marriages.
Game and Fish Commission.
Queen Victoria Niagara Falls Park.
Bureau of Mines.
Provincial Board of Health.
Bureau of Industries.
Forestry.
Accounts of Toronto University.
Registry Offices.
Bills of the Legislature, 1892-7. *In progress.* E.T
Budget Speeches. *Toronto*, 1887-96. *In progress.*   P
Votes and Proceedings, 1892-7. *In progress.* T
Agriculture and Arts Association, Transactions, 1869-96. *In progress.*   P
Agricultural College Bulletins, Nos. 58-98. 1891-96. *In progress.*   P
Agricultural Commission. Report, 5 vols. (append. B.S.). 1881.   P.T
Commission on Municipal Institutions, 1st and 2nd Reports, 1888-9. *Toronto.*

Ontario Gazette. Vols. 1-29, 1868-97. *In progress.*   O.L
   Vols. 17-29, 1884-97. *In progress.* P

Ontario Gazetteer and Business Directory. *Toronto*, 1869, 1871, 1882, 1885, 1887-9, 1892-3. *In progress.*   P

Ontario Medical Journal. Vol. 2. *Toronto*, 1893-4.   C

Ontario Provincial Land Surveyors. *See* Association of Ontario Land Surveyors.

Ontario Teacher. Vols. 1-3. *Strathroy*, 1873-75.   P

Oriental Translation Fund of Great Britain and Ireland. *See* Royal Asiatic Society.

Orientalische Bibliographie. Bd. 1-8. *Berlin*, 1887-95. *In progress.*   U

Orientalist. Vol. 3. *Kandy (Ceylon)*, 1892. C

Ornis. *See* Permanente Internationale ornithologische Comité. Ornis, etc.

Ornithologischer Verein Pommerns. Zeitschrift für Ornithologie und praktische Geflügelzucht. Jahrg. 4-14. *Stettin*, 1880 90. (Wanting Bd. 5.)   U

Ossianic Society. Transactions. Vols. 1-6. 1853-8. *Dublin*, 1855-61.   P

Oswego. School Reports, annual, 1856-69.   E

Ottawa Field-Naturalists' Club. Transactions. Vols. 1 and 2. *Ottawa*, 1880-84. continued as :
Ottawa Naturalist : Transactions of the Ottawa Field-Naturalists' Club. Vols. 1-7. *Ottawa*, 1887-93. *In progress.*   U
Do. Vols. 1-9, *Ottawa*, 1887-96. *In progress.*   C

Ottawa Naturalist. *See* Ottawa Field-Naturalists' Club.

Our Mission News. Continued as : Canadian Church Magazine and Mission News. Vols. 1-11. *Toronto*, 1886-97. *In progress.*   T

Outing. Vols. 7, 21-23, 26-31. *New York*, 1885-98. *In progress.*   P

Overland Monthly. 2nd Series. Vols. 5-6, *San Francisco*, 1885.   L
Do. Vols. 9-22. *San Francisco*, 1887-93.   P

Oxford, Cambridge and Dublin Messenger of Mathematics. 5 vols. *Cambridge* and *London*, 1862-71.
Continued as :
Messenger of Mathematics. Vols. 1-25. *London*, 1872-96. *In progress.*   U

Oxford Historical Society. Publications. Vols. 1-32. *Oxford*, 1884-96. *In progress.*   U

Palaeographical Society. Facsimiles of manuscripts and inscriptions. Vols. 1-6. *London*, 1873-95.   P

Palaeontographica, Beitraege zur Petrefactenkunde. Bd. 1-42, and Supplement, Bd. 1-3. *Cassel*, 1851-95. *In progress.* U
General Register- Bd. 1-20.

Palaeontographical Society. Publications. Vols. 1-49. *London*, 1847-95. *In progress.*   U
(Wanting Vols. 3 and 21).

Palestine Exploration Fund. Quarterly Statement. 11 vols. *London*, 1869-91. *In progress.*   K
Do. *London*, 1875, 1881, 1883, 1890-1892. L
Do. " 1885-96. *In progress.*   C
Do. " 1894-6. "   V
Survey of Palestine, 10 vols. *London.*   K
Do. 7 vols.

Pall Mall Budget. *London*, 1868-82, 1891-5. L

Pall Mall Magazine. Vols. 1-13. *London*, 1893-97. *In progress.*   L.P

Pamphleteer. Vols. 1-29. *London*, 1813-28. E (Wanting Vol. 25.)

Pan-American Medical Congres. Transactions. 1893. 3 vols. *Washington*, 1895. U

Panoplist. Vol. 3. *Boston*, 1808. continued as :
Panoplist and Missionary Magazine. Vols. 9, 11-14. *Boston*, 1813-1818.
New Series. Vols. 2,4-5. *Boston*, 1810-13. Mc

Papers for the School-Master. Vols. 1-4. *London*, 1865-8.   E

Paris Institute. *See* Académie (royale) des Sciences, *and* Académie des Inscriptions et Belles-Lettres.

Parish School Advocate. Vol. 1. *Halifax*, 1858.   E

Parker Society. Publications. 61 vols., including General Index. *Cambridge*, 1841-53.   Mc.
Do. 48 vols. *Cambridge*, 1843-55.   U
Do. 46 vols. *Cambridge*, 1843-55.   K

Parkman Club. Publications. 1st Series, n.p., n.d.   P

Paterson's Scottish Almanac. *Edinburgh*, 1884.   P

Path (The). A magazine devoted to the brotherhood of humanity and Theosophy in America. Vols. 7-11. *New York*, 1892-96. *In progress.* P

Pathological Society of London. Report of the proceedings. Sessions 1 and 6. *London*, 1846-52.   U
Transactions. Vols. 4-46. *London*, 1853-95. U *In progress.* (Wanting Vols. 6, 8-10, 13 and 14). Index, Vols. 1-37, in 3 vols.

Paul and Braune's Beitraege. *See* Beiträge zur Geschichte der deutschen Sprache und Literatur.

Peabody Academy of Science. Annual Report of Trustees. *Salem*, 1869-87. C

Peabody Education Fund. Proceedings of the Trustees. Meetings 1-28 (1867-89). *Boston, Cambridge*, 1875-89. U

Peabody Institute of Baltimore. Annual reports of the Provost. *Baltimore*, 1869-86.   C

Peabody Museum of American Archaeology and Ethnology. Annual Reports of the Trustees. Nos. 1-11 and 21-24. *Cambridge (Mass.)*, 1868-91.   U
Do. Nos. 1-28. *Cambridge (Mass.)*, 1868-95. *In progress.*   C

Pedagogical Seminary. Vols. 2-3. *Worcester (Mass.)*, 1892-5. *In progress.*   E.U

Pennsylvania. Legislative Documents, 1876.   L.
House Journal, 1876.   L.
Adjutant-General. Annual Reports. *Harrisburg*, 1887, 1890, 1892, 1895.   C
Agriculture, Dep't of. Bulletin. Nos. 8-9. *Harrisburg*, 1896.   C
Reports. *Harrisburg*, 1887-93, 1895.   C
Division of Economic Zoology. Bulletin No. 6, *Harrisburg*, 1896.   C
Archives, 1748-90. Vols. 2-12. *Phila.*, 1853. E
Attorney-General. Reports for 1887-92. *Harrisburg*, 1893.   C
Board of Health. Reports. *Harrisburg*, 1886 92, 1894-5.   C

Pennsylvania.

Board of Public Charities and Committee on Lunacy in Pennsylvania. Reports for years 1887-91, 1892, 1894. *Harrisburg.*   C

College. Reports, 1886, 1888-91, 1892, 1895. *Harrisburg.*   C

Department of the Institute of Internal Affairs. Annual Reports. *Harrisburg*, 1886-95. (Imperfect).   C

Factory Inspection of the Commonwealth of Pennsylvania. Reports. *Harrisburg*, 1894-95.   C

Finances of the Commonwealth of Pennsylvania. Report of Auditor-General for years 1887-92, 1895. *Harrisburg.*   C

Report of a joint committee of the Senate and House of Representatives of Pennsylvania upon the conduct of the financial affairs of the Commonwealth from 1838-43. *Harrisburg.*   C

Fire and Marine Insurance Reports. *Harrisburg.* 1887-1892, 1894-5.   C

Fisheries. Report of the State Commissioners. *Harrisburg*, 1887-1891, 1895.   C

Geological Survey of Pennsylvania. Seventh Report on Oil and Gas Fields of West Pennsylvania for years 1887-88. *Harrisburg.*   C

Final Summary Report on Geology in Pennsylvania by J. P. Lesley. State Geologist. 3 vols. *Harrisburg*, 1892-95.   C

General Index with Appendix.   C

Industrial Education, Commission on. Reports. *Harrisburg*, 1887-89.   C

Librarian. Reports. *Harrisburg*, 1887-92-1894-5.   C

Life Insurance. Reports. *Harrisburg*, 1887-92,1894-5.   C

Public Instruction. Reports of Superintendence. 1887, 1889-93, 1895. *Harrisburg.*   C

Public Printing and Binding of Pennsylvania. Annual Report for 1890-92. *Harrisburg.*   C

- School Reports, Annual, 1843-68, 1870-1, 1873, 1875-7, 1880, 1882-3, 1886, 1888, 1891-2.   E

Sinking Fund of the Commonwealth of Pennsylvania. Report of the Commissioners for 1887-1893, '95. *Harrisburg.*   C

Treasurer's Annual and Detailed Reports. *Harrisburg*, 1887-1895.   C

Pennsylvania Historical Society.
See Historical Society of Pennsylvania.

Pennsylvania Magazine of History and Biography. *See* Historical Society of Pennsylvania. · Pennsylvania Magazine, etc.

Pennsylvania School Journal. 34 vols. *Lancaster*, 1844-84, 1886-95. *In progress.*   E

People's Magazine. Vols. 1-10. *London*, 1868-72.   P

Percy Society.
Publications. Vols. 1-30. *London*, 1840-1852. P

Permanente Internationale Ornithologische Comite.
Jahresberichte des Comité für ornithologische Beobachtungs stationen in Oesterreich-Ungarn. (Separat-Abdruck aus "Ornis"). Jahresb. 2-6. (1883-87) *Wien*, 1886-90.   U

Ornis, internationale Zeitschrift für die gesammte Ornithologie. Jahrg. 2-5. *Wien*, 1886-89.   U
Do. Jahrg. 1-7. *Wien*, 1885-91.   C

Petermann's Mittheilungen aus Justus P' stalt.

Pharmaceutical
2nd Series. Vols. 1-7;
London, 1841-1870.

Pharmaceutische
1-20. *Leipzig*, 1830-4
Continued as
Chemisch-Pharmacet
21-26. *Leipzig*, 18
Continued as
Chemisches Central
1856-69.
Neue Folge.   19 J
4 te   "   Ja
Leipzig, 1889-96.

Philadelphia Aca Sciences. *See* Aci
of Philadelphia.

Philadelphia Rec
delphia, 1886, 1888, 18

Philippine Island
Meteorological Repo
Philippine Islands.

Philobiblion. A m
nal. Vols. 1-2. *New*

Philological Mus
1832-33.

Philological Soci
Proceedings. Vols. 1-
Publications, 10 vols.
gress.
Transactions. *Londo*

Index to Proceedin
79.

Philosophical Ma
nal). 68 vols. *Lona*
Continued as
Philosophical Magaz
Mathematics, Astr
General Science.
Continued as
London, Edinburgh
Magazine.
(Third Series).   :
Fourth Series.   5
Fifth Series.   Vc
In progress.

Philosophical Re
1892-96. *In progress*
(Wanting

Philosophical So
Proceedings. Vols.
Do. Vols. 2-4, 6-
1844-96. *In p*

Philosophical Soc
Bulletin. Vols. 1-1:
progress.
Do. Vols. 1-11.
Do. Vols. 1-10.

Philosophische
Berlin, (1868-94).

Philosophische S
zig, 1883-95. *In prog*

Philosophisches Jahrbuch. *See* Görres-Gesellschaft, etc. Philosophisches Jahrbuch.

Phonetische Studien. 6 Bde. *Marburg*, 1888 93.
Continued as :
Neueren Sprachen (Die). Bd. 1-3. *Marburg*, 1894 96. *In progress.* U

Photogram. Vols. 1-4. *London*, 1894-7. *In progress.* P

Photographic Quarterly. Vols. 1-3. *London*, 1889-92. P

Photographic Societies' Reporter. Vol. 2. *London*, 1890. P

Physical Society of London. Proceedings. Vols. 7 14. *London*, 1885-96. *In progress.* C

Physikalisch-Oekonomische Gesellschaft zu Koenigsberg. Schriften. Jahrg. 10-36. *Königsberg*, 1869-95. C
Do. Jahrg. 20-31. " 1879-1891. U

Physikalischer Atlas. Geographisches Jahrbuch zur Mittheilung aller Wichtigern neuen Erforschungen, von H. Berghaus. Nos. 1-4. *Gotha*, 1850-52.
(No. 1 of this work is called No. 19 of " Berghaus' Physikalischer Atlas "). U

Physikalischer Verein zu Frankfurt am Main. Jahresbericht. 1851-90. *Frankfurt am Main*, 1852-91. U

Physiographiske Forening i Christiania for Naturvidenskaberne. *See* Nyt Magazin for Naturvidenskaberne.

Physiologie Experimentale, Travaux du laboratoire de M. Marey. *See* École (pratique) des hautes Études. Physiologie expérimentale.

Physiologische Gesellschaft zu Berlin. Verhandlungen. Jahrg. 1892-3, *Berlin*, 1894-6. *In progress.* C

Pictorial World. Vols. 1-3, 10-20. *London*, 1882-3, 1887-92. P

Pilot, and Journal of Commerce. Vol. 1. *Montreal*, 1844. P

Pipe Roll Society. Publications. Vols. 1-20. *London*, 1884-96. *In progress.* U

Plumber and Decorator. Vols. 6-18. *London*, 1884-1897. *In progress.* P

Poet-Lore. Vols. 1-9. *Philadelphia*, 1889-97. *In progress.*

Poggendorff's Annalen. *See* Annalen der Physik.

Political Science Quarterly. Vols. 1-12 *New York*, 1886-97. *In progress.* L. P
Vols. 1-6. 11-12. *New York*, 1886-97. *In progress.* V
Vols. 5-12. *New York*, 1890-97. *In progress.* U
" 8-11. *New York*, 1893-97. *In progress.* Mc

Polynesian Society. Journal. Vols. 3-5. *Wellington*, 1894-6. *In progress.* C

(Dingler's) Polytechnisches Journal. Bd. 59, 99 274. *Stuttgart*, 1836-89. U
Bd. 279-301. *Stuttgart*, 1891-97. *In progress.* S

Polytekniske Forening. Norsk Teknisk Tidsskrift. Vols. 8 9. *Christiania*, 1890-91. C

Poole's Index to Periodical Literature. (1800-97), 5 vols. *Boston*, 1882-97. *In progress.* P.U

Poor's Manual of the Railroads of the U. S. *See* Manual of the Railroads.

Popular Astronomy. Vols. 2-4. *Northfield, Minn.*, 1894-7. *In progress.* P

Popular Educator. Vols. 10-11. *Boston*, 1892-94. *In progress.* E

Popular Science Monthly. Vols. 1-49. *New York*, 1872-96. *In progress.* L.P
Supplement Nos. 1-20. L.V
" " 13-22. U

Popular Science News. (Commenced as Boston Journal of Chemistry.) *New York*, 1896. *In progress.* P

Portfolio. *London*, 1870-97. *In progress.* P

Portland. School Reports, 1856-77. E

Portugal. Meteorological Reports. *See* Observatories : Portugal.

Positivist Review. Vols 1-5. *London*, 1893-7. *In progress.* P

Postal Microscopical Society. Journal. Vols. 5-8. *London* and *Bath*, 1886-88. C

Practitioner. Vols. 32-57. *London*, 1884-97. *In progress.* Index to Vols. 1-50. P

Prag. K. K. Sternwarte. *See* Observatories : Austria-Hungary.

Presbyterian Church.
Alliance of Reformed Churches, Proceedings, 5th General Council. *Toronto*, 1892. P
Church of Scotland. Annals of General Assembly from 1739 to 1766. 4 vols. *Edinburgh*, 1838 40. K
Church of Scotland Magazine. 5 vols. *Glasgow*, 1834-8. K
Free Church Magazine. 6 vols. *Edinburgh*, 1844-53. K
United Presbyterian Magazine. 16 vols. *Edinburgh*, 1847-62. K
United Secession Magazine. 16 vols. *Edinburgh*, 1833-46. K
CANADA.
Presbyterian Church in Canada in connection with the Church of Scotland. Acts and proceedings of Synod. 4 vols. *Toronto*, 1831-75. K
Historical and Statistical Report, 1866. P
Record. Vols. 14, 16-27. *Montreal*, 1862, 1863-74. K
Do. 7 vols. and Vols. 15-22. *Montreal*, 1852-60, 1862 9. K
Presbyterian Church in Canada. Acts and Proceedings of the General Assembly. *Toronto*, 1875-97. *In progress.* P
Free Presbyterian Church of Canada. Synod Minutes, 1844-61 (MSS.). K
Presbyterian Church of Canada. Ecclesiastical and Missionary Record. *Toronto*, 1844-61. K
United Presbyterian Synod Minutes. 2 vols. 1834-45 (MSS.), K
Do. 5 vols. *Toronto*, 1845-61. K

Presbyterian Church.
Canadian United Presbyterian Magazine. *To-*
ronto, 1851-61.   K
  Do. 5 vols. *Toronto*, 1854-61.   E
  Do.   "   1851-61.   P
Canada Presbyterian Church, Acts and Pro-
ceeds of the Synod. *Toronto*, 1850-54.   P
  Do. Minutes of Synod. *Toronto*, 1863-9. P
Canada Presbyterian Church Pulpit. 2 vols.
Toronto, 1871-3.   E
Home and Foreign Record of the Canada Pres-
byterian Church. Vols. 1-14. *Toronto*, 1861-
1875. (Wanting Vol 1, K).   K.P
  Continued as :
Presbyterian Record. *Toronto*, 1876-92,
1894.   P
Presbyterian Church of the Lower Provinces of
B.N.A. Home and Foreign Record. *Hali-*
fax, 1881-8.   P
  Do. *Halifax*, 1850-56, 1861-66.   K
Presbyterian Church of Nova Scotia. Minutes
of Synod from 1817-42. Copied from original
MS. (only copy). (MS).   K

Presbyterian (The.) Vols. 1-9. *Montreal*,
1852-60.   E

Presbyterian and Reformed Review.
Vols. 1-8. *New York* and *Philadelphia*, 1890-97.
In progress.   K.Mc

Presbyterian Magazine. Vol. 1. *London*,
1843.   P

**Presbyterian Quarterly and Prince-
ton Review.** *See* Biblical Repertory.

Presbyterian Record. Vols. 1-17, 19.
Montreal, 1876-92, 1894.   P

Presbyterian Review. Vols. 1-6, 8. *New*
York, 1880-85, 1887.   K
  Vols. 3-5, 7, 9. *New York*, 1882-1888. K.Mc

Presbyterian Review. 21 vols. *Edin-*
burgh, 1832-48.   K

**Presbyterian Witness and Evangeli-
cal Advocate.** Vols. 3-4. *Halifax, N.S.*,
1850-51.   P

Press (The). Vols. 9,11. *London*, 1861-1863. P

Preussische Jahrbuecher. Bd. 64-86.
Berlin, 1889-96. *In progress.*   U

Prince Edward Island.
Journals of the Assembly, 1868-1896. *In progress.*
                                               L
Educational Report. *Charlottetown*, 1876-95.
In progress.   E
Royal Gazette. Vols. 22-23. *Charlottetown*,
1895-6. *In progress.*   O

**Princeton Contributions to Psychol-
ogy.** Vol. 1. *Princeton*, 1895-6.   C

Princeton Review. *See* Biblical Repertory
and Princeton Review.

Pringsheim's Jahrbuecher. *See* Jahrbücher für wissenschaftliche Botanik.

Process Photogram. Vols. 3-4. *London*,
1896-7. *In progress.*   P

Process Year Book. Vol. 3. *London*, 1897.
In progress.   .

Propugnatore. Studii filologici, storici e bib-
liografici. 20 vols. *Bologna*, 1868-87.
  Nuova Serie. 6 vols. *Bologna*, 1888-93. U

Providence. School Reports, 1865-69.   E

Province. Vols. 1-4. *Victoria, B.C.*, 1894-97.
In progress.   P

Provincial (The) ; or Halifax Monthly Magazine. Vols. 1-2. *Halifax, N. S.*, 1852-3.   P

**Provincial Medical and Surgical
Association.**
Transactions. 12 vols. *London, Worcester,*
1833-44. (Wanting Vol. 5).
  Do. New Series. Vols. 1-4 and 7. *Worcester*,
1845-51.   U

Psyche : Journal of Entomology. Vols. 5-7.
Cambridge, 1894-96. *In progress.*   C

Psychological Review. Vols. 1 and 2.
New York, 1894-95. *In progress.*   E.Mc.U

Public Libraries. Vols. 1-2. *Chicago*, 1896-7.
In progress.   .

Public Opinion. Vols. 4-71. *London*, 1863-
97. *In progress.*   P
  Vols. 1-33. *London*, 1861-77.   E

Publisher's Weekly. Vols. 42-50. *New*
York, 1892-96. *In progress.*   V

Puck. *New York*, 1888, 1890-91.   L

Punch. Vols 1-27, 29-113. *London*, 1841-97,
In progress.   P

Pupil Teacher. Vols. 1-6. *London*, 1857-63. E

Putnam's Magazine. Vols. 1-16. *New*
York, 1853-70.

**Quadro elementar das Relacoes poli-
ticas e diplomaticas de Portugal.**
Tom. 1-18. *Paris, Lisbon*, 1842-60.   U
  (Wanting Tom. 11).

Quarterly Illustrator. Vols. 1-2. *New*
York, 1893-4.
  Continued as :
Monthly Illustrator. Vols. 3-8. *New York*,
1895-7. *In progress.*   P

Quarterly Journal of Economics. Vols.
1-10. *Boston*, 1887-96. *In progress.* (Wanting
Vol. 4, C).   C.U
  Index, Vols. 1-10.   C

Quarterly Journal of Education. *See*
Society for the Diffusion of Useful Knowledge.
Quarterly Journal of Education.

**Quarterly Journal of Microscopical
Science.** Vol. 3. *London*, 1855.   U
  Do. Vols. 1-4, 7. *London*, 1853-9.   C
  Do. New Series. Vols. 1-37. *London*, 1861-96.
In progress. (Wanting Vol. 33).   U

**Quarterly Journal of Pure and Ap-
plied Mathematics.** Vols. 1-27. *London*,
1857-95. *In progress.*   U

**Quarterly Register of Current His-
tory.** Vols. 1-6 (imperfect). *Detroit, Buffalo,*
1892-6. *In progress.*

Quarterly Review. Vols. 1-186. *London*,
1809-97. *In progress.*   P
  Do. Vols. 1-147. *London*, 1809-79.   V
  Do. Vols. 1-119, 170-186. *London* and *New*
York, 1819-97. *In progress.*   U
  Do, Vols. 1-145. *London*, 1809-1878.   O
  Do. Vols. 1-128. *London*, 1809-1870.   T
  Do. Vols. 178-186. *London*, 1894-7. *In pro-*
gress.   E
  Index. Vols. 1-159.   O.P.V

Quebec (Province of)
Journals of the Legislative Assembly, 1867-95.
In progress. L.O
Journals of the Legislative Council, 1867-93.
In progress. L.O
Sessional Papers, 1869-96. *In progress.* O
Do. 1867-96. *In progress.* L
Official Gazette. Vol. 28, 1896. *In progress.* O
Débats de la législature, 2 de Sess., 4e Parl.,
1879. P
Educational Report, 1865-95. *In progress.* E

Quebec Almanac. *Quebec,* 1797, 1799, 1801,
1805, 1807-8, 1810-13, 1816-20, 1822, 1824-6,
1828, 1830-32, 1834-7, 1840-41. P

Quebec City Directory. *Quebec,* 1822. P

Quebec Gazette. *Quebec,* 1768. P
Do. *Quebec,* 1770-1803, 1824-7, 1868-84, 1887,
January-June, 1888. L
See also Canada Gazette.

**Quebec Literary and Historical
Society.** *See* Literary and Historical Society of
Quebec.

Queen (The). Vols. 67-74, 76-102. *London,*
1880 83, 1884-97. *In progress.* P

Queen's College Journal. 8 vols. *Kingston,*
1872 91. E

Queen's Quarterly. Vols. 1-4. *Kingston,*
1893-7. *In progress.* C.E.O.P

Queensland. Official Documents, 1875-6, 1882.
C

Queensland Museum.
Annals. Nos. 1-2. *Brisbane,* 1891-92. C

Quekett Microscopical Club.
Journal. Series 2. Vols. 1-4, 6. *London,* 1881-96.
In progress. C

**Quellen und Eroerterungen zur bayer-
ischen und deutschen Geschichte.**
Bd. 1-9. *München,* 1856-64. U

**Quellen und Forschungen zur Sprach
—und Culturgeschichte der germanischen Voelker.** Heft 1-78. *Strassburg,* 1874-90. *In progress.* U

Quiver. *London,* 1879-97. *In progress.* P

Radcliffe Observatory. *See* Observatories:
England.

Railroad Gazette. Vols. 23-29. *New York,*
1891-7. *In progress.* S

Ray Society.
Publications. 68 vols. *London,* 1848-95. *In
progress.* U

**Real Academia de Ciencias Morales
y Politicas.**
Memorias. *Madrid,* 1884-8, 1891, 1893. C
Resumen de las Actas. *Madrid,* 1862, 1866,
1871, 1876, 1890. C

**Real Academia de Ciencias y Artes
de Barcelona.**
Actas. *Barcelona,* 1883-6. C

Real Academia de la Historia.
Boletin. Tom. 8-11, 13-29. *Madrid,* 1886-96.
In progress. C

Reale Accademia dei Lincei.
Atti. Series 4. Tom. 1-7. *Roma,* 1884-91.
Rendiconti dell' Adunanze Solenne, 1892, 1894.
1896. C

**Reale Accademia delle Belle Arti in
Milano.**
Atti. *Milano,* 1884-94. C

**Reale Accademia delle Scienze dell'
Istituto di Bologna.**
Memorie delle Sezione delle Scienze Nationali.
Serie 4. Tom. 9-10; Serie 5. Tom. 1-3.
Bologna, 1888-1892. C

**Reale Accademia delle Scienze di
Torino.**
Atti. Tom. 14-15, 17, 19-31. *Torino,* 1878-96.
In progress. C
General index to Tom. 11-20 in Tom. 20.
Memorie. Tom. 10-11, 24-40. *Torino,* 1806-38.
Do. Serie 2. Tom. 21-31, 34-43. *Torino,*
1864-96. *In progress.* C

**Reale Accademia di Scienze, Lettere
e Belle Arti di Palermo.**
Atti. Serie 2. Tom. 9-10. *Palermo,* 1887-9.
Do. Serie 3. Tom. 1. *Palermo,* 1891. C

**Reale Accademia Lucchese di Scienze,
Lettere ed Arti.**
Atti. Tom. 25, 27-28. *Lucca,* 1889-1895. *In
progress.* C

Reale Comitato Geologico d'Italia.
Bolletino. Tom. 16-23. *Roma,* 1885-92.
Do. Serie 3. Tom. 6-7, 1895-96. *In progress.* C

**Reale Istituto di Studi superiori
pratici e di Perfezionamento.**
Pubblicazioni. Sezione di Scienze Fisiche e
Naturali. Tom. 1. *Firenze,* 1883-85. C

**Reale Istituto Lombardo di Scienze
e Lettere.**
Memorie. Tom. 10-11. *Milano,* 1869-70. M
Rendiconti. Serie 2. Tom. 19-27, 29. *Milano,*
Napoli and *Pisa,* 1886-96. *In progress.* C

**Reale Istituto Veneto di Scienze,
Lettere ed Arti.**
Atti. Tom. 50-52, 54. *Venice,* 1891-96. *In
progress.* C

Record of American Entomology.
1868-73. *Salem,* 1869-74. U

Record of Modern Engineering. *London,* 1863-1866. L

Records of Literature. *See* Literary and
Annual Register, or Records of Literature, etc.

**Recueil des Travaux chimiques des
Pays-Bas.** Tom. 1-11. *Leide,* 1882-92. U
Do. Tom. 5-14. *Leide,* 1886-95. *In progress.* C

Rede Lectures. *Cambridge,* 1891. P

Religious Tract Society.
Tracts. First Series. Nos. 1-460. *London,* n.d. U
N.S. Vols. 1-7. *London,* 1887-93.
3rd Series. Vol. 1-3. *London,* 1895-7. *In progress.* P

Rensselaer Society of Engineers.
Selected Papers. Vol. 1. *Troy,* 1884-8. C

Repertoire des Travaux historiques.
Contenant l'Analyse des publications faites en
France et à l'Étranger sur l'histoire, les monuments, et la langue de la France. Tom. 1-3 (An-
neès 1881-83). *Paris,* 1882-88. U

Revue Nationale. Vols. 1-4. *Montreal,* 1895-6. *In progress.* P

Revue Philosophique de la France et de l'Etranger. Tom. 1-42. *Paris,* 1887-96. *In progress.* U

Revue Scientifique. Tom. 43-44, 46-47. *Paris,* 1889 91. C

Revue Zoologique. *See* Société Cuvierienne. Revue Zoologique.

Rheinisches Museum fuer Philologie. Neue Folge. Jahrg. 1-51. *Frankfurt am Main,* 1842-96. *In progress.* U (Wanting Bd. 6, Hft. 1 and 2.).

Rhode Island. School Reports, 1636-1876, 1895. *Providence,* 1879-96. *In progress.* E

Rhode Island Historical Society. Collections. Vols. 1-6. *Providence,* 1827-76. P Proceedings. *Providence,* 1883-7, 1889-91. C Publications. N.S. Vol. 3. *Providence,* 1895-6. *In progress.* C

Rhode Island Institute. Journal of Education. 3 vols. *Providence,* 1845-8. E

Rhode Island Schoolmaster. 11 vols. *Providence,* 1855-74. E

Rio de Janeiro Museo Nacional. *See* Museo Nacional de Rio de Janeiro.

Rivista di Filologia Romanza. 2 vols. *Imola, Roma,* 1872-5. U
Continued as:
Giornale di Filologia Romanza. 4 vols. *Roma,* 1878 83.
Continued as :
Studj di Filologia Romanza. Vols. 1-6. *Roma,* 1885-93. *In progress.* U

Rivista di Filosofia scientifica. 10 vols. *Torino, Milano,* 1881-91. U

Rochester. School Reports, annual, 1845-75. E

Rochester Academy of Science. Proceedings. Vols. 1-3. *Rochester,* 1891-6. *In progress.* C.U

Rochester Historical Society. Publications. Vol. 1. *Rochester,* 1892. C.P

Rolls Chronicles. *See* Chronicles and Memorials of Great Britain and Ireland during the Middle Ages.

Romania. Recueil trimestriel consacré à l' étude des langues et des littératures romanes. Années 1-25. *Paris* (1872-96). *In progress.* U Table analytique, 1872-81.

Romanische Forschungen. Bd. 1-8. *Erlangen,* 1883-96. *In progress.* U

Romanische Studien. 6 Bde. *Bonn,* 1870-85. U

Rose Belford's Canadian Monthly. *See* Canadian Monthly.

Roumania. Meteorological Reports. *See* Observatories : Roumania.

Round Table. *New York,* 1865-8. V

Royal Academy of Medicine in Ireland. Transactions. Vols. 7-13. *Dublin,* 1889-95. *In progress.* U (Wanting Vols. 9 and 10).

Royal Agricultural and Commercial Society of British Guiana. Journal [Timehri]. New Series. Vols. 3-7, 10. *London,* 1889-96. *In progress.* C

Royal Agricultural Society of England. Journal. 1st Series. Vols. 1-25. 2nd Series. Vols. 1-25. 3rd Series. Vol. 3. *London,* 1840-92. L

Royal Asiatic Society of Great Britain and Ireland. Journal. Vols. 1-10, 13, 15-20. *London,* 1834-63. C Do. New Series. Vols. 1-9. *London,* 1865-77. C China Branch. Journal. *Shanghai,* 1866-8, 1890-2. C Oriental Translation Fund of Great Britain and Ireland. New Series. 7 vols. *London,* 1891-6. *In progress.* U

Royal Astronomical Society. Monthly Notices. Vols. 1-2, 4-12, 44-49, 51-6. *London,* 1827-96. *In progress.* General Index to Vols. 30-52.

Royal Caledonian Curling Club. Annual. *Edinburgh,* 1876-82. P

Royal Caledonian Curling Club. (Ontario Branch). Annual. *Toronto,* 1876-87, 1889-92. P

Royal Colonial Institute. Proceedings. Vols. 1-28. *London,* 1870-97. *In progress.* C.L.P.U Do. Vols. 8-28. *London,* 1876-97. *In progress.* E (Wanting Vols. 3 and 5, U). (" " 2-6, L). Index, Vols. 1-27, in Vol. 27.

Royal Dublin Society. Journal. Vols. 1 7. *Dublin,* 1856-1878. C Scientific Proceedings. 2nd Series. Vols. 1-6. *Dublin,* 1878-89. U Do. Vols. 1-2, 5-7. *Dublin,* 1878 92. C Scientific Transactions. 2nd Series. Vols. 1-4, *Dublin,* 1877-89. U Do. Vols. 2, 4. *Dublin,* 1880 92. U

Royal Engineers (Corps of). Papers on subjects connected with duties. Vols. 1-8. *London,* 1837-45.

Royal Geographical Society of Australasia. Transactions and Proceedings. Vols. 3-4. *Sydney,* 1885-6. C

Royal Geographical Society of London. Journal. Vols. 1-50. *London,* 1830-80. P Indexes to Vols. 1-50 Proceedings. Vols. 1-22. *London,* 1855-78. C.P Do. N.S. Vols. 1-14. *London,* 1879-92. C.P.U Continued as : Geographical Journal. Vols. 1-8. *London,* 1893-6. *In progress.* C.L.P.U Supplementary Papers. Vols. 1-2. *London,* 1882-89. *In progress.* Do. Vols. 1-4. *London,* 1886-93. *In progress.* P Educational Reports. *London,* 1886. P

Royal Geographical Society of Ireland. *See* Geological Society of Dublin.

Royal Historical and Archæological Society of Ireland. *See* Kilkenny Archæological Society.

Royal Historical Society.
Transactions. Vols. 1-10, (Vol. 1, 2nd ed). *London*, 1875-82.
Do. N.S. Vols. 1-10. *London*, 1884-96. *In progress.* P

Royal Institute of British Architects.
Transactions. Vol. 1, parts 1-2. *London*, 1835-42. C
Journal. 3rd Series. Vols. 1-4. *London*, 1894-7. *In progress.* S

Royal Institution of Cornwall.
Journal. Vols. 9-12. *Truro,* 1886-1895. C

Royal Institution of Great Britain.
Notices of the Proceedings . . . with abstracts of the discourses. Vols. 1-14. *London*, 1851-96. *In progress.* U

Royal Irish Academy.
Proceedings. 10 vols. *Dublin*, 1841-69. U
Do. 2nd Series. 4 vols. *Dublin*, 1877-88. U
Do. 3rd " Vols. 1-3. " 1889-96. *In progress.* C.U
Do. Irish Manuscript Series. Vols. 1-2. *Dublin*, 1870-90. *In progress.* U
Transactions. Vols. 1-30. *Dublin*, 1787-1896. *In progress.* U
(Wanting Vols. 20, 24 and 25).
Do. Vols. 13-17, 19-24. *Dublin*, 1825-64. T
Do. Vols. 24-30. *Dublin*, 1862-96. *In progress.* C
Do. Irish Manuscript Series. Vol. 1. *Dublin*, 1880. *In progress.* C.U
Cunningham Memoirs. Pts. 1-10. *Dublin*, 1880-94. *In progress.* U
(Wanting part 8.)
Do. Pts. 1-4, 6-7, 10. *Dublin*, 1880-94. *In progress.* C
Todd Lecture Series. Vols. 2-6. *Dublin*, 1887-95. *In progress.* U
List of papers published in (1) Cunningham Memoirs, (2) Transactions, (3) Irish Manuscript Series, between years 1786-1886. With an Appendix. *Dublin*, 1887. C

Royal Magazine. Vols. 1-3, 5, 13. *London*, 1759-65. P

Royal Medical Society. *See* Medical and Chirurgical Society.

Royal Microscopical Society.
Journal of Transactions and Proceedings. Vol. 3. *London* and *Edinburgh*, 1880.
Do. Series 2. Vols. 1-6, 7 (Part 1), 8-13, 16, *London*, 1881-1896. *In progress.* C

Royal Military Chronicle. Vols. 1-7. *London*, 1810-1814.
Do. N.S. Vols. 1-2. *London*, 1814-1815. P

Royal Physical Society of Edinburgh.
Proceedings. *Edinburgh*, 1854-96. *In progress.* C

Royal Scottish Society of Arts.
Transactions. Vols. 1-13. *Edinburgh*, 1841-1889. C

Royal Society of Canada.
Proceedings and Transactions. Vols. 1-12, *Montreal, Ottawa,* 1883-95.
Do. 2nd Series. Vol. 1-2. *Ottawa*, 1895-6. *In progress.* C.E.L.Mc.P.T.U.V
(Wanting Vols. 5-8, Mc).

Royal Society of Edinburgh.
Proceedings. Vols. 3-19. *Edinburgh*, 1850-96. *In progress.* U
Do. Vols. 5, 7-14, 16-20. *Edinburgh*, 1869-96. *In progress.* C
Transactions. Vols. 1-38. *Edinburgh*, 1788-96. *In progress.* U
(Wanting Vols. 2, 3 and 26, pt. 2).
Do. Vols. 4-17, 20-38 (Imperfect). *Edinburgh*, 1798-1896. *In progress.* C

Royal Society of Literature of the United Kingdom.
Transactions. Vols. 1-3. *London*, 1827-37. U
Do. 2nd Series. Vols. 1-14. *London*, 1843-87. P

Royal Society of London.
Abstracts of the papers printed in the Philosophical Transactions. 2 vols. (1800-30). *London*, 1832. U
Do. Vols 1-5. *London*, 1800-1850. C
Memoirs . . . . . being a new abridgment of the philosophical transactions from 1665 to 1735 inclusive, by Baddam. 10 vols. *London*, 1738-41. U
Philosophical Transactions. Vols. 1, 44, 56, 68, 70, 74, 117 (1685, 1747, 1765, 1778, 1780, 1784, 1827), and 120-186 (1830-95). *London*, 1685-1896. *In progress.* U
General Index. Vols. 1-70.
Do. *London*, 1817-18, 1821-25 (1-2-3), 1826 (1-4), 1827-32 (1-2), 1833 (1-2). C
Philosophical Transactions (and collections) abridged and disposed under general heads. Vols. 6 and 7 (1719-1733), by Eames and Martin ; Vols. 8-10 (1732-1750), by Martyn. *London*, 1734-51. U
Philosophical Transactions abridged, by Hutton, etc. 18 vols. (1665-1800.) *London*, 1803-09. U
Proceedings. Vols. 8-59. *London*, 1856-96. *In progress.* U
(Wanting Vols. 10-12, 15 and 24).
Do. Vols. 31-44, 48-59. *London*, 1880-96. *In progress.* C

Royal Society of New South Wales.
Journal and Proceedings. Vols. 12-27. *Sydney*, 1878-93. *In progress.* U
Do. Vols. 10-29. *Sydney*, 1876-95. *In progress.* C
Do. Vols. 13-20. *Sydney*, 1879-86. P

Royal Society of Queensland.
Proceedings. Vols. 1, 6 (Pts. 2-5), 9-11. *Brisbane*, 1884-96. *In progress.* C

Royal Society of South Australia.
See Adelaide Philosophical Society.

Royal Society of Tasmania.
Papers, Proceedings and Reports. *Hobart Town*, 1875 85, 1887-9, 1891. M
Do. *Hobart Town*, 1877-87, 1889, 1891. C

Royal Society of Victoria.
Proceedings. Vols. 23-24. *Melbourne*, 1886-1888.

Do. New Series. Vols. 1-7. *Melbourne*, 1888-1895. *In progress.* C
Transactions. Vols. 1-2, 4. *Melbourne*, 1888-1895. C

Royal Statistical Society. *See* Statistical Society.

Russisch-Kaiserliche Mineralogische. Gesellschaft zu St. Petersburg.
Materialen zur Geologie Russlands. Bd. 16-17. *St. Petersburg*, 1893 95. *In progress.* C
Verhandlungen. Series 2. B I. 28-29, 31, 33-35. *St. Petersburg*, 1891-7. *In progress.* C
See also Imperatorskoye Sanktpeterburgskoye Mineralogieskoye Obshchestvo.

Sabbath-School Association of Canada.
Proceedings of Sabbath-School Convention. *Toronto*, 1868-79, 1883. P

Sacred Book of the Buddhists, translated by various Oriental Scholars, and edited by F. Max Müller. Vol. 1. *London*, 1895. *In progress.* U

Sacred Books of the East, translated by various Oriental Scholars, and edited by F. Max Müller. Vols. 1-49. *Oxford*, 1879-96 *In progress.* P.U
Do. Vols. 1-31. *Oxford*, 1875-1885. T
Do. Vols. 1 29. *Oxford*, 1879-1886. K.Mc

Saechsische Gesellschaft der Wissenschaften. *See* Königlich-Sächsische Gesellschaft, etc.

St. Gallische Naturwissenschaftliche Gesellschaft.
Berichte. *St. Gallen*, 1858-63. C

St. George's Hospital.
Reports. Vols. 3 and 4. *London*, 1868-69. U

St. Helena. Observatory. *See* Observatories: St. Helena.

St. James' Magazine. Vols. 1-8. *London*, 1861-63. E

St. Louis Academy of Science. *See* Academy of Science of St. Louis.

St. Paul's Magazine. Vols. 1-14. *London*, 1868-74. P

St. Petersburg Academy of Science. *See* Academia Scientiärum Imperialis Petropolitana.

St. Petersburg Mineralogical Society. *See* Imperatorskoye Sanktpeterburgskoye Mineralogieskoye Obshchestvo.

St. Petersburg—Mining Institute. *See* Gornui Institut.

St. Thomas' Hospital.
Reports. New Series. Vols. 1-10, 19-23. *London*, 1870-96. *In progress.* U

Sale Prices of 1896: Sales by auction of objects of artistic and antiquarian interest. Vol. 1. *London*, 1897. P

San Francisco. School Reports. 1854-81. E

Sanitarian. Vols. 26-29. *Brooklyn*, 1891-1892. L

Sanitary Engineer. Vols. 9-15. *New York*, 1884-87. P
Do. Vols. 5, 8-14. *New York*, 1882-86. L
Continued as :

Engineering and Building Record and Sanitary Engineer. Vols. 16-35. *New York*, 1887-97. *In progress.* P
Do. Vols. 17-35. *New York*, 1888-97. *In progress.* S

Sanitary Engineering. Vols. 10-13. *London*, 1885-88. P

Sanitary Institute of Great Britain. Journal. Vols. 6-8, 10-17. *London*, 1884-97. *In progress.* C

Sanitary Journal. Vols. 1-5. *Toronto*, 1874-83. O.P

Sanitary News. Vols. 3-7. *Chicago*, 1884-86. U
Do. Vols. 9-19. *Chicago*, 1886-1892. L

Sanitary Record. Vols. 5-12. *London*, 1883-1892. L

Santiago—Observatorio. *See* Observatories: Chili.

Saskatchewan Business Directory. *Qu'Appelle, N.W.T.* 1888. P

Saturday Reader. Vols. 1-4. *Montreal*, 1865-67. P

Saturday Review. Vols. 1-84. *London*, 1855-97. *In progress.* P
Do. Vols. 25-58, 61, 65 68, 73-84. *London*, 1868-97. *In progress.* L
Do. Vols. 11-42. *London*, 1861-76. E

Scholastic Journal. Vol. 1. *London*, 1856-7. E

School and Teacher. Vols. 1-8. *London*, 1854-61. E

School Board Chronicle. 16 vols. *London*, 1872-83. E

School Journal. *New York* and *Chicago*, 1871-83, 1888-97. *In progress.* E

School Newspaper. Vols. 2-6. *London*, 1875-79. E

School of Mines Quarterly.
Vols. 5-7, 10-14. *New York* 1883-93. C
" 2-8. " 1880-86. U
Index to Vols. 1-10 in Vol. 10. C

Schoolmaster. *London*, 1873-97. *In progress.* E

Schweizerische Geodaetische Commission.
Arbeiten. 4 vols. *Zürich*, 1879-89. U

Schweizerische Gesellschaft, &c. *See* Allgemeine Schweizerische Gesellschaft, &c.

Science. Vols. 1-22. *Cambridge* and *New York*, 1883-93. (Wanting Vols. 1-2, M). M.P
Do. Vols. 15-22. *New York*, 1890-93. I
Do. N.S. Vols. 1-5. *New York*, 1895-97. *In progress.* M.P.S

Science Sociale. 14 tom. *Paris*, 1886-92. U

Scientific American. Vols. 1-77. *New York*, 1859-97. *In progress.* P
Do. Vols. 28-77. *New York*, 1873-97. *In progress.* I

Scientific American Supplement. Vols. 3-22, 24-44. *New York*, 1877-86, 1887-97. *In progress.* P

Scientific Memoirs. (ed. Richard Taylor), Vols. 1-5. *London*, 1837-52.   C

Scientists' International Directory. *Boston*, 1882-3, 1894.   P

Scotch-Irish Society of America. Proceedings and addresses of the Second Congress at Pittsburg, Pa. *Cincinnati*, 1890.   P

Scots' Magazine. Vols. 1-79. *Edinburgh*, 1739-1817.
    Continued as :
Edinburgh Magazine. Vols. 1-18. *Edinburgh*, 1817-1826.   P

Scottish Arboricultural Society. Transactions. Vol. 1. *Edinburgh*, 1855-58. C

Scottish Art Review. Vols. 1-2. *Glasgow*, 1888-9.   P

Scottish-Celtic Review. *Glasgow*, 1895.   P

Scottish Educational Journal. 1 vol. *Edinburgh*, 1852.   E

Scottish Episcopal Review and Magazine. Vol. 3. *Edinburgh*, 1822.   T

Scottish Geographical Society. Scottish Geographical Magazine. Vols. 1-12. *Edinburgh*, 1885-96. *In progress.* .   C
Do. Vols. 1-5. *Edinburgh*, 1885-9.   U

Scottish History Society. Publications. Vols. 1-26. *Edinburgh*, 1887-96. *In progress.*   P

Scottish Record Publications. 49 vols. *Edinburgh*, 1867-95. *In progress.*   U
    (Wanting one vol. of the series.)

Scottish Review. Vols. 1-30. *London*, 1882-97. *In progress.*   L
Do. Vols. 15-30. *Paisley, London* and *New York*. 1890-97. *In progress.*   U
Do. Vols. 21-30. *London*, 1893-97. *In progress.*   P

Scottish Text Society. Publications. 39 vols. *Edinburgh*, 1884-97. *In progress.*   P

Scribner's Magazine. Vols. 1-22. *New York*, 1887-97. *In progress.*   L.P

Scuola d'Anatomia, Patologica. Archivio. Tom. 1-4. *Firenze*, 1881-6.   C

Seismological Society of Japan. Transactions. Vols. 1-16. *Yokohama*, 1880-92. *In progress.*   U

Selden Society. Publications. Vols. 1-10. *London*, 1887-96. *In progress.*   O.U

Semitistische Studien. *See* Zeitschrift für Assyriologie, etc.

Semper's Arbeiten. *See* Zoologisch-zootomisches Institut in Würzburg. Arbeiten.

Senckenbergische naturforschende Gesellschaft. Berichte. *Frankfurt am Main*, 1883-1896. *In progress.*   C

Shakespeare Society. Publications, 48 nos. *London*, 1841-53.   P.U

Shakesperiana. Vols. 1-10. *Philadelphia*, 1883-93.   P
Do. Vols. 1, 4-6, 9, *New York*, 1883-92.   L

Sidereal Messenger. Vol. 10. *Northfield, Minn.*, 1891.   S

Siebenbuergischer Verein fuer Naturwissenschaften in Hermannstadt. Verhandlungen und Mittheilungen. Bd. 38 45. *Hermannstadt*, 1888-96. *In progress.*   C

Silliman's Journal. *See* American Journal of Science and Arts.

Skandinaviske Naturforskeres Forhandlinger. Tretende Möde. *Christiania*, 1886.   C

Sketch. Vols. 5-9. *London*, 1894-5. *In progress.*   L

Snow Drop. Vols. 1-3. *Montreal*, 1847-50. N. S. Vol. 3. *Montreal*, 1852.   P

Sociedad Cientifica "Antonio Alzate." Memorias. Tom. 1, 3, 5-6, 8-9. *Mexico*, 1885-1896. *In progress.*   C

Sociedad Geografica de Madrid. Boletin. Tom. 20-21, 24-25, 27-35. *Madrid*, 1886-93.   C

Sociedade de Geographia de Lisboa. Actas das sessoes. Tom. 9-15. *Lisboa*, 1889-95. *In progress.*   C
Bolletim. Series 2. Nos. 4-6. *Lisboa*, 1875. M
Do. Series 9-16. *Lisboa*, 1890-97. *In progress.*   C

Sociedade de Geographia do Rio de Janeiro. Tom. 10-11. *Rio de Janeiro*, 1894-5. *In progress.*   C

Societa Adriatica di Scienze Naturali in Trieste. Bollettino. Tom 11-17. *Trieste*, 1889-95. *In progress.*   C

Societa Africana d'Italia, Sezione Fiorentina. Bollettino. Tom. 1-10. *Firenze*, 1885-94.   P

Societa di Letturi. Effemeridi. Anno 2. *Genova*, 1871.   P

Societa Entomologica Italiana. Bollettino. *Firenze*, 1883-1888, 1890, 1892-94.   C

Societa Geographica Italiana. Bollettino. Tom 23-33. *Roma*, 1886-96. *In progress.*   C
Memorie. Tom. 5. *Roma*, 1895-6. *In progress.*   C

Societa Istriana di Archeologia e Storia Patria. Atti e Memorie. Tom. 5-9, 11. *Parenzo*, 1889-95. *In progress.*   C

Societa Italiana di Antropologia, Etnologia e Psicologia Comparata. Archivio per L'Antropologia e L'Etnologia. Tom. 14-25. *Firenze*, 1884-1895. *In progress.*   C

Societa Italiana di Scienze Naturali. Atti. Tom. 29-32, 34-5. *Milan*, 1886-1890, 1892-5. *In progress.*   C

Societa Ligustica di Scienze Naturali e Geografiche. Atti. Tom. 1-3. *Genova*, 1890-92.   C

Societa Siciliana per la Storia Patria. Archivio Storico Siciliano. New Series. Vols. 10-20. *Palermo*, 1885-96. *In progress.*   C

Societa Storica Comense.
Atti. Tom. 1-3. *Como*, 1888-98. *In progress.* C

Societa Storica per la Provincia e Antica Diocesi.
Periodico. Tom. 5-12. *Como*, 1885-98. *In progress.* C

Societa Toscana di Scienze Naturali residente in Pisa.
Atti. Tom. 3-7, 9, 11-13. *Pisa*, 1877-94. C

Societa Veneto-Trentina di Scienze Naturali residente in Padova.
Atti. Tom. 9 12. Serie 2. Tom. 1. *Padova*, 1884-94. C.

Societas Philologa Lipsiensis.
Acta. Tom. 1-6. *Lipsiae*, 1871-76. U

Societas Scientiarum Fennica. *See* Finska Vetenskaps Societet.

Societatum-Litterae. Verzeichniss der in den Publikationen der Akademien und Vereine aller Länder erscheinenden Einzelarbeiten auf dem Gebiete der Naturwissenschaften. Jahrg. 1-10. *Berlin*, 1887-96. *In progress.* U
Do. Jahrg. 3-10. *Berlin*, 1889-96. *In progress.* C

Societe Academique Indo-Chinoise.
Bulletin. Série 2. Tom. 2-3. *Paris*, 1882-90. C
Mémoires. Tom. 1-2. *Paris*, 1872-78. C

Societe Archeologique.
Comptes-Rendus. N. S. Tom. 1. *Agram*, 1895. *In progress.* C

Societe Archeologique du Department de Constantine.
Recueil des Notices et Mémoires. Série 3. Tom. 3-4, 19. *Constantine*, 1886-88, 1894. C

Societe Bretonne de Geographie.
Bulletins. Nos. 33-57, 68. *Lorient*, 1889-93,1896. *In progress.* C

Societe Chimique de Paris.
Bulletin des Séances. 1857-60. *Paris*, 1857-60.
Répertoire de Chimie pure et appliquée. 1859-63. *Paris*, 1859-63.
Bulletin. Années 1861-96. (Nouvelle Série. Tom. 1-50; and 3me Série. Tom. 1-16). *Paris*, 1863-96. Tables, 1875-88. *In progress.* U

Societe Cuvierienne.
Revue Zoologique. Années 1838-48. *Paris*, 1839-48.
United with Magazin de Zoologie, and continued as :
Revue et Magazin de Zoologie pure et appliquée.
2me Série. 23 tom. *Paris*, 1849-72.
3me Série. 7 tom. " 1873-79. U

Societe d'Anthropologie de Paris.
Bulletins. Série 3. Tom. 7-12. *Paris*, 1884-89.
" 4. " 1-4. *Paris*, 1890-93. *In progress.* C
Mémoires. Série 2. Tom. 4. *Paris*, 1893. C

Societe Dauphinoise d'Ethnologie et d'Anthropologie.
Bulletin. Tom. 2. *Grenoble*, 1895. C

Societe de Biologie.
Comptes rendus des Séances, et Mémoires.
1 re Série.	5 tom.	*Paris*,	1850-54.
2 me "	5 "	"	1855-59.
3 me "	5 "	"	1860-64.
4 me "	5 "	"	1865-69.
5 me "	5 "	"	1870-74.
6 me "	5 "	"	1875-79.
7 me "	5 "	"	1880-84.	U

Societe de Chirurgie de Paris.
Mémoires. Tom 3. *Paris*, 1853. U

Societe de Geographie.
Bulletin. Série 6. Tom. 1-6, 8-20. *Paris*, 1871-85.
Do. Série 7. Tom. 1-13, 15-16. *Paris*, 1881-95. *In progress.* C
Compte-rendu des Séances. *Paris*, 1882-6, 1888-9, 1891-3, 1896. *In progress.* C

Societe de Geographie Commerciale de Bordeaux.
Bulletin. Série 2. *Bordeaux*, 1891-1896. *In progress.* C

Societe de Geographie Commerciale de Nantes.
Annés 1890, 1893-7. *Nantes*, [1890-97]. *In progress.* C

Societe de Geographie de Geneve.
Le Globe. Organe de la Société de Géographie de Genève. Série 4. Tom. 3-8. *Genève*, 1883-89.
Do. Série 5. Tom. 1, 3-7. *Genève*, 1889-96. *In progress.*

Societe de Geographie de Lille.
Bulletin. Tom. 10 11, 13-22, 25 6. *Lille*, 1888 96. *In progress.* C

Societe de Geographie de Quebec. *See* Geographical Society of Quebec.

Societe de Geographie et d'Archeologie de la Province d'Oran.
Bulletin Trimestrielle. Tom. 6, 14-16. *Oran*, 1886, 1894-96. *In progress.* C

Societe de Geographie Findlandaise.
Bulletins (Fennia). Tom. 1-9, 11-13. *Helsingfors*, 1889-96. *In progress.* C

Societe de Legislation Comparee.
Annuaire de Législation étrangère. Années 17-18. *Paris*, 1888-89. U
Annuaire de Législation française. Années 7-9. *Paris*, 1888-90.
Bulletin. Années 19-21. *Paris*, 1888-90. U

Societe de l'Enseignement Superieur.
Revue internationale de l'Enseignement. Tom. 1-20. *Paris*, 1881-90. U

Societe de l'Histoire de France.
Annuaire historique. Années 1837-63. *Paris*, 1836-63.
Annuaire-Bulletin. Années 1863-96. *Paris*, 1863-96. *In progress.* U
Publications. 213 vols. *Paris*, 1835 96. *In progress.* U

Societe de Physique et d'Histoire Naturelle de Geneve.
Comptes Rendus des Séances. Tom. 1-13. *Genève*, 1885-96. *In progress.* C

Societe des Anciens Textes Francais.
Bulletin. Années 1-22. *Paris*, 1875-96. U
Publications. 59 vols. *Paris*, 1875-96. *In progress.* U

Societe des Etudes Historiques.
Bulletin des Recherches Historiques. *Levis*, 1895-97. *In prog. ess.* P

Societe des Etudes Indo-Chinoises de Saigon.
Bulletin. 1889, 1895. *Saigon*, 1889 95. *In progress.* C

Societe des Ingenieurs Civils.
Annuaire. *Paris*, 1896 7. *In progress.* C.S
Bulletin. Série 5. Tom. 46-50. *Paris*, 1893-97. *In progress.* S
Do. Série 5. Tom. 47 50. *Paris*, 1894-96. *In progress.* U
Mémoires. *Paris*, 1862-97. *In progress.* S

Societe des Naturalistes.
Mémoires. Tom. 9-11, 13. *Kiew*, 1888-94. C

Societe des Naturalistes a l'Universite Imperiale de Kharkow.
Travaux. Tom. 18-29. *Kharkow*, 1884-95. *In progress.* C

Societe des Recherches Historiques.
See Société des Etudes Historiques.

Societe des Sciences Naturelles de l'Ouest de la France.
Bulletins. Tom. 1, 4. *Nantes*, 1891, 1894. C

Societe d'Ethnographie Americaine et Orientale.
Annuaire. 1878 82. *Paris*, 1878-82. C
Bulletin. 1896-7. *Paris*, 1896-7. *In progress.* C

Societe Finno-Ougrienne.
Journal. Tom. 11-12, 14. *Helsingfors*, 1893 96. *In progress.* C
Mémoires. Tom. 4 6-9. *Helsingfors*, 1892-96. *In progress.* C

Societe Fribourgeoise des Sciences Naturelles.
Bulletin. Années 1-8. *Fribourg*, 1880-88. U

Societe Geologique de Belgique.
Annales. Tom. 20-21. *Liège*, 1892-4. C

Societe Geologique de France.
Bulletin. 2me Série. Tom. 13, 24-25, 28. *Paris*, 1866-71.
3me Série. Tom. 1-2, 4, 6-10, 12-20. *Paris*, 1872-92. C

Societe Geologique de Normandie.
Bulletin. Tom. 6-16. *Havre*, 1879-89. C

Societe Geologique du Nord.
Annales. Tom. 14-20, 24. *Lille*, 1886-92. C

Societe Helvetique des Sciences Naturelles. *See* Allgemeine Schweizerische Gesellschaft für die gesammten Naturwissenschaften.

Societe Historique de Montreal.
Mémoires. Nos. 1-9. *Montreal*, 1859-80. P

Societe Hollandaise des Sciences a Harlem.
Archives Néerlandaises des Sciences exactes et naturelles. Tom. 1-29. *La Haye*, 1866 96. *In progress.* C

Societe Hongroise de Geographie.
Bulletin. Tom. 15-20, 22-23. *Buda Pest*, 1887-92, 1894-5. *In progress.* C

Societe Imperiale des Amis des Sciences Naturelles, d'Anthropologie et d'Ethnographie.
Geognosie. Tom. 1 and 3. *Moscow*, 1894. C

Societe Imperiale des Naturalistes de Moscou.
Bulletin. 1829-89 (imperfect). *Moscou*, 1829-89. U
Do. 1885-87, 1889-95. *Moscou*, 1885-95. C
Mémoires. Tom. 1-5. *Moscou*, 1811-17. U
(Wanting Tom. 2).
Nouveaux Mémoires. Tom. 1-15. *Moscou*, 1829-89. U
(Wanting Tom. 2, 4, 5, and 8).

Societe Imperiale Russe de Geographie.
Bulletins. Tom. 9, 25-27, 29 *Tiflis* and *St. Petersburg*, 1886 93. C
Mémoires de la Section Caucasienne. Tom. 13-15. *Tiflis*, 1890-93. C

Societe Liegeoise de Litterature Wallonne.
Annuaire. Années 1-12. *Liège*, 1863 87. C.U
(Wanting Années 2 and 3, U).
Bulletin. Années 6-13. *Liège*, 1863 72. U
Do. Années 4-12. *Liège*, 1861 69. U
2me Série. Tom. 1-14. *Liège*, 1873-89. U
"   " 1-10, 13-14. *Liège*, 1870-89. C
(Wanting Tom. 9. U)
Mémoires et ouvrages couronnés. 3 vols. *Liège*, 1863-86. U

Societe Linneenne du Nord de la France.
Mémoires. Tom. 7-12. *Amiens*, 1886 94. C

Societe Mathematique de France.
Bulletin. Tom. 1-17. *Paris*, 1873 89. U
"   " Tom. 14-18. *Paris*, 1885-90. C

Societe Meteorologique de France.
Annuaire. *Paris*, 1849-50, 1853-4. M

Societe Nationale des Antiquaires de France.
Mémoires. Série 5. Tom. 5 (or Tome 45 of entire set). *Paris*, 1884. C

Societe Nationale des Sciences Naturelles de Cherbourg.
Mémoires. Tom. 17-29. *Paris*, 1873-95. C

Societe Neerlandaise de Zoologie.
Comptes Rendus des Séances du Troisieme Congrès International. *Leiden*, 1895. C

Societe Neuchateloise de Geographie.
Bulletin. Tom. 1-8. *Neuchatel*, 1885-95. *In progress.* C

Societe Philologique.
Actes. Tom. 16 17, 21-22, 24. *Alençon*, 1886 94. C

Societe Physico-chimique Russe.
Journal. Tom. 18-19, 22, 24, 27. *St. Petersburg*, 1886-96. *In progress.* C

Societe pour l'Etude des Langues Romanes.
Revue des Langues Romanes.

1me Série. 8 tom. *Montpellier, Paris*, 1870-75.
2me " 6 " " " 1876-78.
3me " 16 " " " 1879-86.
4me " 1-9. " " 1887-96.
In progress. U

Societe Royale Belge de Geographie.
Bulletin. *Bruxelles*, 1885-89, 1892-96. *In progress.*

Societe Royale de Botanique de Belgique.
Bulletin. Tom. 1-15, 22-24, 26-34. *Bruxelles,* 1862-95.

Societe Royale des Antiquaires du Nord. See Kongeligt Nordtsk Oldskrift-Selskab.

Societe Royale des Sciences de Liege.
Mémoires. Série 2. Tom. 14, 17-19. *Liège,* 1888-96. *In progress.*

Societe Royale Malacologique de Belgique.
Annales. Tom. 24-27. *Bruxelles*, 1889-92. C
Procès Verbal des Séances. Tom. 19-20, 22 23.
Bruxelles, 1890-94. C

Societe Scientifique de Chili.
Actes. Tom. 2-4. *Santiago*, 1892-4.

Societe Vaudoise des Sciences Naturelles.
Bulletin. Tom. 24-31. *Lausanne*, 1888-95. C

Societe Zoologique de France.
Bulletin. Tom. 1-14. *Paris*, 1876-89. U
" " 1-20. " 1876-95. *In progress.* C
Mémoires. Tom. 1-5. " 1888-92. U

Society for Promoting Christianity among the Jews.
83rd report. *London*, 1891. T

Society for Psychical Research.
Proceedings. Vols. 1-12. *London*, 1883-96. *In progress.* U
Do. Vols. 1-4, 7-10. *London*, 1882-94. C

Society for the Diffusion of Useful Knowledge.
Quarterly Journal of Education. Vols. 1-4. *London*, 1831-2. U
Do. Vols. 1-6. *London*, 1831-33. Mc

Society for the Promotion of Hellenic Studies.
Journal of Hellenic Studies. Vols. 1-16. Plates to Vols. 1-8, and Supplementary Papers 1-2. *London*, 1880-96. *In progress.* U

Society for the Propagation of the Gospel.
Reports and Digests of Records. *London*, 1827, 1832, 1839 40, 1843-45, 1847-55, 1857-8, 1860, 1865. T
Mission Field, a monthly record of the proceedings, 1874-89. *London* [1875-90]. U
Reports 1831 and 1869-88. *London* [1870-89]. U

Society of Antiquaries of London.
Archæologia, or miscellaneous tracts relating to antiquity.
Vols. 1-51. *London*, 1770-1890. U
Vols. 1-53. (Vol. 53, pt. 1 only). *London*, 1770-1892. P
Index to Vols. 1-50. P.U

Proceedings. 2nd Series. Vols. 13 and 14. *London*, 1889-93. U
Do. Vols. 11-14. *London*, 1885-93. C

Society of Antiquaries of Newcastle-upon-Tyne.
Archæologia Æliana. 1st Series. 4 vols. (1822-55).
2nd Series. Vols. 1-18 (1855-96). *Newcastle-upon-Tyne*, 1822 96. *In progress.* PC

Society of Antiquaries of Scotland.
Proceedings. 12 vols. *Edinburgh*, 1851-78. C.P.U
N.S. 12 vols. *Edinburgh*, 1879-90. C.P.U
3rd Series. Vols. 1-3. *Edinburgh*, 1891-3. *In progress.* P
Do. Vols. 1-6. *Edinburgh*, 1891-96. *In progress.* C
Index to 1st and 2nd Series. C
Transactions (Archælogia Scotica, &c.). Vols. 1-5. *Edinburgh*, 1792-1890. *In progress.* P
Do. Vols. 2-4. *Edinburgh*, 1831-33. U

Society (for the Encouragement) of Arts(Manufactures and Commerce).
Journal of the Society of Arts (and of the Institutions in the Union). Vols. 1-37. *London*, 1853-89. U
Vols. 1-6, 37-39, 40-42. *London*, 1852-95. *In progress.* C
Transactions. Vols. 1-3, 5-17, 20-23, 26, 28-30, 32-55. *London*, 1806-44. C
Vol. 26 contains Analytical Index, Vols. 1-25.
Vol. 40 contains Analytical Index, Vols. 26 40.
Vol. 50 contains Analytical Index, Vols. 41-50.

Society of Biblical Archæology.
Transactions. Vols. 1-10. *London*, 1872 96.
Proceedings. Vols. 1-18. *London*, 1878-96. *In progress.* P.U

Society of Comparative Legislation.
Journal. Vol. 1. *London*, 1896. *In progress.* P

Soirees Canadiennes. 5 vols. *Quebec*, 1861-5.
Continued as :
Nouvelles Soirées Canadiennes. Vol. 1-2. *Quebec*, 1882-3. P

Soldiers' Orphans' Institute of Pennsylvania.
Annual Reports, 1887-90, 1892-3, 1895. C

Somerset House Gazette and Literary Museum.
Vols. 1-2. *London*, 1823-4. P

Somerset Record Society.
Publications. Vol. 2. P.P., 1888. U

Somersetshire Archæological and Natural History Society.
Proceedings. Vols. 30-42. *Taunton* and *London*, 1884-96. *In progress.*

South African Philosophical Society.
Transactions. Vols. 5-6. *Cape Town*, 1888-92. C

South America. Meteorological Reports. *See* Observatories : South America.

South Australia. School reports. 1881-91. *Adelaide*. E

Southern Historical Magazine. Vol. 1.
Charleston, 1892.   P

Spain. Meteorological Reports. *See* Observatories : Spain.

Spalding Club.
Miscellany. Vols. 1-5. *Aberdeen*, 1841-52.
Publications. 28 vols. *Aberdeen*, 1842 71.
Continued as :
New Spalding Club. Publications. 13 vols.
Aberdeen, 1888-94. *In progress.*
Hand-list to bibliography of the shires of
Aberdeen, Banff, and Kincardine. *Aberdeen*,
1893.   P

Speaker. *London*, 1893-96.   L

Specola Vaticana. Publicazioni. Vols. 1-4.5+
Roma, 1891-4.   C

Spectator. Vols. 49-56, 60-63, 65-78. *London*,
1876-97. *In progress.*   L
Vols. 57-78. *London*, 1884-97. *In progress.*   P

Spenser Society.
Publications. Nos. 1-34. *London*, 1867-94.
In progress   P

Spiritual Magazine. Vols. 1-13. *London*,
1860-72.   P

Sporting and Dramatic News. Vols.
9-21. *London*, 1878 84.   P

Spottiswoode Society.
Publications. 6 vols. *Edinburgh*, 1844-5.   P

**Staats- und Socialwissenschaftliche
Forschungen.** Bd. 1-10. *Leipzig*, 1879-91.
                                                         U

State Historical Society of Wisconsin.
See Wisconsin State Historical Society.

Statesman's Year Book. *London*, 1865-6,
1868-71, 1873-5, 1877 82, 1884-98. *In progress.* P
Do. *London*, 1889-98. *In progress.*   U

Statist (The). Vols. 35-40. *London*, 1895-7.
In progress.   P

**Statistical Abstract and Record of
Canada.** 1886-88. *Ottawa*, 1887-9.   C
Continued as :
Statistical Year-Book of Canada.   1889-96.
Ottawa, 1890 97. *In progress.*   F.L.O.P.U

(Royal) Statistical Society of London.
Proceedings. *London*, 1834-5.   P
Journal. Vols. 1-59. *London*, 1838-96. *In
progress.*   L.P
Do. Vols. 4-20, 47-59. *London*, 1841-96.
In progress.   U
General indexes to Vols. 1-50, and subject index
to Vols. 28-57 of the Journal.

Stats-Anzeigen. 18 Bde. *Gottingen*, 1782-93.
Register in 3 parts.   U

Stavenger Museum.
Aarsberetning. *Stavenger*, 1890-95.   C

Stock Exchange Year-Book. *London*,
1884.   P

Stockholders' and Investors' Annual.
Montreal, 1893-6. *In progress.*   P

**Stockholm—Royal Swedish Academy
of Science.** *See* Kongliga svenska Vetenskaps
Akademi.

Strand Magazine. Vols. 1-14. *London*,
1891-97. *In progress*   P

**Strassburg — Dissertationes philolo-
gicæ.** *See* Dissertationes philologicæ Argentoratenses selectæ.

Strassburger Studien, Zeitschrift für Geschichte, Sprache und Litteratur des Elasses. 2
Bde. *Strassburg*, 1883-4.   U

Stryker's American Register. Vol. 4.
Trenton, N.J., 1850.   E

Student (The). 6 vols. *New York*, 1848-55. E

Student and Schoolmaster. 6 vols.
New York, 1855-58.   E

**Studien zur griechischen und latein-
ischen Grammatik** (hrsg. von G. Curtius).
Bd. 1-10. *Leipzig*, 1868-78.   U

Studj di Filologia Romanza. *See* Rivista
di Filologia Romanza.

**Stuttgart—Verein fuer Vaterlaendi-
sche Naturkunde in Wuertemberg.**
See Verein für Vaterländische Naturkunde.

Sunday at Home. *London*, 1854-97. *In
progress.*   P

Sunday School Banner. 6 vols. *Toronto*,
1872-82.   E

Sunday School Teachers' Magazine.
15 vols. *London*, 1855-70.   E

Sunday School Times. *London*, 1866 68. Mc

Surtees Society.
Publications. Vols. 1-97. *Newcastle*, 1835 97.
(Wanting Vol. 36).   U
Do. Vols. 1-97. *London*, 1834-97. *In pro-
gress.*   U
(Wanting Vols. 81, 89).

Sussex Archæological Society.
Sussex Archæological Collections. Vols. 26-37.
London, 1876-90.   U

**Svensk Saellskapet foer Antropologi
och Geografi.**
Tidskrift. *Stockholm*, 1884-86, 1888-90, 1892 96.
In progress.   C

Swarthmore Conferences.
Proceedings. *Philadelphia*, 1896.   P

Sweden. Meteorological Reports. *See* Observatories : Sweden.

**Swedish Academy of Belles Lettres,
&c.** *See* Kongliga Vitterhets, Historie, och Antiqvitets Akademi.

Swedish Academy of Science. *See*
Kongliga svenska Vetenskaps Akademi.

Switzerland.
School Reports. Annual. *Zurich*, 1887-91. E
Statistics. *Zurich*, 1881.   E

Sword and Trowel. *London*, 1865-73, 1875-
80, 1882.   Mc

Sydenham Society.
Publications. 33 vols. *London*, 1843-57. (Wanting 7 vols. to complete the series).   U

**Syllogue Litteraire Grec de Constan-
tinople.** Tom. 19-22. *Constantinople*, 1884-91.
                                                         C

Syracuse. School Reports. 1876-80, 1883.   E

Tagore Law Lectures. 1870-87. *Calcutta*,
1870-87.   U

Tasmania.
Legislative Council Journals, 1875-84; House of Assembly Journals, 1875-83 (Imperfect); Journals and Papers of Parliament, 1884-91 (Imperfect).
Reports on Education. Annual. *Hobart Town*, 1885-95. *In progress.* E

Teachers' Institute. Vols. 15-17. *New York*, 1892-95. *In progress.* E

Technical Society of the Pacific Coast. Transactions. Vols. 3-8. *San Francisco*, 1886-91. C

Technisch-chemisches Jahrbuch. Jahrg. 8-11 (1885-89). *Berlin*, 1887-90. U

Telegraphic Journal and Electrical Review. Vols. 21-39. *London*, 1888-96 *In progress.* P

Temple Bar. Vols. 1-112. *London*, 1861-97. *In progress.* P

Tennessee. School reports. *Nashville*, 1869-77, 1888-92. E

Texas. School Reports. *Austin*, 1886-90. E

✗ **Texas Academy of Science.** Transactions. Vol. 1. *Austin*, 1892-96. *In progress.* C

Texas Sanitarian. Vol. 1. *Austin*, 1891-2. L

Texts and Studies. Vols. 1-3. *Cambridge*, 1891-5. P

Thalia. *See* Neue Thalia.

Theatre. Vols. 1-3. *London*, 1878-9. N.S. Vols. 1-30, *London*, 1883-97. *In progress.* P

Themis (La). Vols. 2-5. *Montreal*, 1881-83. E

Theologian (The). Nos. 1-8; N S., 1-10. *London*, 1844-47. (Incomplete). T

Theological Critic. Vol. 1. *London*, 1851. T Do. Vols. 1, 11. *London*, 1851-61. Mc.

Theological Eclectic. Vols. 1-7. *Cincinnati*, 1864-71. Mc

Theological Monthly. Vols. 1-4. *Toronto*, 1889-90. P

Theological Review. Vols. 10-14. 16. *London*, 1873-77, 1879. Mc.

Theologische Literatur-Zeitung. Bd. 11-19. *Leipzig*, 1876-94. T

Theologische Studien und Kritiken. *Gotha*, 1828-70, 1882, 1884-5, 1895-7. *In progress.* Mc Do. *Gotha*, 1854, 1884-97. *In progress.* T

Theosophy. Vol. 11. *New York*, 1897. *In progress.* P

Therapeutic Gazette. Vols. 9-16. *Detroit*, 1865-92. L

Thinker. Vols. 1-8. *London*, 1892-95. V

Thurgauischer naturforschender Verein. Mittheilungen. Heft. 6-9. *Frauenfeld*, 1884-90. U Do. Heft. 10-12. *Frauenfeld*, 1892-96. *In progress.* C

Tijdschrift voor Indische Taal-, Land-, en Volkenkunde. *See* Bataviaasch Genootschap van Kunsten en Wetenschappen. Tijdschrift, &c.

Times (The). *London*, 1805-97. *In progress.* O Do. *London*, 1859-87. U Palmer's Index, 1829-96. *In progress.* O

Times (The) Register of Events. *London*, 1883-9. P

Tokyo Anthropological Society. Bulletin. Vols. 5, 7, 9. *Tokyo*, 1889-93. C ✗

Tomahawk (The). Vols. 1-6. *London*, 1867-70. P

Toronto Almanac and Royal Calendar. *See* York Almanac.

Toronto.
Board of Trade Reports. *Toronto*, 1886-96. P
By-laws. 1885, 1887-89, 1891. P
Consolidated By-laws. 1834-91. P
City Council By-laws. Minutes. 1859-97. P
City Directory. *Toronto* and *York*, 1833-4, 1837, 1846-7, 1850-51, 1856, 1859-98. *In progress.* P
City Engineer. Reports. 1882-97. P
Water-works Reports. 1872-92. P
City Mission Reports. 1 vol. *Toronto*, 1849-58, 1862-64. P
City Treasurer. Reports. 1860-63, 1874-5, 1877-86, 1888-90. P
Eye and Ear Infirmary. Reports Nos. 1, 3-10. 1869-78.
House of Industry Reports. 1852-82. E.P
Industrial Refuge. Reports. 1854-87. E
Infants' Home. Reports. 1876-88. E
Local Board of Health. Report. 1891. P
Observatory. *See* Observatories : Canada.
Orphans' Home. Reports. *Toronto*, 1853-87. E
Public School Board. Minutes. 1875-92, 1894-6.
By-laws. 1890. P
Hand-book. 1890, 1893, 1897.
Reports. 1859-77, 1879-94.
Relief Society. Reports. 1879-87. E
Sick Children's Hospital. Reports. 1876-87. E
Voters' Lists. 1886-90, 1893.
Assessment roll. 1890. P

Tour (Le) du Monde. Tom. 66-68. *Paris*, 1893-4. ✗

Toronto University. *See* University of Toronto.

Toynbee Record. Vols. 3-5 (imperfect). *London*, 1890-93. U

Tracts for the Times. Vols. 1-5. *London*, 1838. T

Trade Review. Vols. 1-2. *Montreal*, 1866. P

Treble Almanac. *See* Gentleman's and Citizen's Almanack.

Trenton Natural History Society. Journal. Vols. 1-2. *Trenton*, 1886-91. C

Tribune Almanac. *New York*, 1838-78, 1892. L

Triest –Zoologische Station. *See* Zoologisches Institut der Universität Wien und der zoologischen Station in Triest.

Trinity University Review. Vols. 8-9. *Toronto*, 1895-6. *In progress.* P

Tromso Museum.
Aarshefter. Vols. 1, 11-17. *Tromso*, 1878-94. C
Aarsberetning. *Tromso*, 1881, 1892-3. C
Truth. *London*, 1881, 1882, 1892. L
Tschermak's Mittheilungen. *See* Mineralogische und Petrographische Mittheilungen.
Turin Academy of Science. *See* Accademia delle Scienze.
Turkey. Meteorological Reports. *See* Observatories : Turkey.
Ulster Journal of Archæology. Vols. 1-9. *Belfast*, 1853-62. L.P
Union Geographique du Nord de la France.
Bulletin. Tom. 7-10. *Douai*. 1886-89. U
Do. Tom. 12-13. *Douai*, 1891-2. M
Do. Tom. 15-16. *Douai*, 1894-5. C
Unitarian Review. Vols. 31-36. *Boston*, 1889-91. P
U. E. Loyalist. Vols. 1-2. *York*, 1826-7. (Printed with Upper Canada Gazette). L.P
Continued as :
Loyalist. Vol. 1. *York*, 1828-9. P
United Service Journal and Naval and Military Magazine. *London*, 1829-43.
Continued as :
Colburn's United Service Magazine. *London*, 1843-45, 1847-63. P
United States.
Congress.
Abridgment of Debates. Vols. 1-16. *New York*, 1789-1850. L.P
American Arch ves. 4th Series. Vols. 1-6.
5th Series. Vols. 1-3. (1774-76). *Washington*, 1837-53. L.P
American State Papers. 39 vols. 1832-67.
Contents:--Finance, 5 vols.; Foreign Relations, 6 vols.; Military Affairs, 7 vols.; Claims, 1 vol. Miscellaneous, 2 vols.; Indian Affairs, 2 vols.; Naval Affairs, 4 vols. ; Post Office. 1 vol. Commerce and Navigation, 3 vols.; Public Lands, 8 vols. L.P
(Wanting Commerce and Navigation, Vol. 3, L).
Annals of Congress. 1797-1807. Vols. 1-16. *Washington*, 1834-52. T
Do. 1789-1824. L
Congressional Globe. 1850-65, 1869-77. L
Congressional Record. 1878-94. L
Register of Debates. Vol. 1. 1824-37. L
Reports of Committees of Congress. 1851-2. Vol. 1. *Washington*, 1852. L
Senate.
Executive documents. 1851-52. Vols. 1-19. *Washington*, 1852. T
Do. 1854-95. L
Journal. 1857-94. L
Miscellaneous Documents. 1854-95. L
Reports. 1859-95 L
House of Representatives.
Executive documents. 1851-2. *Washington*, 1852. T
Do. 1853-94. L
Journals. 1851-2. *Washington*, 1852. T
Do. *Washington*, 1857-94. L

House of Representatives.
Miscellaneous documents. 1851-2. *Washington*, 1852. T
Do. *Washington*, 1854-95. L
Reports. 1857-93. L
Department of Agriculture.
Report upon an examination of wools and other animal fibres. *Washington*. 1882. P
Fibre investigations. Report No. 4. *Washington*, 1892. C
Reports. *Washington*, 1862, 1864-69, 1871-2, 1875. P
Do. *Washington*, 1881-2, 1886-95. C
Secretary of Agriculture. Report. 1896. C
Statistic-. Reports Nos. 41-68, 70-95, 97-112, 115-117, 119-128, 131-133. *Washington*, 1887-95. C
Miscellaneous Reports. Nos.1-7. *Washington*, 1890-93. C
Animal Industry, Bureau of. Annual reports. *Washington*, 1887-90. C
Bulletin. No. 1. Texas fever. *Washington*, 1893. P
Animal parasites of sheep. 2nd edition. *Washington*, 1890. P
Sheep industry of the U.S. *Washington*, 1892. P
Botany, Division of. Illustrations of North American Grasses. 2 vols. *Washington*, 1891-93. P
Chemistry, Division of. Bulletin, Nos. 8-23, 32, 39. *Washington*, 1886-94. C
Entomology, Division of.
Bulletin, Nos. 1-2. *Washington*, 1877. P
Do. Nos. 13-17, 19-21, 25, 27-30, 32. *Washington*, 1887-94. C
Insect Life. Vols. 1-8. *Washington*, 1888-96. In progress. P.U
Periodical Bulletin, Nos. 1-6. *Washington*, 1888-94. C
Report of Entomologist. *Washington*, 1885. C
Farmers' Bulletins. Nos. 3, 4, 7, 9-10, 12. 14-15. 17, 20, 22-23, 25, 28, 31. *Washington*, 1891-95. C
Foreign Markets, Sections of. Bulletins, Nos. 1-5. 1895. C
Forestry Division.
Annual Report. 1877. *Washington*,1878. P
Do. 1886. *Washington*, 1887. C
Bulletins, Nos. 1-5. *Washington*, 1887-91. C
Report on Timber. *Washington*, 1895. T
Microscopy, Division of. Report of Microscopist. *Washington*, 1891. C
Ornithology and Mammalogy. Bulletin, Nos. 1-4. *Washington*, 1888-93. C
Department of Interior.
Census. 7th Census, 1850, Statistics,1 vol., 1853. 10th Census, 1880. Vols. 1-22. 1883-8. 11th Census, 1890. Vols. 1-24. 1892-7. In progress. P
Census Bulletin Nos. 1-379. (Wanting Nos. 98, 180, 182, 199, 201, 211, 213, 217, 226, 229, 254, 257, 260, 329, 332). 1890-93. C
Extra Census Bulletin on Indians. 1892-4. C
Education, Bureau of. Circular of Information, 1891, Nos. 1, 4, 7 ; 1892, No. 1 ; 1893, No. 4. V

United States.
Department of Interior.
Education—
Report of the Commissioner of Education,
1867-8, 1870-85, 1890-96. *In progress.* P
1870 96. *In progress.* E
1882-96 *In progress.* Mc
1883-94. V
1887 91. T
1890-96. *In progress.* O
Reports of the Commissioner of Industrial
Education, 1887-9. (With appendices). C
National Education Association. Proceed-
n g., 1871-7, 1879-82, 1884-86, 1888 94.
In progress. E
Entomological Commission, 2nd report, 1878-9,
relating to Rocky Mountain Locust and the
Western Cricket. *Washington,* 1880. I'
Indian Affairs, Report of Commissioner, 1856,
1869, 1871, 1875-8. C
Do. 1854, 1867, 1872-92. E
Do. 1855, 1857-8, 1860-61, 1863, 1882, 1888,
1890-96. *In progress.* P
Report of Board of Indian Commissioners,
1870-71. C
Labor, Report of Commissioner, 1886-95. V
Do. 1886-91. L
Do. 1890-96. *In progress.* P
Bulletin of the Department of Labor. Nos. 1-
8. 1895 7. *In progress.* V
Land Office. Report of Commissioners. *Wash-
ington,* 1866, 1890 96. *In progress.* P
Miscellaneous Reports. 1890-96. *In progress.* P
Patent Office. Official Gazette. Vols. 1-77.
Washington, 1872-97. *In progress.*
Index. 1790-1873. 3 vols.
Index. Annual, 1872-96. *In progress.*
Report of Commissioner of Patents. *Wash-
ington,* 1847-1851-8. T
Do. *Washington,* 1854-55, 1858, 1860. M
Do. *Washington,* 1890-96. *In progress.* P
Surveys.
Boundary between the Territory of the United
States and the possessions of Great Britain,
from the Lake of the Woods to the Summit of
the Rocky Mountains, in 1872. *Washington,*
1878. P.V
Exploration and Surveys for Railroad route from
Mississippi River to the Pacific Ocean, Report.
1853-5. 12 vols. *Washington,* 1855-60. C.E.P
(Wanting Vol. 12, C.)
Exploration of the Valley of the Amazon. Parts
1-2. *Washingt n,* 1853-4. P
Explorations across the Great Basin of Utah in
1859. *Washington,* 1876. C
Geographical and Geological Survey of the
Rocky Mountain Region. Vol. 3. *Washington,*
1877. L
Contributions to North American Ethnology.
Vols. 1 7, 9. *Washington,* 1877 93. P
Geological and Geographical Survey of the
Territories.
Annual Report. Nos. 1-3,8-11,1867-9. *Wash-
ington,* 1872-9. P
Do. Nos. 5, 7, 9, 11-12, 1873-78. L
Do. No. 12. 1878. C
Bulletin. No. 1. *Washington,* 1873. L
" Vol. 4, No. 4. } *Washington,* 1878'
" Vol. 5, No. 3. }
1879. C

Department of Interior.
Miscellaneous publications. No. 8. *Washing-
ton,* 1877. P
Geological and Geographical Survey of the
Territories of Wyoming and Idaho. Reports
for the year 1878 in 2 volumes. *Washington,*
1883. C
Geological and Natural History Survey of Min-
nesota. Vols. 1-3. *Washington,* 1872-92. P
Geological Exploration of the 40th Parallel.
Vols. 1-7. *Washington,* 1870-80. P
Vols. 1-5, 7. *Washington,* 1870-80. L
Vols. 2, 5-7, 9. *Washington,* 1881-93. C
Geological Report of Wisconsin, Iowa and Min-
nesota. *Philadelphia,* 1852. C
Geological Survey. Preliminary Report of
Wyoming, (being a second annual report of
progress). *Washington,* 1871. P
Preliminary Report of Montana, (being a 5th
annual report of progress). *Washington,*
1872. P
Annual Reports, 1880-96. *Washington,* 1882-
97. *n -1- 5*. P.C
Bulletin. Vols. 1-8.5 *Washington,* 1883 89.
Also Nos. 55-86, 90-134. *Washington,*
1889-96. C
Mexican Boundary Survey. *Emory.* 2 vols.
Washington, 1857. E.P
Mineral resources of the U.S. Reports, 1868,
1883 93. P
Do. 1883-4. P
Lands of the arid region. *Washington.* C
Monographs. Vols. 3-9, 11. *Washington,*
1882-85. P
Do. Vols. 1-24. *Washington,* 1890-94. C
Geological Survey of Nebraska. Final Report,
1871. C
Geology of Tennessee. *Safford,* 1869. P
Geology of the Black Hills of Dakota. *Wash-
ington,* 1880. L
Geology of the Henry Mountains. *Washington,*
1880. L.P
Geology of the High Plateaus of Utah. *Wash-
ington,* 1880. L
Survey of the North and North Western Lakes,
Report. *Washington,* 1863. C

Department of State.
Diplomatic correspondence, 1862, 1864 (4 parts),
1865 (parts 1, 3 4), 1867 (parts 1-2). P
Report of the International Penitentiary Con-
gress of London. *Washington,* 1872. P
Report on commercial relations of the U.S. with
foreign nations 4 vols. *Washington,* 1857. E
Do. 2 vols. 1861, 1865. P

Department of the Navy.
Armored Vessels, Report on. *Washington,*
1864. P
Naval astronomical expedition to the southern
hemisphere. 1849-52. Vols. 1, 6. *Washing-
ton.* C
Do. Vols. 1-2. *Washington.* L
Do. Vols. 1-3, 6. *Washington.* C
Naval Institute. Proceedings. Vols. 8-16 (im-
perfect). *Annapolis,* 1883-90. U
Do. Vols. 12-22. *Annapolis,* 1886-96. C
Navy Register. *Washington,* 1855-58. C
Transit of Venus. Papers relating to. Part 1.
Washington, 1872. L

United States.
Department of War.
Army Register. *Washington*, 1855.   C
Art of War in Europe in 1854-56. Report on.
 Washington, 1860.   C.P
Artillery Journal. Vols. 1-6. *Fort Munro*,
 1894-96.   C
Chief of Engineers. Report. *Washington*,
 1840.   T
Chief Signal Officer. Reports. 1887-90.
 Washington.   C
Exploring expedition from Santa Fé to the
 junction of the Grand and Green Rivers.
 Washington, 1876.   P
Geographical surveys west of the 100th meri-
 dian. 7 vols. *Washington*, 1875-89.   P
Military commission to Europe in 1855-6.
 Washington, 1857-60.   C.P
Secretary of War. Report. Vol. 4. *Washing-
 ton*, 1892.   C
Statistical report on sickness and mortality in
 the army of the U.S. 1839-60. 2 vols.
 Washington, 1856-60   P
 Do. 1839-55. *Washington*, 1856.   C
Statistics, medical and anthropological. Vols.
 1-2. *Washington*, 1875.   P
Surgeon-General. Report. *Washington*, 1887-
 91.   C
Fish Commission.
 Bulletin. Vols. 1-8. *Washington*, 1881-8.   P
 (Wanting Nos. 5-6).   U
 Vols. 1-7, *Washington*, 1881-9.
 (Wanting Vol. 2).
 Vols. 7-15. *Washington*, 1887-95.   C
Reports for 1850, 1854-9, 1861 71, 1873, 1875-
 94.   M
 Do. 1875-7, 1879, 1881, 1883-6, 1889.   P
 Do. Pts. 2-15. *Washington*, 1874 91.   U
Fisheries and Fishery Industries of the U.S. Sec-
 tions 1-5. 6 vols. *Washington*, 1884-87.   P.U
 (Wanting Plates to Section 1. U).
 Sections 3-5 and plates. *Washington*, 1887. C
Smithsonian Institution.   U
 Annual report of the Board of Regents. *Wash-
 ington*, 1854-95. *In progress*.   P
 Do. *Washington*, 1863 87.   Mc
Bureau of Ethnology. Annual reports, 1-14.
 (1879-93). *Washington*, 1881-96. *In progress*.
 (Wanting No. 9, U.).   C.P.U
Smithsonian Contributions to Knowledge. Vols.
 5-26. *Washington*, 1853 90. *In progress*. U
 Vols. 1-26, 28.30 *Washington*, 1848-92. *In
 progress*.   C
 Vols. 1-26, 28, 30 32. *Washingtoń*, 1848-90,
 1892, 1895. *In progress*.   P
Smithsonian Miscellaneous Collections. Vols. 1-
 39. *Washington*, 1862-93. *In progress*.   P.U
United States National Museum.
 Bulletin. Nos. 1-16. *Washington*, 1877-82. P
 Nos. 14. 21, 40, 42-49. *Washington*,
 1879-96. *In progress*.   C
 Special bulletin. Nos. 1-3. *Washington*,
 1892-5.   C
 Proceedings. Vols. 1-4. *Washington*, 1878-81.
          P
 Vols. 10-18. *Washington*, 1887-
 95. *In progress*.   C
 Reports. *Washington*, 1886-96. *In progress*. P
 Do. 1886-94. *In progress*.   C

Treasury Department.
Andrews' report on Colonial and Lake Trade.
 Washington, 1852.   P
Coast Survey. Reports for years 1851-54,
 1856-58, 1862-67. *Washington*.   C
 Do. 1851-62, 1864-1877. *Washington*.   P
Sketches accompanying Annual Report of
 Survey for 1851. *Washington*.   C
Coast and Geodetic Survey.
 Bulletin. Nos. 8-35. *Washington*, 1889-96.
 In progress.   C
 Do. Nos. 19, 25-30, 34-35. *Washington*.   T
Reports. *Washington*, 1851-1895.   T
 Do. *Washington*, 1878-95. [Pt. 2 only
 of 1891-4]. *In progress*.   P
 Do. *Washington*, 1873 95. *In progress*. S
 Do. *Washington*, 1880-95. [Pt. 2 only
 of 1891-4].   C
Commerce and Navigation. Report. *Washing-
 ton*, 1868-9, 1871-2.   P
 Do. *Washington*, 1886-7.   C
Comptroller of the Currency. Report. *Wash-
 ington*, 1887-8, 1893.   P
Internal Commerce. Report. *Washington*,
 1885.   P
Navigation, Bureau of. Report. *Washington*,
 1887.   C
Statistics, Bureau of. Statistical Abstract,
 No. 9. *Washington*, 1889.   C
National Board of Health. Bulletin. *Wash-
 ington*, 1879-82.   U
United States. Catalogue of Public Documents
 (monthly). 1895-96. *In progress*.   O
 Do. 1889-95. *In progress*.   P
Catalogue of U.S. Government Publications
 (by Hickcox). Vols. 1-10. *Washington*,
 1885-94.   P
United States Official Postal Guide. *Washington*,
 1890-91.   P
United States Sanitary Commission, Documents
 and Bulletin. Vols. 1-3. *Washington*, 1863-
 65.   T

United States Almanac. *Philadelphia*,
 1843.   P
United States Catholic Magazine.
 Vols. 2-7. *Baltimore*, 1843-8.   P
**Universal Magazine of Knowledge
 and Pleasure.** Vols. 25, 26 and 30. *London*,
 1759-62.   U
Universal Review. Vols. 1-8. *London*,
 1888-90.   P
Universidad de Quito.
 Anales. Tom. 11. *Quito*, 1894.   C
Universite Catholique de Louvain.
 Annuaire. *Louvain*, 1884 97. *In progress*.   C
 Liber Memorialis. *Louvain*, 1887.   C
Universite d' Aix Marseilles.
 Annales de la Facul é des Sciences. Tom. 1-5,
 7-8. *Marseilles*, 1893-97. *In progress*.   C
Universite de France.
 Travaux et Mémoires des Facultés de Lille.
 Tom. 1-3. (Mémoires 1-14). *Lille*, 1889-
 94.   U
 (Wanting Mémoire 4).
Universities Commission, England.
 3 vols. *London*, 1872.   E

University Extension. Vols. 1-3. *Phila-delphia*, 1891-94. E
Do. Vols. 2-4. *Philadelphia*, 1892-4. P

University Magazine. Vols. 1-5. *London*, 1878-80. L
Do. Vols. 1-4. *London*, 1878-9. Mc

University Monthly. Vol. 2. *New York*, 1872. E

University of California.
Agricultural Experimental Station. Reports. *Sacramento*, 1886-92. C
College of Agriculture. Reports. 1883-90. *Sacramento*. C
Department of Geology. Bulletin. Vol. 1. *Berkeley*, 1893-6. C

University of Nebraska.
Agricultural Experimental Station. Annual reports. Vols. 4-5, 7. *Lincoln*, 1890-94. C
Bulletins. Nos. 16-17, 25-27, 38-39, 41, 43-45. *Lincoln*, 1891-6. C

University of Pennsylvania.
Department of History.
Translations and reprints from the original sources of European history. Vols. 1-3. *Philadelphia*, 1894-96. P

University of the State of New York.
Annual report. Nos. 56-66, 78, 91-93, 99-108. *Albany*, 1845-94. E
Nos. 68, 71, 76. *Albany*, 1855-63. C
Nos. 87-100, 105-108. *Albany*, 1874-94. L
Regents' Bulletin. No. 21. *Albany*, 1893. C
Extension Bulletin. Nos. 1-2, 4, 24, 27, 29. 1891-4. *Albany*, 1891-4. C

University of Tokyo.
Abhandlungen. No. 10. *Tokyo*, 1883. C
Memoirs. Vol. 11. *Tokyo*, 1885. C

University of Toronto Quarterly. Vols. 1-2. *Toronto*, 1895-6. P

University of Toronto Studies.
Biological Series. No. 1. *Toronto*, 1898.
Economic Series. No 1. *Toronto*, 1898.
History, 1st Series. Vols. 1 and 2. *Toronto*, 1897-8.
Do. 2nd Series. No. 1. *Toronto*, 1897.
Psychological Series. No. 1. *Toronto*, 1898. C.P.U.
In progress.

University of Wisconsin.
Bulletin. Vol. 1 (1894-96). *Madison*, 1897. *In progress* P

University Quarterly Review. *Toronto*, 1890. P

Unsere Zeit. Jahrbuch zum Conversations-Lexikon. 8 Bde. *Leipzig*, 1857-64.
Continued as :
Unsere Zeit, Deutsche Revue der Gegenwart. 27 Jahrg. *Leipzig*, 1865-91. U

(Woechentliche) Unterhaltungen fuer Dilettanten und Freunde der Astro-nomie Geographie und Witterung-skunde. Jahrg, 3, 7-8. *Leipzig*, 1849-54. U

Untersuchungen zur deutschen Staats und Rechtsgeschichte. Heft. 1-37. *Breslau*, 1878-91. U

Untersuchungen zur Naturlehre des Menschen und der Thiere (hrsg. von J. Moleschott). Bd. 12 and 13. *Giessen*, 1881-88. U

Upper Canada Almanac and Provin-cial Calendar. *York, U.C.*, 1831. P

Upper Canada Gazette. *See* Canada Gazette.

Upper Canada Journal. 1 vol. *Toronto*, 1852-53. E

Upper Canada Journal of Medical, Surgical and Physical Science. Vol. 3. *Toronto*, 1853-4. P

Upper Canada Jurist. 2 vols. *Toronto*, 1844-48 (1877). U

Upper Canada Law Directory. *Toronto*, 1858. P

Upper Canada Law Journal. Vols. 1-10. *Toronto*, 1855-64.
Continued as :
Canada Law Journal. New Series. Vols. 1-31. *Toronto*, 1865-95. *In progress.* E

Upper Canada Law List. *Toronto*, 1860-62.
Continued as :
Ontario Law List. *Toronto*, 1870, 1873, 1876, 1882-3. P

Upsala Universitet. Arsskrift. 1861-94. *Upsala* [1861-94]. *In progress.* U
(Wanting Vols. for 1868 and 1884).
Do. 1881-95. *Upsala*, 1881-95. *In progress.* C
Redogörelse för 1885-90. C

V. P. Journal. Vols. 1-2. *Cobourg*, 1883-4.
Continued as :
Kosmos. Vols. 3-4. *Cobourg*, 1885-6. P.V

Van Nostrand's Eclectic Engineering Magazine. Vols. 1-35. *New York*, 1869-86. P.S
Do. Vols. 1-6. *New York*, 1869-72. L

Vanity Fair. Vols. 1-8, 11-14, 25-30. *London*, 1868-83. L
Vol-. 32-40, 48-49. *London*, 1884-94. P

Vanity Fair Album. *London*, 1869-80. L

Varsity. Vols. 1-16. *Toronto*, 1880-96. *In progress.* (Vols. 6 and 8 imperfect.) U

Vassar Brothers Institute.
Transactions. Vols. 1-4. (1881-87.) *Pough-keepsie*, [1881-87]. U

Verein fuer Erdkunde zu Dresden.
Jahresbericht. Bd. 1-21. *Dresden*, 1865-85.
Festschrift. *Dresden*, 1888. U

Verein fuer Erdkunde zu Halle.
Mittheilungen. *Halle*, 1889-96. *In progress.* C

Verein fuer Erdkunde zu Leipzig. *See* Verein von Freunden der Erdkunde zu Leipzig.

Verein fuer Geschichte der Deutschen in Boehmen.
Mittheilungen. Bd. 27-28, 31-34. *Prag*, 1888-96. *In progress.* C

Verein fuer Hansische Geschichte.
Hansische Geschichtsblätter. Jahrg. 1872-77. *Leipzig*, 1873-79. U

Verein fuer Nassauische Naturkunde. *See* Nassauischer Verein.

Verein fuer Naturkunde zu Cassel.
Berichte. 26-39. *Cassel*, 1880-94. C
Do. 29-35. *Cassel*, 1883-89. U

Continued as :
Abhandlungen und Berichte. Nos. 40-41.
   Cassel, 1894-6. *In progress.* C
   Festschrift. *Cassel*, 1886. U

Verein fuer Naturkunde zu Zwickau.
Jahresberichte. 1871-2, 1875-86, 1888-9.
  Zwickau, 1872-90. U

Verein fuer Naturwissenschaft zu Braunschweig.
Jahresberichte 2-6. *Braunschweig*, 1881-91. U
   Do. 1-6. *Braunschweig*, 1879-91. C

Verein fuer naturwissenschaftliche Unterhaltung zu Hamburg.
Verhandlungen, 1871-85. *Hamburg*, 1875-87. U
   Do. *Hamburg*, 1876-97. C

Verein fuer niederdeutsche Sprachforschung.
Jahrbuch, 1875-83. *Bremen*, 1876-84.
Niederdeutsche Denkmäler. Bd. 1-5. *Bremen*,
  Norden and *Leipzig*, 1876-93.
Drucke, 1-3. *Norden* and *Leipzig*, 1885-89. U

Verein fuer oeffentliche Gesundheitspflege im Herzogthum Braunschweig.
Monatsblatt für öffentliche Gesundheitspflege.
  Jahrg. 10-14. *Braunschweig*, 1887-91. U

Verein fuer Schlesische Insektenkunde.
Zeitschrift für Entomologie. Neue Folge. Heft
  1-21. *Breslau*, 1870-96. *In progress.* U
   (Wanting Heft 15-17).

Verein fuer Thueringische Geschichte und Alterthumskunde.
Zeitschrift. N. F. Bde. 2-8. *Jena*, 1882-92.

Verein fuer vaterlaendische Naturkunde in Wuerttemberg.
(Also entitled Württembergische naturforschende
  Jahreshefte.)
Jahreshefte 1-46. *Stuttgart*, 1845-90. U
   Do. 49, 51. *Stuttgart*, 1893, 1895. C

Verein fuer Volkskunde.
Zeitschrift. Jahrg. 1-6. *Berlin*, 1891-96. *In progress.*

Verein "Lotos."
"Lotos" Jahrbuch für naturwissenschaft. N.F.
  Bd. 6-15. *Prag*, 1885-95. *In progress.* C

Verein von Alterthumsfreunden im Rheinlande.
Jahrbücher. Hft. 69-88. *Bonn*, 1880-89. U

Verein von Freunden der Erdkunde zu Leipzig (afterwards : Verein für Erdkunde zu Leipzig).
Jahresbericht. Bd. 1-4. *Leipzig*, 1861-64. U
Mittheilungen, nebst dem Jahresbericht. 1875-
  89. *Leipzig*, 1875-89. U
   Do. 1883-92. *Leipzig*, 1883-92. C

Verein zur Befoerderung des Gewerbefleisses in Preussen.
Verhandlungen. Jahrg. 22-63. *Berlin*,1843-8. U

Verein zur Verbreitung Naturwissenschaftlicher Kenntnisse in Wien.
Schriften. Bde. 2-5, 8-10. *Wien*, 1861-70. U

Vermont.
Geology of Vermont. Report. Vols. 1-2. *Claremont*, *N.H.*, 1857-61. C
School Reports. 1857-67, 1872-80, 1884, 1888.
  1890. E

Vermont Historical Society.
Collections. Vols. 1-2. *Montpelier*, 1870-1. P

Vermont School Journal. Vols. 1-5. *Montpelier*, 1859-63. E

Veterinary Journal. Vols. 24-45. *London*, 1887-97. *In progress.* P

Victoria.
Minutes of the Proceedings of the Legislative
  Council 1875-96 (imperfect).
Votes and Proceedings of the Legislative Assembly, with Papers, etc., 1875-96. L
Abstracts of Specifications of Patents : Metals.
  Parts 1-2. *Melbourne*, 1872-76. P
Patents applied for. 1854-66. *Melbourne*, 1870. P
Patents and Patentees. Vols. 5-22, 24-5. 1870-
  87, 1889-90. *Melbourne*, 1872-92, 1894-5 *In progress.* P
School Reports. Annual. *Melbourne*, 1854-96.
  In progress. E

Victoria Institute ; or, Philosophical Society of Great Britain.
Journal of Transactions. Vols. 2, 6-27. *London*, 1867-94. C
  Index to Vols. 1-27 in Appendix of Vol. 27.

Victoria Magazine. Vol. 1. *Belleville*, 1847-8. P

Victoria Zoological and Acclimatisation Society. *See* Zoological and Acclimatisation Society of Victoria.

Victorian Year Book. *Melbourne*, 1876-94. O
  Do. *Melbourne*, 1885-92, 1894. O
  Do. 1878-89. *Melbourne*, 1879-89. C

Videnskabs-Selskab i Christiania.
Förhandlinger. *Christiania*, 1860-61, 1863-81, 1884-1887, 1889-94. C
Skrifter. Historisk-Filosofisk Klasse. *Christiania*, 1894. C
Do. Mathematisk-Naturvidenskabelige Klasse. *Christiania*, 1894. C

Vienna Academy. *See* Kaiserliche Akademie der Wissenschaften.

Vienna—Aerztlicher Verein. *See* Aerztlicher Verein zu Wien.

Vienna—K.K. Gesellschaft der Aerzte.
See Kaiserlich-königliche Gesellschaft der Aerzte zu Wien.

Vienna—K.K. zoologisch-botanische Gesellschaft. *See* Kaiserlich-königliche zoologisch-botanische Gesellschaft zu Wien.

Vienna University. *See* Zoologisches Institut der Universität Wien and der zoologischen Station in Triest.

Vierteljahrsschrift fuer Litteraturgeschichte. 6 Bde. *Weimar*, 1888-93.
Continued as :
Euphorion, Zeitschrift f. Litteraturgeschichte.
  Bd. 1-3. *Bamberg*, 1894-96. *In progress.* U

Vierteljahrsschrift fuer wissenschaftliche Philosophie. Jahrg. 1-20. *Leipzig*, 1877-96. *In progress.* U

Virginia.
Calendar of Virginia State Papers, and other MSS. Vols. 1-9. 1652-1807. *Richmond*, 1875-90.   P
School Reports. *Richmond*, 1880, 1887, 1890-91, 1894-5.   E

Virginia Historical Society.
Collections. N.S. Vols. 1-11. *Richmond*, 1882-92. *In progress.*   P
Virginia Magazine of History and Biography. Vols. 1-5. *Richmond*, 1893-8. *In progress.* P

Volunteer Review. Vol. 1. *Ottawa*, 1867. P

Vox Stellarum, or a Loyal Almanac for 1858. *London*, 1858.   U

Wagner Free Institute of Science of Philadelphia. *f.s.*
Transactions. Vols. 1-3. *Philadelphia*, 1887-92.   C

Washington (City). School Reports, 1864-75, 1879-80.   E

Washington Biological Society. *See* Biological Society of Washington.

Washington Philosophical Society. *See* Philosophical Society of Washington.

Week (The). Vols. 1-13. *Toronto*, 1883-96. P
Do.   Vols 7-11. *Toronto*, 1889-94.   E

Weekly Magazine, or Edinburgh Amusement. *Edinburgh.* 1777.   T

Weekly Medical Review. Vols. 15-26. *St. Louis*, 1887-92.   L

Weekly Notes. *London.* 1881-82.   L

Weekly Oracle, or Universal Library. Nos. 2-66. *London*, 1734-36.   U

Weekly Political Register (Cobbett). Vols. 12-13, 16-18. *London*, 1807-10.   L

Weekly Register. Vols. 1-8. *Baltimore*, 1811-15.   T

Wesleyan (The). Vols. 1-3. *Montreal*, 1840-42.   P

Wesleyan Methodist Magazine. *London*, 1865-73.   E
Do.   *London*, 1822-29, 1831-37, 1839-40. Mc

Wesleyan Sunday School Magazine. *London*, 1857-64.   E
Do.   *London*, 1867-76.   V

West-American Scientist. Vols. 1-3. *San Diego*, 1885-87.   C

Western (The). 3 vols. *St. Louis*, 1873-76. E

Western Australia.
Reports on Education, Annual. *Perth*, 1890-94. *In progress.*   E
Year-Book. *Perth*, 1893-95. *In prog. ess.* M

Western Educational Journal. Vol. 1. *Chicago*, 1881.   E

Western Reserve Historical Society. Historical and Archaeological Tracts. Nos. 1-4. *Cleveland*, 1870-71.   P

Western Review of Science and Industry. (After Vol. 2: Kansas City Review, etc.). Vols. 2-9. *Kansas City*, 1878-85.   U

Westfaelischer Provinzial-Verein fuer Wissenschaft und Kunst.
Jahresberichte 1-24. *Münster*, 1872-96. *In progress.*   U
Do. *Münster*, 1887-96. *In progress.*   C

Westminster Papers. Vols. 1-6. *London*, 1868-74.   P

Westminster Review. Vols. 1-29, 32-126, 128-148. *London*, 1824-97. *In progress.* L
Vols. 33-34, 36-39, 41-43, 45-47, 50-52, 54-55, 59-66, 69-70, 72-75, 77-8, 83-148. *London* and *New York*, 1839-97. *In progress.* P
Vols. 74-87, 91-98, 131-136. *London, New York* and *Philadelphia*, 1860-91.   U
Vols. 103-108, 113-114. *New York*, 1875-7, 1880.   E
Vols. 60-64, 71-94, 101, 111-118, 121, 123, 125-6. *London* and *Philadelphia*, 1853-86.   V

Wetterauische Gesellschaft fuer die gesammte Naturkunde zu Hanau.
Jahresberichte (after 1863 : Berichte). 1851-89. *Hanau*, 1851-89.   U

Whitaker's Almanac. *London*, 1871, 1887, 1890-98. *In progress.*   C
Do. *London*. 1872-74, 1876, 1878-90, 1892, 1894-98. *In progress.*   L
Do. *London*, 1884-98. *In progress.*   P

Whitaker's Journal. *London*, 1876.   P

Whitaker's Titled Persons. *London*, 1897.   P

White's Celestial Atlas, or a new and improved Ephemeris. 1835-56. *London*, [1835-56].   U

Who's Who. 1898. *London*, 1898. *In progress.*   P

Wiedemann's Annalen. *See* Annalen der Physik.

Wisconsin.
Geological Survey of the State of Wisconsin. Report. Vols. 19, 27, 31. *Madison*, 1862.   C
School reports. *Madison*, 1850-81, 1883-8.   E

Wisconsin Academy of Sciences, Arts and Letters.
Transactions. Vols. 1-7. *Madison*, 1872-89. U
Vols. 4, 6-10. *Madison*, 1876-95. *In progress.*   C

Wisconsin Journal of Education.
4 vols. *Madison*, 1858-65.   E

Wisconsin State Agricultural Society. Transactions. Vol. 8. *Madison*, 1869.   C
Do. Vols. 13-27. *Madison*, 1875-89.   U

Wisconsin State Historical Society.
Reports and Collections. Vols. 2-3, 10-11. *Madison*, 1856-88.   U
Do. Vols. 1-13. *Madison*, 1854-95. *In progress.*   P
General index to Vols. 1-10.   C P
Proceedings. Meetings 28-43. *Madison*, 1882-96. *In progress.*   U
    (Wanting Nos. 33, 35 and 40).
Do. Meetings 32-43. *Madison*, 1886-96.   C
Do. Meetings 41-44. *Madison*, 1894-7. *In progress.*   P

Wisconsin, University of. *See* University of Wisconsin.

Wissenschaftlicher Club in Wien.
Jahresbericht. Nos. 11-13, 15-21. *Wien*, 1886-
97. *In progress.*   C
Monatsblätter. Bd. 8-10, 12-14, 16-17. *Wien,*
1887-96. *In progress,*   C
Witness. 24 vols. *Edinburgh*, 1840-62.   K
Wodrow Society.
Publications. 6 vols. *Edinburgh*, 1845.   U
Do. 28 vols. *Edinburgh*, 1842-50.   P
Do. 28 vols. *Edinburgh*, 1842 47.   K
Do. 26 vols. *Edinburgh*, 1842-49.   Mc
Woman at Home. Vols. 1-2. *London*, 1894.   P
Woman's World. *London*, 1889-90.   P
Wonderful and Scientific Museum; or
Magazine of remarkable characters. Vols. 1-6.
London, 1803-20.   P
Woodstock College Monthly. *Woodstock,*
1890 91.   Mc
Worcester (Mass.) School reports, 1855-80.
(Wanting 1867-68).   E
Worcester Society of Antiquity.
Collections. Vols. 1-10. *Worcester*, 1881-93. C
Proceedings. *Worcester*, 1891-95.   C
Publications. Vol. 11. *Worcester*, 1893.   C
Work. Vols. 1-4. *London*, 1889-93.   P
Working Man. Vol. 1. *London*, 1866.   P
Workshop (The). Vol. 17. *New York*, 1884.   P
Do. N.S. 1 vol. *London*, n.d.   P
World. *London*, 1876, 1882, 1888, 1889.   L
World Almanac and Encyclopædia.
New York, 1894-5.   P
Writer. Vols. 1-2. *Boston*, 1887-88.   L
**Wuerttembergische naturforschende
Jahreshefte.** *See* Verein für Vaterlandische
Naturkunde in Württemberg.
**Wuerzburg — Zoologisch - zootomis-
ches Institut.** *See* Zoologisch-zootomische
Institut in Würzburg.
Wyclif Society.
Publications. *London*, 1882-96.   T
Do. 18 vols. *London*, 1883 94.   L
Yale Lectures. *London*, 1891.   P
**Year Book and Almanac of British
North America.** *Montreal*, 1867-8.   P
Year Book and Almanac of Canada.
Montreal, 1864, 1867-9, 1877, 1879.   P
Do. *Montreal*, 1866 75.   E
**Year Book of Facts in Science and
Art.** 1839-62. *London*, 1839-62.   P
Do. 1844 51 and 1881. *London*, 1844-81.   U
Do. 1839-54, 1866. *London*. 1839-66.   P
Year Book of Pharmacy. 1870-72.
London, 1870-72.   U
Yellow Book. Vols. 1-13. *London*, 1894 7. P
York (County). Council Minutes, Reports, By-
laws, etc. 1867-73, 1875-77, 1879 94. *In progress.*
          O
York and Peel. Council of the United Coun-
ties of. Minutes, Reports, By-laws, etc. 1860 66.
          O

York (Township).
Assessment Roll,1834,Council Minutes,1860 71. P
York Almanac and Royal Calendar.'
York, U.C., 1824-6.
Continued as :
Toronto Almanac and Royal Calendar. *Toronto,*
1839.   P
**Yorkshire Archaeological and Topo-
graphical Association.**
Record Series. Vols. 1-8. P.P. 1885-90.   U
Young Canadian. Vol. 1. *Montreal*, 1891. P
Young's Annals of Agriculture. Vols.
2-28. *London*, 1784-1797.   L
Zeitschrift fuer analytische Chemie.
Jahrg. 1-35. *Wiesbaden*, 1862-96. *In progress.* U
Register, Jahrg. 1-30, in 2 vols.   U
**Zeitschrift fuer Anatomie und Ent-
wickelungsgeschichte.** Bd. 1 and 2.
Leipzig, 1875-76.
(Continuation in Anatomische Abtheilung in
Archiv für Anatomie und Physiologie).   U
Zeitschrift fuer anorganische Chemie.
Bd. 1-11. *Hamburg* and *Leipzig*, 1892-96. *In
progress.*   . U
**Zeitschrift fuer Assyriologie und ver-
wandte Gebiete.** Bd. 1-11, *Berlin, Leipzig*
and *Weimar*, 1886-96. *In progress.*   U
Semitistische Studien, Ergänzungshefte zur Zeit-
schrift für Assyriologie. Hft. 1-9. *Berlin* and
Weimar, 1894 95. *In progress.*   U
Zeitschrift fuer Biologie.   Bd. 1-32.
München, 1865-96. *In progress.*   U
Zeitschrift fuer Chemie.   *See* Kritische
Zeitschrift für Chemie, etc.
**Zeitschrift fuer das Berg-, Huetten-,
und Salinenwesen in den preuss-
ischen Staate.** Bd. 1-17. *Berlin*, 1854-69. U
**Zeitschrift fuer den deutschen Unter-
richt.** Bd. 7-10. *Leipzig*, 1893-96. *In pro-
gress.*   U
Zeitschrift fuer deutsche Philologie.
Bd. 1-28 and Ergänzungsband. *Halle*, 1869-96.
In progress.   U
Zeitschrift fuer deutsches Alterthum
(und deutsche Literatur). Bd. 1-40. *Leipzig* and
Berlin, 1841-96. *In progress.*   U
**Zeitschrift fuer die alttestamentliche
Wissenschaft.** Jahrg. 1-16 *Giessen*, 1881-
96. *In progress.*   U
**Zeitschrift fuer die gesammte Staats-
wissenschaft.** Bd. 44-52. *Tübingen*, 1888-
96. *In progress.*   U
**Zeitschrift fuer die gesamte Straf-
rechtswissenschaft.** Bd. 1-9. *Berlin,
Leipzig* and *Wien*, 1881-89.   U
**Zeitschrift fuer die oesterreichischen
Gymnasien.** Jahrg. 34,35. 44-47, (1883, 1884, 1893 96).
Wien, [1883-96]. *In progress.*   U
Zeitschrift fuer Entomologie. *See* Verein
für Schlesische Insektenkunde. Zeitschrift für
Entomologie.
Zeitschrift fuer Ethnologie. *See* Berliner
Gesellschaft für Anthropologie.

Zeitschrift fuer exacte Philosophie im Sinne des neuern philosophischen Realismus. Bd. 1-20. *Leipzig, Langensalza,* 1861-94. U

Zeitschrift fuer franzoesische Sprache und Litteratur. *See* Zeitschrift für neufranzösische Sprache, etc.

Zeitschrift fuer Instrumentenkunde. Jahrg. 7-15. *Berlin,* 1887-95. U
General-Register, Jahrg. 1-10.

Zeitschrift fuer Keilschriftforschung und verwandte Gebiete. 2 Bde. *Leipzig,* 1884-85. U

Zeitschrift fuer Kirchengeschichte. Bd. 1-3, 7. *Gotha,* 1877-85. Mc

Zeitschrift fuer Krystallographie und Mineralogie. Bd. 16-25. *Leipzig,* 1890-96. *In progress.* U
General Register, Bd. 11-20.

Zeitschrift fuer Lutherische Theologie und Kirche. *Leipzig,* 1840-44, 1848-74. Mc

Zeitschrift fuer (die gesammte) Naturwissenschaften. *See* Naturwissenschaftlicher Verein für Sachsen und Thüringen. Zeitschrift, etc.

Zeitschrift fuer neufranzoesische Sprache und Litteratur (after Bd. 10: Zeitschrift für französische Sprache, etc.). Bd. 1-18. *Oseln, Leipzig* and *Berlin,* 1879-96. *In progress.* U

Zeitschrift fuer Ornithologie und praktische Gefluegelzucht. *See* Ornithologischer Verein Pommerns. Zeitschrift für Ornithologie.

Zeitschrift fuer Pflanzenkrankheiten. Bd. 1-6. *Stuttgart,* 1891-96. *In progress.* U

Zeitschrift fuer Philosophie und Paedagogik. Jahrg. 2-3. *Langensalza,* 1895-96. *In progress.* U

Zeitschrift fuer Philosophie und Spekulative Theologie (after Bd. 16: Zeitschrift für Philosophie und Philosophische Kritik). Bd. 1-108. *Bonn, Tübingen* and *Halle,* 1837-96. *In progress.* U

Zeitschrift fuer physikalische Chemie, Stochiometrie, und Verwandtschaftslehre. Bd. 1-19. *Leipzig,* 1887-96. *In progress.* U

Zeitschrift fuer physiologische Chemie. Bd. 1-21. *Strassburg,* 1877-96. U *progress.*
(Wanting Bd. 13-17).
Do. Bd. 10-14. *Strassburg,* 1866-90. C

Zeitschrift fuer Psychologie und Physiologie der Sinnesorgane. Bd. 3-9. *Leipzig,* 1892-96. *In progress.*

Zeitschrift fuer romanische Philologie. Bd. 1-20 and Supplementheft 16. *Halle,* 1877-96. *In progress.* • U

Zeitschrift fuer vergleichende Litteraturgeschichte und Renaissance-Litteratur. Neue Folge. Bd. 1-9. *Berlin,* 1887-96. *In progress.*

Zeitschrift fuer vergleichende Sprachforschung auf dem Gebiete des Deutschen, Griechischen und Lateinischen. (After Bd. 22 : Zeitschrift, etc., auf dem Gebiete der indogermanischen Sprachen). Bd. 1-34. *Berlin,* 1852-96. *In progress.* U
Gesammtregister, Bd. 1-20.

Zeitschrift fuer Vermessungswesen. Bd. 19-23. *Stuttgart,* 1890-96. *In progress.* S

Zeitschrift fuer Voelkerpsychologie und Sprachwissenschaft. 20 Bde. *Berlin,* 1860-90. U
Continued as :
Zeitschrift des Vereins für Volkskunde. *See* Verein für Volkskunde.

Zeitschrift fuer wissenschaftliche Geographie. Bd. 1-5. *Lahr* and *Wien,* 1880-84. U

Zeitschrift fuer wissenschaftliche Mikroskopie und fuer mikroskopische Technik. Bd. 1-13. *Braunschweig,* 1884-96. *In progress.* U
(Wanting Bd. 7 and 8).

Zeitschrift fuer wissenschaftliche Theologie. Vols. 26-40. *Leipzig,* 1883-97. *In progress.* T

Zeitschrift fuer wissenschaftliche Zoologie. Bd. 1-60. *Leipzig.* 1848-96. *In progress.* U
Namen und Sach-Register. Bd. 31-45.

Zoological and Acclimatisation Society of Victoria.
Proceedings and Reports. Vols. 1-5. *Melbourne,* 1872-78. U

Zoological Record. *See* Zoological Society of. London. Record of Zoological Literature.

Zoological Society of London.
Proceedings of the Committee of Science and Correspondence. 2 parts. *London,* 1831-32. U
Proceedings. 28 parts. *London,* 1833-60. U
(Wanting Part 15).
Proceedings of the Scientific Meetings. For the years 1861-96. *In progress.* U
Index 1830-90, in 5 vols.
Transactions. Vols. 1-13. *London,* 1835-95. *In progress.* U
Record of Zoological Literature. Vols. 1-6 (1864-69). *London,* 1865-70.
Continued as :
Zoological Record. Vols. 7-32 (1870-95). *London,* 1871-96. *In progress.* U
Reports of the Council and Auditors, 1830, 1843-50, 1852-55. *London,* 1831-55. U
List of the vertebrated animals, now or lately living in the Gardens. 5 vols. *London,* 1872-83. U

Zoologisch-botanischer Verein.
Verhandlungen. Vols. 3-9. *Wien,* 1853-59.
Continued as :
Kaiserlich—Königliche-Zoologisch-botanische Gesellschaft in Wien. Verhandlungen. Vols. 10-46. *Wien,* 1860-96. *In progress.* C

Zoologisch-zootomisches Institut in Wuerzburg.
Arbeiten. Bd. 1-10. *Würzburg* and *Wiesbaden*, 1874-95. *In progress.*   U

(Neue) Zoologische Gesellschaft zu Frankfurt-am-Main.
Zoologischer Garten. Jahrg. 1-30. *Frankfurt am Main*, 1859-89.   U

Zoologische Jahrbuecher, Zeitschrift fuer Systematik, Geographie und Biologie der Thiere. Bd. 1-8. *Jena*, 1886-95. *In progress.*   U

Zoologische Station zu Neapel.
Fauna und Flora des Golfes von Neapel und der angrenzenden Meeres-Abschnitte. Bl. 1-25. *Leipzig, Berlin*, 1880-96. *In progress.*   U
Mittheilungen. Bl. 1-11. *Leipzig, Berlin*, 1878-95. *In progress.*
Zoologischer Jahresbericht. For the years 1879-95. *Leipzig, Berlin*, 1880-96. *In progress.* U

Zoologischer Anzeiger. Bl. 1-19. *Leipzig*, 1878-96. *In progress.* (Wanting Bd. 14).   U
Register, Jahrgang 11-15.

Zoologischer Garten. *See* Zoologische Gesellschaft zu Frankfurt am Main.

Zoologischer Jahresbericht. *See* Zoologische Station zu Neapel. Zoologischer Jahresbericht.

Zoologisches Institut der Universitaet Wien und der zoologischen Station in Triest.
Arbeiten. Bd. 1-10. *Wien*, 1878-93. *In progress.*   U

Zoologist. 1st Series. 23 vols. *London*, 1843-65.
　　　　　　2nd " 11 vols. *London*, 1866-76.
　　　　　　3rd " 20 vols. *London*, 1877-96.
　　　　　　4th " Vol. 1. *London*, 1897. *In progress.*   P

Zwickau –Verein fuer Naturkunde.
See Verein fur Naturkunde zu Zwickau.

ADDENDA.

Akademia Umiejetnosci.
Pamietnik Akademii Umiejetnosci w Krakowie.
Wydziat Matematyczno-Przyrodniczy. Tom. 16-18. *Krakow*, 1889-91.   C
Wydziat Matematyczno-Przyrodniczy.
Serga 1. Tom. 19-20. *Krakow*, 1889-90. C
Serga 2. Tom. 1-9. *Krakow*, 1891-95. *In progress.*   C
Rozprawy Akademii Umiejetnosci.
Wydziat Historyczno-Filozaficzny.
Serga 1. Tom. 22-25. *Krakow*, 1888-91.
Serga 2. Tom. 1-5, 7. *Krakow*, 1891-95. *In progress.*
Wydziat Filologiczny.
Serga 1. Tom. 13-14. *Krakow*, 1889-91.
Serga 2. Tom. 1-6, 9. *Krakow*, 1892-95. *In progress.*
Wydziat Filologiczny i Historyczno-Filozoficzny. Tom. 7-8, *Krakow*, 1889 90. C
Rocznik Zarzadu Akademii Umiejetnosci w Krakowie. *Krakow*, 1888 93. C
Wydawmictwo Akademii Umiejetnosci w Krakowie Naczynia Limfatyczne w Staniowacinie zbadal i opisal Ludwik Teichmann. *Krakow*, 1892.

Allgemeiner Verein fuer vereinfachte Rechtschreibung.
Zeitschrift. 1885-87. *Wiesbaden*, 1885-7.   P

Zeitschrift des Allgemeinen Vereins fuer Vereinfachte.
Rechtschreibung. *Wiesbaden*, 1885-7.   P

Architectural Review. Vols. 1-3. *Boston*, 1888-90.   S

Board of Arts and Manufactures for Upper Canada. *See* Journal of the Board, etc.

Cambridge Camden Society (afterwards Ecclesiological Society.)
Ecclesiologist. *See* Ecclesiologist.

Figaro in London. Vol. 1. *London*, 1832.   P

Forening til Norske Fortidsmindesmerkers Bevaring.
Aarsberetning. *Kristiania*, 1863-84.   C

Historical Manuscripts Commission.
Reports Nos. 1-14. *London*, 1870 95. *In progress.*   P
Calendar of the Manuscripts of the Marquis of Salisbury. Parts 1-5. *London*, 1883 94.

Kongeligt Nordisk Oldskrift - Selskab.
(Société Royale des Antiquaires du Nord.)
Aarsberetning. *Copenhague*, 1848.   P
Bulletin. *Copenhague*, 1843-45.   P
Mémoires. *Copenhague*, 1845-49.   P
Do. *Copenhague*, 1850-60.   C
Do. Nouv. Sér. *Copenhague*, 1866 7, 1878-89.   P
Do.　　Do.　　*Copenhague*, 1866-69, 1877-84, 1886.   C

Mexico.
Anuario de Estadistico. Vols. 1-2. *Mexico*, 1893-4.   C

INDEX.

Univ. of California, Agric. Exper. Station.
Univ. of Nebraska, Agric. Exper. Station.
Wisconsin State Agric. Soc.
Young's Annals of Agric.

Almanacs and Ephemerides.

Alman. Américain.
Alman. de Gotha.
Alman. Royal.
Amer. Alman. and Reposit.
Amer. Alman. and Treasury.
Amer. Church Alman.
Amer. Ephem. and Naut. Alman.
Armana Prouvencau.
Astron.-meteor. Jahrbuch f. Prag.
Astron. Jahrb. f. phys. u. naturhist. Himmelsforscher.
Ranking Alman.
Boston Alman.
Brit. Alman. and Companion.
Brit. North Amer. Alman.
Canad. Alman.
Caroline Alman.
Dietrichsen and Hannay's Royal Almanac, etc.
Eason's Alman. for Ireland.
Edinburgh Alman.
Illust. Canad. Alman.
Ladies' Diary.
Lady's and Gentleman's Diary.
Legitimist Calendar.
Nautical Almanac and Astron. Ephemeris.
Oliver and Boyd, New Edinburgh Almanac.
Paterson's Scott. Alman.
Philadelphia Record Alman.
Quebec Alman.
Tribune Alman.
United States Alman.
Upper Canada Alman.
Vox Stellarum.
White's Celestial Atlas.
World Alman.
Year-Book and Alman. of Brit. Amer.
Year-Book and Alman. of Canada.
York Alman.

Anatomy. See *Biology*.

Anthropology and Ethnology (including Folk-lore).

Aborig. Protect. Soc.
Amer. Ethnol. Soc.
Amer. Folk-lore Soc.
Anthrop. Inst. of Gt. Brit. and Ireland.
Anthrop. Rev.
Anthrop. Soc. of London.
Anthrop. Soc. of Washington.
Anthrop. Gesells. in Wien.
Banner of Israel.
Berliner Gesells. f. Anthrop., Ethnol., etc.
Canad. Indian.
Colonial Intell. and Aborigines' Friend.
Deutsche anthrop. Gesells. in Nürnberg.
Deutsche Gesells. f. Anthrop. Ethnol. u. Urgeschichte.
Folk-lore.
Folk-lore Espanol.
Indian.
Instit. hist. geog. e ethnog. de Brazil.
Jl. of Amer. Ethnol. and Archaeol.
Jl. of Amer. Folk-lore.
Königl. zool. (und anthropol.-ethnograph.) Museum zu Dresden.
Museum f. Völkerkunde.

Peabody Mus. of Amer. Archaeol. and Ethnol.
Soc. ital. di Antropol. Etnol. e Psicol. compar.
Soc. d'Anthrop. de Paris.
Soc. dauphinoise d'Ethnol. et d'Anthrop.
Soc. d'Ethnog. Amér. et orient.
Svensk. Sällskap för Antropol. och. Geog.
Tokyo Anthrop. Soc.
U.S. Bureau of Ethnology.
Zeits. f. Völkerpsych.
    See also *Archaeology*.

Archaeology.

Acad. d'Hippone.
Amer. Antiquar. and Orient. Jl.
Amer. Antiquar. Soc.
Amer. Jl. of Archaeol.
Antiquar. Mag. and Bibliog.
Antiquar. Gesells. in Zürich.
Antiquar. Tidssk. för Sverige.
Antiquary.
Archaeol. Inst. of Amer.
Archaeol. Inst. of Gt. Brit. and Ireland.
Archaeol. Rev.
Brit. Archaeol. Ass.
Cambrian Archaeol. Ass.
Canad. Antiquar. and Numis. Jl.
Celtic Soc.
Comité des Trav. Hist. et Sci., Bull. Archéol.
Commission Sci. du Mexique.
Cumberland and Westmoreland Antiquar. and Archeol. Soc.
Dumfriesshire and Galloway Nat. Hist. and Antiquar. Soc.
Ecclesiologist.
Egyptian Explor. Fund.
Forening til Norske Fortidsmind. Bevaring (*in Addenda*).
Germania.
German. National-Museum.
Illust. Archaeologist.
Indian Antiquary.
Institut. Archéol. Liégeois.
Institut Égyptien.
Irish Archaeol. Soc.
Jl. of Amer. Ethnol. and Archaeol.
Kilkenny Archaeol. Soc.
Kongel. Nordisk Oldskrift-Selskab (*and in Addenda*).
Musée Guimet.
Palestine Explor. Fund.
Peabody Mus. of Amer. Archeol. and Ethnol.
Reliquary.
Royal Asiat. Soc.
Soc. Istriana di Archeol. e Storia patria.
Soc. Archéol. (*Agram.*)
Soc. Archéol. du Département de Constantine.
Soc. de Géog. et. d'Archéol. de la Province d'Oran.
Soc. Nat. des Antiquaires de France.
Soc. of Antiquaries of London.
Soc. of Antiquaries of Newcastle-Upon-Tyne.
Soc. of Antiquaries of Scotland.
Soc. of Biblical Archaeol.
Somersetshire Archaeol. and Nat. Hist. Soc.
Sussex Archaeol. Soc.
Ulster Jl. of Archaeol.
Worcester Soc. of Antiquity.
Yorkshire Archaeol. and Topograph. Ass.
Zeits. f. deut. Alterthum.

Architecture.

Amer. Archit. and Build. News.
Architect.

Archit. Publ. Soc.
Archit. Rec.
Archit. Rev. (*and in Addenda*).
Archit. Soc. (Assoc.)
Archit. and Building.
Builder.
Canad. Archit. and Builder.
Civil Engin. and Archit. Jl.
Encyclop. d'Archit.
Inland Archit. and News Rec.
Matériaux et Documents d'Archit. et de Sculpt.
Oesterreich. Ingenieur- und Architektenverein.
Royal Instit. of Brit. Architects.

Art. See *Fine Arts*.

Asia.

Asiat. Annual Reg.
Asiat. Soc. of Bengal.
Asiat. Soc. of Japan.
Calcutta Rev.
Deut. Gesells. f. Natur- u. Völkerkunde Ostasiens.
Imper. and Asiat. Quart. Rev.
Indian Antiquary.
Koninkl. Instit. voor de Taal- Land- en Volkenkunde
van Nederlandsch-Indie.
Royal Asiat. Soc.
Soc. Acad. Indo-Chinoise.
Soc. des Études Indo-chinoises de Saigon.
  See also executive publications under Hong-
  Kong.

Assyriology. See *Oriental Languages, etc.*

Astronomy.

Astron. and Phys. Soc. of Toronto.
Astron. Papers prep. for Amer. Ephem.
Astron. Soc. of London.
Astron. Nachrichten.
Astron. and Astro-Phys.
Astrophys. Jl.
Observatories.
Observatory.
Popular Astron.
Royal Astron. Soc.
Sidereal Messenger.
Specola Vaticana.
Unterhaltungen f. Dilettanten u. Freunde d. Astron.,
etc.
  See also *Almanacs*.

Australasia.

Australia Year-Book.
Geog. Soc. of Australasia.
New South Wales, Hist. Rec.
New South Wales Statist. Reg.
Polynesian Soc.
Victorian Year-Book.
Western Australia Year-Book.
  See also the parliamentary and executive publi-
  cations under New Zealand, Queensland,
  Tasmania and Victoria.

Austria. See *Germany*.

Bacteriology.

Centralb. f. Bact.
Jahresb. üb. d. Fortschritte in d. Lehre von. d. path-
ogenen Mikroorganismen.
Jl. of Pathol. and Bacteriol.
  See also *Biology* and *Medical Sciences*.

Banking. See *Finance*.

Bees.

Canad. Bee Jl.

Biblical Interpretation, etc.

Bible Soc. Recorder.
Biblical Repert. and Class. Rev.
Deutscher Palästina-Verein.
Expositor.
Expository Times.
Jewish Quart. Rev.
Jl. of Sacred Lit.
National Soc.
Old Test. Student.
Soc. of Biblical Archæol.
Sunday School Teachers' Mag.
Sunday School Times.
Wesleyan Sunday School Mag.
Zeits. f. d. alttest. wiss.
  See also *Theology*.

Bibliography.

Amer. Newspaper Cat.
Amer. Newspaper Directory.
Annual Lit. Index.
Antiquar. Mag. and Bibliog.
Bibliographer.
Bibliographica.
Calendars of State Papers.
Canada, Rep. on Canad. Archives.
Cat. of Canad. Publ.
Centralbl. f. Bibliothekswesen.
Courrier du Livre.
English Cat. of Books.
Histor. Manus. Commiss. (*and in Addenda*).
Index Soc.
Jahresb. f. Geschichtswiss.
Library.
Library Chron.
Library Jl.
Naturae Novitates.
Newspaper Press Directory for the United Kingdom.
Oriental. Bibliog.
Philobiblion.
Poole's Index to Period. Lit.
Public Libraries.
Publishers' Weekly.
Societatum Litterae.

Biology (including Microscopy and Morphology).

Amer. Monthly Micros. Jl.
Amer. Quarterly Micros. Jl.
Anatom. Anzeiger.
Annales des Sci. Nat.
Archiv f. Anat., Phys., u. wiss. Med.
Archiv f. mikros. Anat.
Archiv f. Naturges.
Archives de Biol.
Biol. Soc. of Washington.
Biol. Centralblatt.
Birmingham Nat. Hist. and Micros. Soc.
Boston Soc. of Nat. Hist.
Cellule.
Internat. Monatsschrift f. Anat. u. Histol.
Jahresb. üb. d. Fortschritte d. Anat. u. Physiol.
Jl de l'Anat. et de la Physiol.
Jl. de Micrographie.
Jl. of Anat. and Physiol.
Jl. of Morphology.
Kommission zur wiss. Untersuchung d. deut. Meere.
Linnean Soc.

Linnean Soc. of New South Wales.
Linnean Soc. of New York.
Liverpool Biol. Soc.
Marine Biol. Ass. of the United Kingdom.
Medizin.- naturwiss. Gesells. zu Jena.
Microscop. Soc. of London.
Morphol. Jahrbuch.
New York Microscop. Soc.
New Zealand, Colon. Mus. and Geol. Survey.
Postal Microscop. Soc.
Quart. Jl. of Microscop. Sci.
Quekett Microscop. Club.
Ray Soc.
Revue biol. du nord de la France.
Royal Microscop. Soc.
Soc. de Biol.
Soc. Linnéenne du Nord de la France.
Zeits. f. Anat. u. Entwickelungsgesch.
Zeits. f. Biol.
Zeits. f. wissen. Mikroskopie.
Zool.-botan. Verein.
Zool. Station zu Neapel.

Botany.

Annals of Bot.
Bayer. Bot. Gesell.
Bot. Gazette.
Bot. Mag.
Bot. Soc. of Canada.
Bot. Soc. of Edinburgh.
Bot. Zeitung.
Bot. Jahresb.
Bot. Centralbl.
Jahrb. f. wiss. Botanik.
Missouri Bot. Garden.
Nederland. bot. Vereeniging.
Soc. royale de Bot. de Belgique.
Zeits. f. Pflanzenkrankheiten.

See also *Biology*.

Brazil.

Brazilian Biog. Annual.
Instituto Hist. Geog. e Ethnog. de Brazil.

Bremen.

Bureau f. Bremische Statistik.
Kunstlerverein, Abth. f. Bremische Gesch.

Browning.

Boston Browning Soc.

Buenos Aires.

Annuaire Statist. de la Province de Buenos Aires.

Business.   See *Commerce*.

Canada.

Annuaire de Québec.
Canad. Antiquar. and Numismat. Jl.
Canad., Brit. Amer., and West Indian Mag.
Canadiana.
Celtic Soc. of Montreal.
Dominion Annual Reg.
Geog. Soc. of Quebec.
Geol. and Nat. Hist. Survey of Canada.
Glasgow Colon. Soc.
Grand Annuaire de Québec.
Hist. and Sci. Soc. of Manitoba.
Lit. and Hist. Soc. of Quebec.
Lundy's Lane Hist. Soc.
Nova Scotia Hist. Soc.

Soc. des Études Histor.
Soc. Hist. de Montréal.
Statist. Abstract and Record of Canada.

See also the parliamentary and executive publications under Canada and the names of the various provinces.

Celtic Philology.

Celtic Mag.
Celtic Soc.
Celtic Soc. of Montreal.
Ossianic Soc.
Scottish-Celtic Rev.

Charities.   See *Sociology*.

Chaucer.

Chaucer Soc.

Chemistry and Pharmacology.

Amer. Analyst.
Amer. Chem. Jl.
Amer. Pharmac. Ass.
Ann. d. Chem. u. Pharm.
Chem. Gazette.
Chem. News.
Chem. Soc. of London.
Chem. and Druggist.
Deutsche Chem. Gesells.
Gazzetta Chim. ital.
Jahrb. d. Chemie.
Jahresb. üb. d. Fortschritte d. Chemie.
Jahresb. üb. d. Fortschritte d. Thierchemie.
Jahresb. üb. d. Leistungen d. chem. Technol.
Jl. f. prakt. Chemie.
Krit. Zeits. f. Chemie.
Monatshefte f. Chemie.
Pharmaceut. Jl.
Pharmaceut. Centralblatt.
Recueil des Trav. Chim. des Pays-Bas.
Soc. chim. de Paris.
Technisch-chem. Jahrbuch.
Year-Book of Pharmacy.
Zeits. f. analyt. Chemie.
Zeits. f. anorgan. Chemie.
Zeits. f. physikal. Chemie.

See also *Physical Science*.

China.   See *Asia*.

Classical Philology and Antiquities.

Amer. Jl. of Philol.
Archiv f. latein. Lexik. y. Gram.
Ass. pour l'encour. des Ét. Grecques.
Attisches Museum.
Biograph. Jahrbuch f. Alterthumskunde.
Class. Jl.
Class. Museum.
Class. Rev.
Dissertat. philolog. Argentorat.
École franç. d'Athènes et de Rome.
École franç. d'Athènes.
Ephemeris Epigraph.
Harvard Studies in Class. Philol.
Hermes.
Jahresb. üb. d. Fortschritte d. class. Alterthümswiss.
Jl. of Class. and Sacred Philol.
Jl. of Philol.
Mnemosyne.
Museum Criticum.
Philolog. Museum.
Rheinisches Mus. f. Philol.

Soc. for the Promotion of Hellenic Studies.
Studien zur griech. u. latein. Gram
Syllogue littéraire grec de Constantinople.
    See also *Archaeology.*

College Journals.
Acta Victoriana.
Etonian.
Hartford Seminary Rec.
Knox College Monthly.
McMaster Univ. Monthly.
Queen's Coll. Jl.
Queen's Quarterly.
Trinity Univ. Rev.
University Mag.
Univ. of Toronto Quarterly.
V. P. Journal.
Varsity.
Victoria Mag.
Woodstock Coll. Monthly.

Commerce and Business.
Adress-Buch deut. Export-Firmen.
British Columbia Bd. of Trade.
Canada Business Directory.
Canad. Merchants' Mag.
Colonial Enterprise.
Colonial Mag.
Commercial Year-Book.
Co-operative Wholesale Soc.
Hunt's Merchant's Mag.
Jl. of Commerce.
New York Chamber of Commerce.
New York Produce Exchange.
Pilot and Jl. of Commerce.
Royal Agric. and Commercial Soc. of Brit Guiana.
Statist.
Stockholders' and Invest. Annual.
Trade Review.
    See also *Economics, Finance, Statistics.*

Conchology and Malacology.
Conchologist.
Soc. royale Malacol. de Belgique.
    See also *Biology.*

Crystallography. See *Geology.*

Dante.
Dante Soc.

Denmark. See *Sweden.*

Dentistry.
Dental Cosmos.

Ecclesiastical History (including Missions and Church Reviews).
Amer. Cath. Hist. Soc.
Brit. and For. Bible Soc.
Bull. d'Hist. Ecclés.
Bulwark.
Canada Ecclés.
Canad. Baptist.
Canad. Church Miss. Gleaner.
Canad. Church Press.
Canad. Eccles. Gazette.
Canad. Independent.
Canad. Independent Mag.
Canad. Presbyter.
Catholic Weekly Reg.
Christian Guardian.
Christian Mirror.
Christian Witness.

Christian Work.
Church.
Church Bells.
Church Chronicle.
Church Missionary.
Church of England.
Clergy Lists.
Colon. Church Chron.
Crockford's Clerical Directory.
Evangel. Christendom.
Evangel. Mag.
Fliegende Blätter aus d. Rauhen Hause zu Horn.
General Baptist Reposit.
Hartford Seminary Rec.
Indian Evangel. Rev.
Knox Coll. Monthly.
Lambeth Conferences.
Mag. of Christian Lit.
Massachusetts Miss. Mag.
Methodist Church.
Miss. Herald.
Miss. Mag.
Miss. Mag. and Chronicle.
Miss. Reg.
Miss. Rev. of the World.
Morning Watch.
National Church.
News of the Churches.
Our Mission News.
Panoplist.
Presbyt. Church.
Presbyterian.
Presbyt. Rec.
Sabbath-School Ass. of Canada.
Scottish Episcop. Rev. and Mag.
Soc. for Promoting Christ. among the Jews.
Soc. for the Propag. of the Gospel.
Sunday School Banner.
Swarthmore Conferences.
United States Cath. Mag.
Wesleyan.
Wesleyan Meth. Mag.
Zeits. f. Kirchengesch.
    See also *Theology.*

Economics.
Amer. Econ. Ass.
Brit. Econ. Ass.
Christ. Social Union.
Cobden Club.
Columbia Coll. Univ. Stud.
Comité des Trav. Hist. et Sci., Section des Sci. Écon.
École libre des Sci. Polit.
Economist.
Jahrb. f. National-ökon. u. Statistik.
Journal des Écon.
Quarterly Jl. of Econ.
Revue d'Écon. Polit.
    See also *Political Science* and *Sociology.*

Education.
Amer. Educ. Monthly.
Amer. Jl. of Educ.
Amer. Teacher.
Austral. Jl. of Educ.
Brit. Mothers' Jl.
Butler's Educat. Rev.
California Teacher.
Canada Educat. Directory.

Canada Educat. Monthly.
Canada School Journal.
Central-Organ f. d. Interessen d. Realschulwesens.
Child Garden.
Connecticut Common School Jl.
Dominion Educat. Ass.
Education.
Educat. Expositor.
Educat. Jl.
Educat. Rec.
Educat. Rev.
Educat. Times.
Educat. Weekly.
Educationalist.
English Jl. of Educ.
Home and School.
Illinois Teacher.
Indiana School Jl.
Iowa School Jl.
Journal de l'Instruction Pub.
Jl. of Education.
Jl. of Educ. and Agriculture.
Jl. of Educ. for Iowa.
Jl. of Educ. for Lower Canada.
Jl. of Educ. for New England.
Jl. of Educ. for Upper Canada.
Kindergarten.
Maine Jl. of Educ.
Maine Teacher.
Massachusetts Common School Jl.
Massachusetts Teacher.
Michigan Jl. of Educ.
Michigan Teacher.
Missouri Educator.
Mother's Mag.
National Teacher's Monthly.
Neue deutsche Schule.
New Brunswick Educat. Rev.
New Hampshire Jl. of Educ.
New Popular Educator.
New York School Jl.
New York State Educat. Jl.
New York Teacher.
Ohio Jl. of Educ.
Ohio School Jl.
Ontario Teacher.
Papers for the Schoolmaster.
Parish School Advocate.
Peabody Educ. Fund.
Pedagog. Seminary.
Pennsylvania School Jl.
Popular Educator.
Pupil Teacher.
Revue de l'Enseignement, etc.
Revue de l'Instruct. pub.
Rhode Island Institute.
Rhode Island Schoolmaster.
Scholast. Jl.
School and Teacher.
School Board Chron.
School Jl.
School Newspaper.
Schoolmaster.
Scottish Educat. Jl.
Soc. de l'Enseignement Supér.
Soc. for the Diffusion of Useful Knowledge.
Student.
Student and Schoolmaster.
Teachers' Institute.
University Extension.

University Monthly.
Vermont School Jl.
Western Educat. Jl.
Wisconsin Jl. of Educ.
Zeits. f. Philos. u. Pädagogik.
See also school and educational reports under
names of various cities, provinces, states,
and countries.

Egypt.
Egyptian Explor. Fund.
Institut Égyptien.

Engineering.
Amer. Engin. and Railroad Jl.
Amer. Machinist.
Amer. Soc. of Civil Engin.
Annales des Ponts et Chaussées.
Appleton's Mechan. Mag.
Ass. of Engin. Soc.
Canad. Elect. News and Steam Engin. Jl.
Canad. Engineer.
Canad. Soc. of Civil Engin.
Civil Engin. and Archit. Jl.
Elect. Engin.
Elect. World.
Electrician.
Engineer.
Engineering.
Engin. and Mining Jl.
Engin. Mag.
Engin. News.
Engin. Rec.
Engin. Soc. of the School of Pract. Sci.
English Mechanic.
Giornale del Genio Civile.
Indian Engineering.
Instit. of Civil Engin.
Instit. of Civil Engin. of Dublin.
Instit. of Engin. and Shipbuilders in Scotland.
Instit. of Mechan. Engin.
Iron and Steel Institute.
Manchester Ass. of Employers, Foremen and
Draughtsmen.
Manchester Ass. of Engineers.
Mechan. News.
Mechanics' Mag.
Mechanics' Mag. and Engineers' Jl.
Midland Instit. of Mining, Civil and Mechan. Engi-
neers.
Mining World and Engin. Rec.
North of England Instit. of Mining and Mechan.
Engin.
Oesterreich. (Ingenieur-und) Architekten-Verein.
Record of Modern Engin.
Rensselaer Soc. of Engin.
Royal Engineers, Papers.
Sanitary Engineer.
Sanitary Engineering.
Scient. American.
Scient. American Supplement.
Technical Soc. of the Pacific Coast.
Telegraphic Jl. and Elect. Rev.
Van Nostrand's Eclectic Engin. Mag.
See also *Mines, Railways, Technology.*

England. See *Great Britain.*
English Philology.
Aelfric Soc.
Amer. Dialect Soc.
Anglia.

Ballad Soc.
Boston Browning Soc.
Chaucer Soc.
Deut. Shakespeare-Gesells.
Early Eng. Text Soc.
Englische Studien.
English Dialect Soc.
Haliburton Club.
New Shakespeare Soc.
Percy Soc.
Scottish Text Soc.
Shakespeare Soc.
Shakesperiana.
Spenser Soc.

Entomology.
Canad. Entomologist.
Entomol. Forening i Stockholm.
Entomologist.
Massachusetts, State Entomologist, Rep.
Psyche.
Record of Amer. Entomol.
Soc. Entomol. Ital.
U.S., Dep. of Agric.
Verein f. Schlesische Insektenkunde.
See also *Biology*.

Ephemerides. See *Almanacs*.
Ethics. See *Philosophy*.
Ethnology. See *Anthropology*.
Fashions.
Harper's Bazar.
Lady's Pictorial.
Queen.
Woman's World.

Finance (Including Banking).
Banking Alm.
Banking Law Jl.
Banks and Sav. Inst. of Philadelphia.
Financial Rev.
Finanz-Archiv.
Institute of Bankers.
Investor's Rev.
Merchants' and Bankers' Almanac.
Monetary Times.
Statist.
Stock-Exchange Year-book.
Stockholders' and Investors' Annual.

Fine Arts.
Amer. Art. Rev.
Art.
Art Amateur.
Art Decorator.
Art for All.
Art Interchange.
Art Jl.
Art pour Tous.
Art. Japan.
Art. Reposit. and Drawing Mag.
Arundel Soc.
Chromolithograph.
Connoisseur.
Curio.
Decoration.
Decorator and Furnisher.
Ex Libris Soc.
Exposition des Beaux Arts.
Grip Cartoons.
Jl. of Decorative Art.

Mag. of Art.
Matériaux et Documents d'Archit. et de Sculpture.
Moderne Kunst.
Portfolio.
Process Year-Book.
Quarterly Illustrator.
Real Accad. d. Belle Arti in Milano.
Scottish Art Rev.
Vanity Fair Album.
Work.

Finland.
Finska Vetenskaps Soc.
Soc. de Géog. Findlandaise.
Soc. Finno-Ougrienne.

Folklore. See *Anthropology*.
Forestry and Lumbering.
Canada Lumberman.
Garden and Forest.
Scottish Arboricult. Soc.

France.
Collection de Doc. inéd. sur l'hist. de France.
École des Chartes.
Répertoire des Trav. hist.
Soc. de l'Hist. de France.
See also *Archæology* and *Geography*.

Frankfurt.
Frankfurter Verein f. Geog. u. Statistik.
Freemasons. See *Friendly Societies*.
French Philology.
Franzós. Studien.
Moliériste.
Revue des Patois.
Revue des Patois Gallo-Romains.
Soc. des Anciens Textes.
Soc. liègeoise de litt. Wallonne.
Zeits. f. neufranzós. Sprache u. Lit.

Friendly Societies.
Ancient Order of For. Friend. Soc.
Ashlar.
Canad. Jl. of Oddfellowship.
Craftsman and Brit. Masonic Rec.
Freemason's Mag. and Masonic Mirror.
Freemason's Quart. Rev.
Grand Lodge of Anc. Free and Accepted Masons of Canada.
Grand Priory of the United Orders of the Temple and Hospital.
Masonic Rev.

Geodesy and Surveying.
Ass. géodés. internat.
Ass. of Dominion Land Surveyors.
Ass. of Prov. Land Surveyors.
Königl. (preuss.) geodät. Institut.
Norske Gradenaalings-Komm.
Norweg. Commiss. d. Europä. Gradmessung.
Oesterreich. Gradmessungs-Commission.
Schweizer. geodät. Commission.
U.S. Coast and Geodetic Survey.
Zeits. f. Vermessungswesen.
See also *Engineering*.

Games. See *Sports*.
Geography.
Amer. Geog. Soc.
Amer. Geog. and Statist. Soc.

Année Géog.
Comité des Trav. Hist. et Sci., Bull. de géog.
Cosmos di Guido Cora.
Geog. Soc. of Australasia.
Geog. Soc. of California.
Geog. Soc. of Quebec.
Geog. Abhandlungen.
Geog. Gesells. f. Thuringen.
Geog. Gesells. in Bern.
Geog. Gesells. in München.
Geog. Gesells. zu Bremen.
Geog. Gesells. zu Hannover.
Geol. and Nat. Hist. Survey of Canada.
Gesells. f. Erdkunde zu Berlin.
Globus.
Hakluyt Soc.
Instituto fisico-geog. (*San José.*)
Instituto Geog. Argentino.
Instituto hist. geog. e. ethnog. de Brazil.
Internat. Polarforschung.
Istituto fisico-geog. y Museo Nac. (*Costa Rica.*)
Kaiserl.-königl. geograph. Gesells. (*Vienna*).
Liverpool Geog. Soc.
Manchester Geog. Soc.
Mittheilungen aus Justus Perthes' geog. Anstalt.
Physikal. Atlas.
Polynes. Soc.
Revue géog. internat.
Royal Geog. Soc. of London.
Scottish Geog. Soc.
Soc. Geog. de Madrid.
Soc. de Geog. de Lisboa.
Soc. de Geog. do Rio de Janeiro.
Soc. Geog. Italiana.
Soc. bretonne de Géog.
Soc. de Géog.
Soc. de Géog. Commerciale de Bordeaux.
Soc. de Géog. Commerciale de Nantes.
Soc. de Géog. de Génève.
Soc. de Géog. de Lille.
Soc. de Géog. et d'Archéol. de la Province d'Oran.
Soc. de Géog. Findlandais-.
Soc. Hongroise de Géog.
Soc. impér. russe de Géog.
Soc. Neuchateloise de Géog.
Soc. roy. belge de Géog.
Svensk Sällskap för Antrop. och Geog.
Tour du Monde.
Union géog. du Nord de la France.
U.S., Surveys.
Verein f. Erdkunde zu Dresden.
Verein f. Erdkunde zu Halle.
Zeits. f. wiss. Geog.

Geology and Mineralogy.

Amer. Geologist.
Annuaire géol.
Comité géol. de Russie.
Edinburgh Geol. Soc.
Geol. and Nat. Hist. Survey of Canada.
Geol. Mag.
Geol. Rec.
Geol. Soc. of America.
Geol. Soc. of Dublin.
Geol. Soc. of Glasgow.
Geol. Soc. of London.
Geol. Forening i Stockholm.
Geologist.
Imperat. Sanktpeterburg. Mineralog. Obshchestvo.
Kaiserl.-königl. geolog. Reichsanstalt (*Vienna*).

Manchester Geol. Soc.
Mineralog. u. petrograph. Mittheilungen.
Neues Jahrb. f. Mineral. Geol. u. Paläontol.
Palæontographica.
Palæont. Soc.
Reale Comitato geol. d'Italia.
Russ.-kaiserl. Mineral. Gesells. zu St. Petersburg.
Seismolog. Soc. of Japan.
Soc. géol. de Belgique.
Soc. géol. de France.
Soc. géol. de Normandie.
Soc. géol. du Nord.
Univ. of California, Dep. of Geol.
Zeits. f. Krystallog. u. Mineral.
    See also geological surveys of various countries and states under India, Michigan, Minnesota, Missouri, New South Wales, New York, New Zealand, Ohio, Pennsylvania, United States, Vermont, Wisconsin.

German Philology.

Alemannia.
Beit. zur Gesch. d. deut. Spr. u. Litt.
Beyt. zur krit. Hist. d. deut. Spr., etc.
Deutsche Mundarten.
Germania.
Germanist. Abhandlungen.
Gesells. f. deut. Philol.
Goethe-Gesells.
Goethe-Jahrb.
Jahresb. f. neuere deut. Literaturgesch.
Lit. Verein in Stuttgart.
Quellen u. Forschungen zur (Sprach- u. Culturgesch.) d. german. Völker.
Strassburger Studien.
Verein f. niederdeut. Sprachforschung.
Zeits. f. deut. Philol.
Zeits. f. deut. Alterthum.

Germany (including Austria).

Frankfurter Verein f. Geog. u. Statistik.
Geog. Gesells. f. Thuringen.
Germania.
German. National-Museum.
Hist. Gesells. f. d. Provinz Posen.
Hist. Verein f. Niedersachsen.
Hist. Verein f. Steiermark.
Institut f. österreich. Geschichtsforchung.
Künstlerverein, Abtheilung f. Bremische Geschichte.
Neues Lausitzisches Mag.
Quellen u. Erört. zur bayer. u. deut. Geschichte.
Verein f. Gesch. d. Deutschen in Böhmen.
Verein f. Hansische Gesch.
    See also *Archaeology* and *Geography*.

Goethe.

Goethe-Gesells.
Goethe-Jahrb.

Great Britain and Ireland (History).

Abbotsford Club.
Calendars of State Papers.
Cambrian Jl.
Cambrian Reg.
Camden Soc.
Chetham Soc.
Chronicles and Memorials of Gt. Brit. and Ireland.
Eng. Hist. Soc.
Grampian Club.
Great Brit., State Papers.
Great Brit., Record Com.

Harleian Soc.
Hist. Manuscripts Commission (*and in Addenda.*)
Hist. Soc. of Lancashire and Cheshire.
Irish Record Publ.
Lit. and Statist. Mag. for Scotland.
Maitland Club.
Manx Soc.
Navy Records Soc.
Oxford Hist. Soc.
Pipe Roll Soc.
Royal Hist. Soc.
Scottish Hist. Soc.
Scottish Record Pub.
Somerset Record Soc.
Spalding Club.
Spottiswoode Soc.
Surtees Soc.
See also *Archaeology*, and parliamentary and executive publications under Great Britain and Ireland.

Greek Philology, etc. See *Classical Languages and Antiquities.*

Haliburton.
Haliburton Club.

History (General.)
Acad. des. Inscrip. et Belles-Lettres. (*Paris*)
Amer. Hist. Ass.
Amer. Hist. Rev.
Annuaire des Deux Mondes.
Annuaire hist. univ.
Annual Reg.
Colonial Jl.
Columbia Coll., Univ. Studies.
Comité des Trav. Hist. et Sci., Bull. hist.
Current History.
École franç. d'Athènes et de Rome.
Edinburgh Annual Reg.
English Hist. Rev.
Hist. Mag.
Hist. Reg.
Hist. Zeitschrift.
Hist. Taschenbuch.
Hist. of the year.
Imper. and Asiat. Quarterly Rev.
Jahresb. d. Geschichtswiss.
Johns Hopkins Univ. Stud.
Mag. f.d. neue Hist. u. Geog.
Quart. Reg. of Current Hist.
Revue Hist.
Royal Colon. Institute.
Royal Soc. of Lit.
Stats-anzeigen.
Univ. of Pennsylvania, Dep. of Hist.

Horticulture.
Amer. Garden.
Bon Jardinier Alm.
California, State Hort. Commiss.
Garden.
Garden and Forest.
Gardener's Chron.
Horticult. Soc.
Meehan's Monthly.
Scottish Arboricult. Soc.

Hygiene. See *Medical Sciences.*
Hypnotism. See *Psychology.*
Imperial Federation.
Imperial Federation.

India. See *Asia.*
Insurance.
Assur. Mag.
Instit. of Actuaries.
Insur. Soc. and Firemen's Rev.
Insur. Year-book.
Investments. See *Finance.*
Ireland. See *Great Britain.*
Italian Philology.
Archiv. glottolog. ital.
Dante Soc.
Giornale storico della lett. ital.
Propugnatore.
Italy.
Istituto storico ital.
Soc. Istriana di Archeol. Storia Patria.
Soc. Siciliana per la Storia Patria.
Soc. Storica Comense.
Soc. Storica per la Provincia e antica diocesi.
Jamaica.
Canad., Brit. Amer. and West Ind. Mag.
Handbook of Jamaica.
Institute of Jamaica.
Japan. See *Asia.*
Latin Philology, etc. See *Classical Languages, etc.*
Law.
Allgem. Verein f. vereinfachte Rechtschreibung (*in Addenda*).
Amer. Law Rev.
Archiv. f. soziale Gesetzgeb.
Bibl. du Code Civil, Québec.
Canad. Law Times.
Centralbl. f. Rechtswiss.
Columbia Coll., Univ. Stud.
Giurisprudenza internaz.
Green Bag.
Harvard Law Rev.
Institut de Droit internat.
Jahrb. f. Gesetzgebung, etc.
Law Quart. Rev.
Lower Canada Jurist.
Revue de Législat. et de Jurisprud.
Selden Soc.
Soc. de Législat. comparée.
Soc. of Compar. Legislation.
Tagore Law Lectures.
Untersuch. zur deut. Staats- u. Rechtsgeschichte.
Upper Canada Jurist.
Upper Canada Law Directory.
Upper Canada Law Jl.
Upper Canada Law List.
Weekly Notes.
Zeits. f.d. gesammte Straf-rechtswissenschaft.

Literary and General (including Magazines.)
Abeille Canad.
Academy.
Album des Fam.
Album litt. et mus.
All the Year Round.
Almanac der Bellett.
Almanac des Maris.
Amer. Cath. Quart. Rev.
Amer. Monthly Mag.

Amer. Pub. Circular.
Amer. Quart. Reg.
Amer. Quart. Rev.
Amer. Rev.
Analectic Mag.
Anglo-Amer. Mag.
Anti-Jacobin Rev.
Appleton's Jl.
Archiv f. Litteráturgesch.
Arcturus.
Arena
Argosy.
Arrow.
Atalanta.
Athenæum.
Atlantic Monthly.
Band of Hope Rev.
Bay State Monthly.
Beeton's Boy's Annual.
Belfast Mag.
Belgravia.
Biblical Repert. and Class. Rev.
Bibliothek der schönen Wiss.
Bibliothèque Canad.
Bizarre Notes and Queries.
Blackwood's Mag.
Bookman.
Brit. American.
Brit. Amer. Jl.
Brit. Amer. Mag.
Brit. Colon. Mag.
Brit. Critic.
Brit. Mag.
Brit. Quart. Rev.
Brit. Rev.
Brit. Workman.
Californian.
Canada.
Canada Français.
Canad. Gem and Family Visitor.
Canad. Mag.
Canad. Mag. and Lit. Repository.
Canad. Monthly.
Canad. Rev.
Canadien illustré.
Cassell's Family Mag.
Cassell's Mag.
Catholic World.
Century Mag.
Chambers's Jl.
Chap-Book.
Chapman's Mag. of Fiction.
Chautauquan.
Chercheur.
Christ. Jl. and Lit. Reg.
Christ. Mag.
Christ. Observer.
Christ. Remembrancer.
Church Club Lect.
Churchman's Family Mag.
Contemp. Rev.
Continent.
Cornhill Mag.
Cosmopolis.
Cosmopolitan.
Critic.
Critical Rev.
Current Lit.
Day of Rest.
Demorest's Monthly Mag.

Deutsche Literaturzeitung.
Deutsche Rundschau.
Diario de los Literatos en Espana.
Dolman's Mag.
Dominion Illust. Monthly.
Dominion Rev.
Douglas Jerrold's Shilling Mag.
Dublin Mag.
Dublin Penny Jl.
Dublin Univ. Mag.
Écho de la France.
Écho du Cabinet de Lecture paroissial.
Eclectic Mag.
Eclectic Rev.
Edinburgh Rev.
Encyclopéd. Canad.
English Illust. Mag.
English Rev.
Euphorion.
Europa.
Exeter Hall Lectures.
Family Herald.
Foreign Quart. Rev.
Fortnightly Rev.
Forum.
Foyer Canad.
Foyer Domestique.
Fraser's Mag.
Gartenlaube.
Gegenwart.
General Mag.
Gentleman's Mag.
Good Words.
Grand Mag. of Mag.
Harper's Mag.
Harvard Mag.
Home.
Horen.
Household Words.
Howitt's Jl.
Independent Whig.
Internat. Mag.
Journal des Savants.
Kermesse.
Lake Mag.
Leisure Hour.
Lippincott's Mag.
Literar. Centralbl. f. Deutschland.
Literarium.
Liter. and Educat. Year-book.
Liter. and Statist. Mag. for Scotland.
Liter. Annual Reg.
Liter. Digest.
Liter. Garland.
Liter. Gazette.
Liter. Jl.
Liter. Opinion.
Liter. World.
Liter. Year-Book.
Literature.
Littell's Living Age.
London Quart. Rev.
London Society.
Longman's Mag.
Macmillan's Mag.
Mag. f. Literatur.
Mag. of Poetry.
Manhattan Mag.
Maple Leaf.
Massey's Mag.

Metropolitan.
Mirror of Literature, etc.
Monthly Mag.
Monthly Rev. and Liter. Miscell. of the U.S.
Monthly Rev. (or Liter. Jl.)
Monthly Visitor.
Munsey's Mag.
Murray's Mag.
Musen-Almanach.
Museum.
National Mag.
National Repository.
National Rev.
Neue Thalia.
New Dominion Monthly.
New Engländer.
New Monthly Mag. and Universal Reg.
New Rev.
Newgate Monthly Mag.
Nineteenth Century.
Nord u. Süd.
North Amer. Rev.
North Brit. Rev.
Norton's Literary Guide.
Notes and Queries.
Nuova Antologia.
Once a Week.
Overland Monthly.
People's Mag.
Poet Lore.
Positivist Review.
Preussische Jahrbücher.
Provincial.
Putnam's Mag.
Quarterly Rev.
Quiver.
Répertoire National.
Rev. of Reviews.
Revista Contemporanea.
Revue Canad.
Revue de Montréal.
Revue de Paris.
Revue des Deux Mondes.
Revue Nationale.
Round Table.
Royal Mag.
Royal Soc. of Lit.
St. James' Mag.
St. Paul's Mag.
Saturday Reader.
Scots' Mag.
Scottish Rev.
Scribner's Mag.
Snowdrop.
Soirées Canad.
Somerset House Gazette, etc.
Strand Mag.
Sunday at Home.
Temple Bar.
Universal Mag. of Knowledge and Pleasure.
Universal Rev.
University Mag.
University Quart. Rev.
Unsere Zeit.
V. P. Journal.
Vierteljahrsschrift f. Literaturgesch.
Western.
Westminster Rev.
Whitaker's Jl.
Writer.

Yellow Book.
Young Canadian.
Zeits. f. vergleich. Literaturgesch.
Lumbering. See *Forestry.*
Manufactures. See *Technology.*
Mathematics.
Acta Math.
Amer. Jl. of Math.
Amer. Math. Soc.
Ann. of Math.
Arch. d. Math. u. Phys.
Boilet. di Bibliog. e di Storia delle Sci. Mat. e Fis.
Cambridge Math. Jl.
Circolo Matemat. di Palermo.
Gentleman's Diary.
Jl. de Mathémat. élément. et spéciales.
Jl. de Mathémat. pures et appliques.
Jl. f.d. reine u. angewandte Math.
Ladies' Diary.
Lady's and Gentleman's Diary.
London Math. Soc.
Math. and Phys. Soc. of the Univ. of Toronto.
Math. Monthly.
Math. Questions and Solutions.
Math. Repos.
Math. Annalen.
New York Math. Soc.
Nouv. Annales de Math.
Oxford, Cambridge and Dublin Messenger of Math.
Quart. Jl. of Pure and Applied Math.
Soc. Math. de France.
Medical Sciences.
Acad. (Roy.) de Méd.
Aerztl. Verein zu Wien.
Allgem. Zeits. f. Psychiatrie.
Amer. Jl. of Obstet.
Amer. Jl. of the Med. Sci.
Amer. Lancet.
Amer. Med. and Philos. Reg.
Amer. Med. Ass.
Amer. Med.-Surg. Bull.
Amer. Practitioner.
Amer. Pub. Health Ass.
Ann. d. Char.-Krank. zu Berlin.
Ann. d'Hyg. pub.
Ann. Méd.-Psychol.
Ann. f. Hyg.
Arch. f. Anat. Phys. u. wiss. Med.
Arch. f. path. Anat.
Arch. f. Psychiatrie.
Arch. de Méd. expériment.
Arch. de Phys. norm. et path.
Arch. Gén. de Méd.
Asylum Jl. of Mental Science.
Beit. zur path. Anat.
Bibl. d. deut. Med. u. Chirurg.
Brit. Amer. Jl.
Brit. Amer. Jl. of Med. and Phys. Sci.
Brit. and For. Med. Rev.
Brit. and For. Med.-Chirurg. Rev.
Brit. Med. Ass.
Canada Lancet.
Canada Med. Ass.
Canada Med. Jl.
Can. Jl. of Med. Sci.
Centralbl. f. Allgem. Path.
Centralbl. f.d. med. Wiss.
Clinical Soc. of London.

Congrès périod. internat. des Sci. Méd.
Dominion Med. Monthly and Ontario Med. Jl.
Dublin Quart. Jl. of Med. Sci.
Edinburgh Med. Jl.
Half-yearly Abstract of the Med. Sci.
Hall's Jl. of Health.
Internat. Sanitary Conference.
Jahresb üb. d. Leistungen u. Fortschritte in d.
    gesammten Medicin.
Johns Hopkins Hospital Rep.
Journal d'Hygiène.
Jl. of Compar. Med. and Surg.
Jl. of Nervous and Mental Disease.
Jl. of Pathol. and Bacteriol.
Kaiserl.-konigl. Gesells. d. Aertzte zu Wien.
Kaiserl.-königl. Allgem. Krankenhaus.
King's College Hospital.
Lancet.
Laws of Life.
London Med. Press and Circular.
Mag. f. d. gesammte Heilkunde.
Med. and Chirurg. Soc. of London.
Med. and Phys. Soc. of Bombay.
Med. Bulletin.
Med. Chronicle.
Med. Circular, etc.
Med. News.
Med. Record.
Med. Times and Gazette.
Med.-Chirurg. Soc. of Edinburgh.
Med.-Legal Jl.
Med.-Naturwiss. Gesells. zu Jena.
Med. National-Zeitung f. Deutschland.
Monatsschrift f. Geburtskunde u. Frauenkrankheiten.
Montreal Med. Jl.
Naturhist.-med. Verein zu Heidelberg.
New Sydenham Soc.
New York Med. Jl.
Niederrhein. Gesells. f. Natur- u. Heilkunde.
Oberhess. Gesells. f. Natur- u. Heilkunde.
Obstet. Soc. of London.
Ontario Med. Jl.
Pan-Amer. Med. Congress.
Pathol. Soc. of London.
Practitioner.
Provincial Med. and Surg. Ass.
Retrospect of pract. Med. and Surg.
Revista Chilena de Hijiene.
Revue Méd. Franç. et Étrangère.
Royal Acad. of Med. in Ireland.
St. George's Hospital Rep.
St. Thomas' Hospital Rep.
Sanitarian.
Sanitary Engineer.
Sanitary Engineering.
Sanitary Instit. of Gt. Brit.
Sanitary Jl.
Sanitary News.
Sanitary Record.
Scuola d'Anat. patol.
Soc. de Chirurgie de Paris.
Sydenham Soc.
Texas Sanitarian.
Therapeutic Gazette.
Upper Canada Jl. of Surg. and Phys Sci.
Verein f. öffentl. Gesundheits-pflege im Herzogthum
    Braunschweig.
Weekly Med. Rev.

Metallurgy. See *Mines and Mining*.

Meteorology.
Brit. Meteor. Soc.
Jahrbuch.
Observatories.
Soc. Météor. de France.
Unterhaltungen f. Dilettanten u. Freunde d. Astron.
Geog. u. Witterungskunde.

Mexico.
Commission Sci. du Mexique.
Mexico, Anuario de Estadistico   (*in Addenda.*)

Microscopy. See *Biology*.

Military and Naval.
Canad. Milit. Institute.
Hart's Army List.
Naval and Milit. Mag.
Navy and Army Illustrated.
Navy Annual.
Royal Milit. Chron.
United Service Jl.
Volunteer Rev.

Mineralogy. See *Geology*.

Mines and Mining (including Metallurgy). ·
Amer. Inst. of Mining Engin.
Berg- u. Hütten. Zeitung.
Canad. Min. Manual.
Canad. Min. Rev.
Engin. and Mining Jl.
Escola de Minas de Ouro Preto.
Gornozavodskaya.
Gornui Institut.
Journal des Mines.
Mexico, Boletin de Agricult. Mineria, etc.
Mineral Industry.
Mining Jl., etc.
Mining Soc. of Nova Scotia.
Mining World, etc.
School of Mines Quarterly.
Zeits. f. d. Berg-, Hütten-. u. Salinenwesen.
    See also *Engineering, Geology*.

Moliere.
Moliériste.

Morphology. See *Biology*.

Music.
Album Litt. et Mus.
Musical Jl.
Musical World.

Natural Sciences (including Biology, Palæ-
    ontology, Geology and Mineralogy).
Aargau. Naturforsch. Gesells.
Acad. de la Rochelle.
Acad. of Nat. Sci. of Philadelphia.
Allgem. Schweiz. Gesells. f. d. ges. Naturwiss.
Amer. Mus. of Nat. Hist.
Amer. Naturalist.
Annaes de Sci. Nat.
Annals of Nat. Hist.
Belfast Nat. Field Club.
Bristol Nat. Soc.
Buffalo Soc. of Nat. Soc.
Bull. Univ. des Sci.: Sci. Nat. et Géol.
Cincinnati Soc. of Nat. Hist.
Colorado Sci. Soc.
Davenport Acad. of Nat. Sci.
Dumfriesshire and Galloway Nat. Hist. and Antiquar.
    Soc.

Edinburgh New Jl.
cinburgh New Philos. Mag.
Feuille des Jeunes Nat.
Geol. and Nat. Hist, Survey of Canada.
Gesells. naturforsch. Freun le zu Berlin.
Illinois, State Lab. of Nat. Hist.
Iowa State Univ.
Kaiserl.-königl. naturhist. Hofmuseum (*Vienna*).
Lyceum of Nat. Hist. (*New York*).
Mag. of Nat. Hist. and Jl. of Zool., etc.
Midland Union of Nat. Hist. Soc.
Musée Royal d'Hist. Nat. de Belgique.
Museo civico di Storia Nat. (*Trieste*).
Museo de La Plata.
Museo Nacional (*Costa Rica*).
Mus. Nac. de Buenos Aires.
Mus. Nac. de Mexico.
Mus. Nac. de Montevideo.
Mus. Nac. de Rio de Janeiro.
Muséum d'Hist. Nat. de Paris.
Nassauischer Verein f. Naturkunde.
Nat. Hist. Rev.
Nat. Hist Soc. of Dublin.
Nat. Hist. Soc. of Glasgow.
Nat. Hist. Soc. of Montreal.
Nat. Hist. Soc. of New Brunswick.
Nat. Sci.
Naturalist.
Naturaliste Canadien.
Naturforsch. Gesells. in Bern.
Naturforsch. Gesells. in Dantzig.
Naturforsch. Gesells. in Emden.
Naturforsch. Gesells. in Zürich.
Naturforsch. Gesells. zu Freiburg.
Naturforsch. Gesells. zu Görlitz.
Naturforsch. Gesells. zu Leipzig.
Naturhist.-med. Verein zu Heidelberg.
Naturhist. Gesells. zu Hannover.
Naturhist. Gesells. zu Nürnberg.
Naturhist. Verein d. preuss. Rheinlande u. West-
phalens.
Naturhist. Museum zu Hamburg.
Naturhistorisk Tidskrift.
Naturwiss. Gesells. "Isis."
Naturwiss. Wochenschrift.
Naturwiss. Verein d. Regierungsbezirks Frankfurt.
Naturwiss. Verein f. Sachsen u. Thuringen.
Naturwiss. Verein in Hamburg.
Naturwiss. Verein in Bremen.
Naturwiss. Verein f. Schleswig-Holstein.
Naturwiss. Verein zu Hamburg-Altona.
Natuurkundig Vereen. in Nederl.-Indië.
New York Mus. of Nat. Hist.
Newport Nat. Hist. Soc.
Niederrhein. Gesells. f. Natur- u. Heilkunde.
Nova Scotian Inst. of (Nat.) Sci.
Nyt Mag. f. Naturvidenskaberne.
Oberhess. Gesells. f. Natur- u. Heilkunde.
Offenbacher Verein f. Naturkunde.
Ottawa Field-Naturalists' Club.
Revista Argentina de Hist. Nat.
Royal Phys. Soc. of Edinburgh.
St. Gallische Naturwiss. Gesells.
Senckenberg. naturforsch. Gesells.
Siebenbürg. Verein f. Naturwiss. in Hermannstadt.
Skandin. Naturforsk. Forhandlinger.
Soc. Adriat. di Sci. Nat. in Trieste.
Soc. Ital. di Sci. Nat.
Soc. Ligustica di Sci. Nat. e Geog.
Soc. Toscana di Sci. Nat.

Soc. Veneto-Trentina di Sci. Nat.
Soc. des Naturalistes (*Kief*).
Soc. des Naturalistes à l'Univ. impér. de Kharkow.
Soc. des Sci. Nat. de l'Ouest de la France.
Soc. Fribourgeoise des Sci. Nat.
Soc. Impér. des Amis des Sci. Nat., etc.
Soc. Impér. des Nat. de Moscou.
Soc. Nation. des Sci. Nat. de Cherbourg.
Soc. Vaudoise des Sci. Nat.
Somersetshire Archæol. and Nat. Hist. Soc.
Thurgauischer naturforsch. Verein.
Trenton Nat. Hist. Soc.
Tromso Museum.
Verein f. Naturkunde zu Cassel.
Verein f. Naturkunde zu Zwickau.
Verein f. Naturwiss. zu Braunschweig.
Verein f. Naturwiss. Unterhaltung zu Hamburg.
Verein zur Verbreitung naturwiss. Kenntnisse in
Wien.
Wetterauische Gesells. f. d. gesammte Naturkunde
zu Hanau.

Naval. See *Military.*

Navigation.
Nautical Mag.
See also *Astronomy* and *Almanacs.*

Neurology. See *Psychology* and *Physiology.*

**Newspapers and Journals of current
political events.**
Adventurer.
Albion.
Ballou's Pictorial.
Banner.
Black and White.
Britannic Mag.
Brit. Chronicle.
Bystander.
Canad. American.
Canad. Illust. News.
Colon. Gazette.
Companion to the Newspaper, etc.
Diogenes.
Dominion Illustrated.
Frank Leslie's Illust. Paper.
Fun.
Gentlewoman.
Graphic.
Grinchuckle.
Grip.
Grumbler.
Harper's Weekly.
Illust. London News.
Illust. Times.
Instructor and Select Weekly Advertiser.
Judge.
Judy.
Lady's Newspaper.
Lady's Pictorial.
Lanterne.
League.
London Mag.
Loyalist and Conservative Advocate.
Manitoban.
Monthly Rev. (*Montreal*).
Montreal Register.
Montreal True Witness.
Montreal Witness.
Moonshine.
Nation.

New York Daily Graphic.
Niles' Weekly Reg.
North American.
Pall Mall Budget.
Pictorial World.
Press.
Province.
Public Opinion.
Puck.
Punch.
Queen.
Saturday Rev.
Sketch.
Speaker.
Spectator.
Times.
Times Register of Events.
Tomahawk.
Truth.
U.E. Loyalist.
Vanity Fair.
Week.
Weekly Oracle.
Weekly Polit. Reg.
Weekly Reg.
World.

Norway. See *Sweden.*

Oriental Philology and Antiquities.

Amer. Antiquar. and Orient. Jl.
Amer. Orient. Soc.
Asiat. Soc. of Bengal.
Asiat. Soc. of Japan.
Babylon. and Orient. Record.
Beit. zur Assyriologie.
Deutsche morgenländ. Gesells.
École des Langues Orient. vivantes.
Hebraica.
Orientalist.
Royal Asiat. Soc.
Sacred Books of the Buddhists.
Sacred Books of the East.
Soc. Finno-Ougrienne.
Zeits. f. Assyriologie.
Zeits. f. Keilschriftforschung.
     See also *Archæology.*

Ornithology.

Allg. deut. ornith. Gesell. zu Berlin.
Ibis.
Nuttall ornith. Club.
Ornithol. Verein Pommerns.
Permanente internat. Ornithol. Comité.
Zeits. f. Ornithol. u. praktische Geflügelzucht.
     See also *Biology.*

Palæography.

Palæograph. Soc.

Palæontology. See *Geology.*

Patents.

Canada, Patent Office.
Great Brit., Patents.
Inventor's Advocate and Patentee's Recorder.
Repertory of Arts, Manufactures, etc.
U.S., Patent Office.
Victoria, Patents.

Pathology. See *Medical Sciences.*

Pharmacology. See *Chemistry.*

Philology (General).

Acad. des Inscript. et Belles-Lettres   (*Paris*).
Amer. Philol. Ass.
Anecdota Oxon.
Archiv f. d. Stud. d. neueren Spr. und Lit.
Beit. zur Kunde d. indogerm. Spr.
Cambridge Philol. Soc.
Fonetic Herald.
Internat. Zeits. f. allgemein. Sprachwiss.
Jahrb. f. roman. u. engl. Spr. u. Lit.
Literaturblatt f. german. u. roman. Philol.
Maître phonétique.
Mod. Lang. Notes.
Neue Jahrb. f. Philol. u. Pädagogik.
Neu. philolog. Centralblatt.
Nordisk Tidskrift f. Filol. og Pædagogik.
Philol. Soc.
Phonet. Studien.
Revue de Linquistique.
Royal Soc. of Lit.
Soc. Philol. Lipsiensis.
Soc. Philologique.
Texts and Studies.
Zeits. f. deut. Unterricht.
Zeits. f. österreich. Gymnasien.
Zeits. f. vergleich. Sprachforschung.

Philosophy (including Metaphysics, Ethics and Theosophy).

Advocate of Moral Reform.
Archiv. f. Gesch. d. Philos.
Critical Rev.
Ethical Rec.
Gifford Lect.
Isis Moderne.
Jl. of Speculative Philos.
Lamp.
Lucifer.
Metaphys. Mag.
Mind.
Monist.
Path.
Philos. Rev.
Philos. Monatshefte.
Philos. Studien.
Real Acad. de Ciencias Morales y Polit.
Revue philos.
Rivista di Filos. Scient.
Spiritual Mag.
Theosophy.
Vierteljahrsschrift f. wiss. Philos.
Zeits. f. exacte Philos.
Zeits. f. Philos u. Pädagogik.
Zeits. f. Philos. u. spekul. Theol.
     See also *Psychology* and *Theology.*

Phonetics. See *Philology (General).*

Photography.

Amateur Photog.
Amer. Annual of Photog.
Anthony's Photog. Annual.
Brit. Jl. of Photog.
Brit. Jl. Photog. Alm.
Canad. Photog. Jl.
Photogram.
Photog. Quarterly.
Photog. Societies' Reporter.
Process Photogram.
     See also *Fine Arts.*

Physical Sciences.
Ann. d. Physik (u. Chem.).
Ann. de Chimie (et de Phys.).
Physikal. Verein zu Frankfurt.
Soc. Phys.-chim. Russe.
Zeits. f Instrumentenkunde.
See also *Chemistry* and *Physics*.

Physics.
Arch. d. Math. u. Phys.
Astron. and Phys. Soc. of Toronto.
Bollet. di Bibliog. e di Stori delle Sci. Mat. e Fis.
Jl. de Physique.
Math. and Phys. Soc. of the Univ. of Toronto.
Phys. Soc. of London.
Repertorium d. Physik.
See also *Mathematics* and *Physical Sciences*.

Physiology.
Archiv. f. Anat., Physiol., u. wiss. Med.
Archiv. f. d. gesammt. Physiol.
Archives. de Physiol. norm. et path.
Centralbl. f. Physiol.
Jahresb. üb. d. Fortschritte d. Anat. u. Physiol.
Jahresb. üb. d. Fortschritte d. Physiol.
Jl. de l'Anat. et de la Physiol.
Jl. of Anat. and Physiol.
Jl. of Physiol.
Physiol. Gesells. zu Berlin.
Zeits. f. physiol. Chemie.
Zeits. f. Psychol. u. Physiol. d. Sinnesorgane.
See also *Biology* and *Medical Sciences*.

Political Science.
Amer. Acad. of Polit. and Social Sci.
Amer. Jl. of Politics.
École Libre des Sci. Polit.
Government Year-book.
Harvard Univ. Publ.
Harvard Hist. Stud.
Jahrb. f. Gesetzgebung, etc.
Johns Hopkins Univ. Stud.
Polit. Sci. Quarterly.
Real Acad. de Ciencias Morales y Polit.
Staats- u. socialwiss. Forschungen.
Statesman's Year-book.
Untersuch. zur deut. Staats- und Rechtsgeschichte.
Zeits. f. d. gesammte Staats- wissenschaft.
See also *Economics* and *Sociology*.

Portugal.
Quadro element. das Relacoes polit. e. diplomat. de Portugal.

Poultry.
Canad. Poultry Chron.

Psychology (including Psycho-physics, Hypnotism and Mental Diseases).
Allgem. Zeits. f. Psychiatrie.
Amer. Jl. of Psychol.
Amer. Soc. for Psych. Research.
Ann. Méd.-psychol.
Arch. f. Psychiatrie.
Asylum Jl. of Ment. Sci.
Brain.
Jl. of Compar. Neurology.
Jl. of Nervous and Mental Disease.
Princeton Contrib. to Psychol.
Psychol. Rev.
Revue de l'Hypnotisme.
Soc. for Psych. Research.

Zeits. f. Psych. u. Physiol. d. Sinnesorgane.
See also *Philosophy*.

Railways.
Amer. Engin. and Railroad Jl.
Amer. Railway Master Mech. Ass.
Manual of the Railroads of the U.S.
Mining Jl., Railway and Commerc. Gazette.
Railroad Gazette.
See also *Engineering*.

Religion. See *Theology*.

Romance Philology.
Bibliograph.-krit. Anzeiger f. roman. Spr. u. Lit.
Jahrb. f. roman. u. engl. Spr. u. Lit.
Literaturbl. f. german. u. roman. Philol.
Rivista di Filol. rom.
Romania.
Roman. Forschungen.
Roman. Studien.
Soc. pour l'Étude des Langues Rom.
Zeits. f. roman. Sprachforschung.

Sanitary Science. See *Medical Sciences*.

Science (General).
Acad. Cæsarea Nat. Curios.
Acad. Nacional de Cienc. de la Repub. Argentina en Cordoba.
Acad. Real das Sci. de Lisboa.
Acad. Sci. imper. Petropol.
Acad. des Sci. (*Paris.*)
Acad. of Sci. of St. Louis.
Adelaide Philos. Soc.
Albany Institute.
Amer. Acad. of Arts and Sci.
Amer. Ass. for the Adv. of Sci.
Amer. Jl. of Sci. and Arts.
Amer. Med. and Philos. Reg.
Amer. Philos. Soc.
Annual of Sci. Discovery.
Annual Rec. of Sci. and Industry.
Assoc. franç. pour l'Av. des Sci.
Austral. Ass. for the Adv. of Sci.
Bibl. univ.: Archives des Sci. phys. et nat.
Brit. Ass. for the Adv. of Sci.
Bull. Sci. de la France et de la Belgique.
California Acad. of Sci.
Cambridge Philos. Soc.
Carlsberg Laboratori.
Chicago Acad. of Sci.
Comité des Travaux Hist. et Sci., Revue des Trav. Sci.
Connecticut Acad. of Arts and Sci.
Cosmos.
Denison Univ.
École centrale des Trav. pub.
École Normale Sup.
École polytech. de Delft.
Elisha Mitchell Sci. Soc.
Field Columbian Museum.
Geol. and Polytech. Soc. of the West Riding of Yorkshire.
Greenock Philos. Soc.
Helios.
Hollandsche Maatsch. d. Weten.
Imperial Univ. of Japan, Coll. of Sci.
Indiana Acad. of Sci.
Institut.
Institut Royal Grand-Ducal de Luxembourg.
Institute of Jamaica.

Jahrb. d. Hamburg. wiss. Anstalten.
Jamaica Soc. of Arts.
Journal des Soc. Sci.
Kansas Acad. of Sci.
Knowledge.
Kongl. Svenska Vetenskaps Akad.
Mag. of Popular Sci.
Math. und naturwiss. Berichte aus Ungarn.
Meriden Sci. Ass.
Mondes.
Nat. Acad. of Sci. (*Ashington*).
Nature.
New South Wales Philos. Soc.
New York Acad. of Sci.
Peabody Acad. of Sci.
Philos. Mag.
Philos. Soc. of Glasgow.
Philos. Soc. of Washington.
Physikalisch-ökonom. Gesells. zu Königsberg.
Popular Sci. Monthly.
Popular Sci. News.
Queensland Museum.
Reale Accad. delle Sci. dell' Istituto di Bologna.
Reale Istituto di Studi Super. prat., etc. (*Florence*).
Revue des Cours Sci. de la France et de l' Étranger.
Revue des Soc. Savantes.
Revue des Soc. Savantes des Départements.
Revue Scientifique.
Rochester Acad. of Sci.
Royal Dublin Soc.
Royal Instit. of Gt. Brit.
Royal Soc. of Edinburgh.
Royal Soc. of London.
Royal Soc. of New South Wales.
Royal Soc. of Queensland.
Royal Soc. of Tasmania.
Royal Soc. of Victoria.
Science.
Scientific Memoirs.
Soc. Cientif. "Antonio Alzate."
Soc. de Phys. et d'Hist. nat. de Genéve.
Soc. Hollandaise des Sci. à Harlem.
Soc. Royale des Sci. de Liège.
Soc. Scient. de Chili.
South African Philos. Soc.
Texas Acad. of Sci.
U. S., Smithsonian Instit.
Univ. d'Aix-Marseilles.
Victoria Instit.
Wagner Free Instit. of Sci. of Philadelphia.
West-American Scientist.
Western Rev. of Sci. and Industry.
Wissen. Club in Wien.
Year-book of Facts in Sci. and Art.
    See also *Academies.*

Scotland. See *Great Britain.*

Seismology. See *Geology.*

Shakespeare.

Deutsche Shakespeare-Gesells.
New Shakespeare Soc.
Shakespeare Soc.
Shakesperiana.

Sociology.

Amer. Acad. of Polit. and Social Sci.
Arch. f. soziale Gesetzgeb.
Charity Organiz. Soc.
Conference of Char. and Corrections.
Englishwoman's Rev.

Herald of Peace.
Humanitarian.
Meliora.
National Ass. for the Promotion of Social Sci.
Science Sociale.
Soldiers' Orphans' Instit. of Pennsylvania.
Staats- u. socialwiss. Forschungen.
Toynbee Record.
Zeits. f. d. gesammte Strafrechtswissenschaft.
    See also *Political Science* and *Economies.*

Spain.
Real Acad. de la Hist.

Sports and Amusements.
Badminton Mag.
Conjurer's Mag.
Field.
Forest and Stream.
Grand Nat. Curling Club Annual.
Kennel Club Stud Book.
Kennel Gazette.
Outing.
Royal Caledonian Curling Club.
Sporting and Dram. News.
Westminster Papers.

Statistics.
Amer. Geog. and Statist. Soc.
Amer. Statist. Ass.
Annuaire de Québec.
Annuaire Statist. de la Prov. de Buenos Aires.
Barker's Facts and Figures.
Bureau f. Bremische Statist.
Canada, Bd. of Regist. and Statist.
Canada, Census.
Colonial Office List.
Financial Reform Almanac.
Frankfurter Verein f. Geog. u. Statistik.
Gentleman's and Citizen's Almanac.
Globe Annual.
Grand Annuaire de Québec.
Handbook of Jamaica.
Imperial Instit. Year-book.
Institut internat. de Statistique.
Internat. Statist. Congress in Berlin.
Jahrb. f. Nationalökon. u. Statistik.
Lit. and Statist. Mag. for Scotland.
Mexico, Anuario de Estadistico (*in Addenda*).
National Almanac and Annual Rec.
New South Wales Statist. Reg.
Statesman's Year-book.
Statist. Abstract and Record of Canada.
Statist. Soc. of London.
U.S., Census.
Whitaker's Almanac.
Year-book and Alman. of Brit. Amer.
Year-book and Almanac of Canada.

Surgery. See *Medical Sciences.*

Surveying. See *Geodesy.*

Sweden and Norway.
Antiquarisk Tidsk. för Sverige.
Forening til Norske Fortidsmind. Bevaring (*in Addenda*).
Kongl. Nord. Oldskrift-Selskab (*and in Addenda*).

Technology and Useful Arts.
Amer. Institute.
Amer. Jl. of Sci. and Arts.
Annual Rec. of Sci. and Indust.
Artizan.

Bollett. Indust. del Regno d'Italia.
Canad. Manufacturer.
Farmer and Mechanic.
Franklin Institute.
Geolog. and Polytech. Soc. of the West Riding of
   Yorkshire.
Industries.
Iron and Steel Institute.
Jahresb. über d. Leistungen d. chem. Technol.
Jl. of the Board of Arts and Manufactures for Upper
   Canada.
Liverpool Polytech. Soc.
Manufacturer and Builder.
Massachusetts Inst. of Technol.
Mechanics' Mag.
Neue Zeits. f. Rübenzuckerindustrie.
Polytechnisches Journal.
Polytekniske Forening.
Royal Scott. Soc. of Arts.
Soc. (for the Encouragement) of Arts, etc.
Technisch-chem. Jahrbuch.
Western Rev. of Sci. and Industry.
Working Man.
Workshop.
Year-book of Facts in Sci. and Arts.
   See also *Engineering.*

Theatrical.

Sporting and Dram. News.
Theatre.

Theology and Religion.

Andover Rev.
Arminian Mag.
Baird Lectures.
Baldwin Lectures.
Bampton Lectures.
Bibliotheca Sacra.
Boyle Lectures.
Brit. and For. Evangel. Rev.
Brit. Controversialist.
Brit. Critic.
Calvin Trans. Soc.
Canada Baptist Mag.
Canad. Christ. Examiner.
Canad. Method. Mag.
Canad. Method. Quarterly.
Catholic.
Catholic Presbyterian.
Catholic World.
Christ. Advocate.
Christ. Examiner and Theol. Rev.
Christ. Miscell. and Family Visitor.
Christ. Recorder.
Christ. Rev.
Christ. Thought.
Christ. World Pulpit.
Church of England Mag.
Church of England Quart. Rev.
Church Quart. Rev.
Churchman's Remembrancer.
Congregat. Lectures.
Critical Rev.
Cunningham Lect.
Dublin Rev.
Edinburgh Christ. Instructor.
Evangel. Mag. and Theol. Rev.
Gifford Lect.
Gospel Mag.
Gospel Tribune.
Guardian of Educat.

Hanserd Knollys Soc.
Hibbert Lect.
Homiletic Quarterly.
Homiletic Rev.
Homilist.
Hulsean Lect.
Irish Congregat. Mag.
Jahrb. f. deut. Theologie.
Messenger of the Sacred Heart.
Methodist Mag.
Methodist (Quart.) Rev.
Modern Rev.
Monthly Repository.
New World.
Parker Soc.
Presbyt. and Reformed Rev.
Presbyt. Mag.
Presbyt. Rev.
Presbyt. Witness, etc.
Rede Lect.
Relig. Tract Soc.
Theologian.
Theol. Critic.
Theol. Eclectic.
Theol. Monthly.
Theol. Rev.
Theol. Literatur-Zeitung.
Theol. Studien u. Kritiken.
Thinker.
Tracts for the Times.
Unitarian Rev.
Witness.
Wodrow Soc.
Wyclif Soc.
Yale Lect.
Zeits. f. Lutherische Theol.
Zeits. f. Philos. u. spekul. Theol.
Zeits. f. wiss. Theol.
   See also *Biblical Interpretation*, *Ecclesiastical
   History*, and *Philosophy.*

Theosophy. See *Philosophy.*

Trades and Trade Jls.

Amateur Work.
Amer. Book-maker.
Amer. Cabinet-maker.
Brit. Lithographer.
Builder and Wood-worker.
Canad. Shoe and Leather Directory.
Carpentry and Building.
Decorator and Furnisher.
Furniture Gazette.
Gewerbehalle.
Illust. Carpenter and Builder.
Metal Worker.
Plumber and Decorator.
   See also *Commerce* and *Technology.*

United States.

Amer. Annual Reg.
Amer. Cath. Hist. Soc.
Amer. Hist. Reg.
Amer. History.
Amer. History Leaflets.
Amer. Pioneer.
Buffalo Hist. Socy.
Chicago Hist. Soc.
Connecticut, Colonial Rec.
Connecticut Hist. Soc.
Geog. Soc. of California.

Georgia Hist. Soc.
Harvard Hist. Studies.
Hist. Coll. of Louisiana.
Hist. Mag.
Hist. Reg.
Hist. Soc. of Pennsylvania.
Iowa Hist. Rec.
Jefferson County Hist. Soc.
Kansas State Hist. Soc.
Mag. of Amer. Hist.
Mag. of Western Hist.
Maine Hist. Soc.
Massachusetts Hist. Soc.
Michigan Pioneer and Hist. Soc.
Minnesota Hist. Soc.
Missouri Hist. Soc.
Narragansett Club.
National Alman. and Annual Rec.
Nebraska State Hist. Soc.
New Hampshire Hist. Soc.
New Jersey, Archives.
New Jersey Hist. Soc.
New York, Archives.
New York Hist. Soc.
Old South Leaflets.
Oneida Histor. Soc.
Parkman Club.
Rhode Island Hist. Soc.
Rochester Hist. Soc.
Scotch-Irish Soc. of America.
Southern Hist. Mag.
Stryker's Amer. Mag.
Vermont Hist. Soc.
Virginia, Calendar of State Papers.
Virginia Hist. Soc.
Western Reserve Hist. Soc.

Wisconsin State Hist. Soc.
  See also *Archæology*, *Geography* and parliamentary and executive publications under United States and the names of the various States.

Useful Arts. See *Technology*.

Veterinary Science.
Veterinary Jl.

Weights and Measures.
Bureau Internat. des Poids et Mes.
Internat. Standard.

Zoology.
Archives de Zool. expér. et. gén.
Jl. de Zoologie.
Königl. zool. Museum zu Dresden.
Koninkl. zool. Genootschap.
Mag. de Zoologie.
Museum of Compar. Zool. at Harvard College.
Nederland. dierkund. Vereeniging.
Niederländ. Archiv f. Zool.
Soc. Cuviérienne.
Soc. néerland. de Zoologie.
Soc. Zool. de France.
Untersuch. zur Naturlehre d. Menschen u. d. Thiere.
Zeits. f. wissen. Zool.
Zool. and Acclimat. Soc. of Victoria.
Zool. Soc. of London.
Zool.-zootom. Institut in Würzburg.
Zool. Gesells. zu Frankfurt.
Zool. Jahrbücher.
Zool. Anzeiger.
Zool. Institut d. Univ. Wien u. d. zool. Station in Triest.
Zoologist.
  See also *Biology*.

www.ingramcontent.com/pod-product-compliance
Lightning Source LLC
Chambersburg PA
CBHW032355280326
41935CB00008B/580